GEORGE FRIEDMAN

THE NEXT DECADE

George Friedman is the CEO and founder of Stratfor, the world's leading private intelligence company. He is frequently called upon as a media expert in intelligence and international geopolitics, and is the author of six books, including the *New York Times* bestseller *The Next 100 Years*, as well as numerous articles on national security, international affairs, and the intelligence business. He lives in Austin, Texas.

www.stratfor.com

D0359391

THE

NEXT

DECADE

EMPIRE AND REPUBLIC IN
A CHANGING WORLD

GEORGE FRIEDMAN

ANCHOR BOOKS
A DIVISION OF RANDOM HOUSE, INC.
NEW YORK

FIRST ANCHOR BOOKS EDITION, JANUARY 2012

Copyright © 2011, 2012 by George Friedman

All rights reserved. Published in the United States by Anchor Books, a division of Random House, Inc., New York, and in Canada by Random House of Canada Limited, Toronto. Originally published in hardcover in slightly different form in the United States by Doubleday, a division of Random House, Inc., New York, in 2011.

Anchor Books and colophon are registered trademarks of Random House, Inc.

The Library of Congress has cataloged the Doubleday edition as follows:
Friedman, George.
The next decade / George Friedman.
p. cm.
1. World politics—21st century—Forecasting. I. Title
D863.F75 2011
909.83'1—dc22 2010043116

Anchor ISBN: 978-0-307-47639-5

Author photograph © Celeste Casas
All maps created by STRATFOR

www.anchorbooks.com

Manufactured in the United States of America
10

For Don Kuykendall,
Friend

I hope to have God on my side, but I must have
Kentucky.

—Abraham Lincoln

Rules are not necessarily sacred, principles are.

—Franklin Roosevelt

We cannot play innocents abroad in a world that is
not innocent.

—Ronald Reagan

It is necessary for a prince who wishes to maintain his
position to learn how not to be good, and to use this
knowledge or not to use it according to necessity.

—Niccolò Machiavelli

CONTENTS

LIST OF ILLUSTRATIONS

This book is about the relation among empire, republic, and the exercise of power in the next ten years. It is a more personal book than *The Next 100 Years* because I am addressing my greatest concern, which is that the power of the United States in the world will undermine the republic. I am not someone who shuns power. I understand that without power there can be no republic. But the question I raise is how the United States should behave in the world while exercising its power, and preserve the republic at the same time.

I invite readers to consider two themes. The first is the concept of the unintended empire. I argue that the United States has become an empire not because it intended to, but because history has worked out that way. The issue of whether the United States should be an empire is meaningless. It is an empire.

The second theme, therefore, is about managing the empire, and for me the most important question behind that is whether the republic can survive. The United States was founded against British imperialism. It is ironic, and in many ways appalling, that what the founders gave us now faces this dilemma. There might have been exits from this fate, but these exits were not likely. Nations become what they are through the constraints of history, and history has very little sentimentality when it comes to ideology or preferences. We are what we are.

It is not clear to me whether the republic can withstand the pressure of the empire, or whether America can survive a mismanaged empire. Put differently, can the management of an empire be made compatible with the requirements of a republic? This is genuinely unclear to me. I know the United States will be a powerful force in the world during this next decade—and for this next century, for that matter—but I don't know what sort of regime it will have.

I passionately favor a republic. Justice may not be what history cares about, but it is what I care about. I have spent a great deal of time thinking about the relationship between empire and republic, and the only conclusion I have reached is that if the republic is to survive, the single institution that can save it is the presidency. That is an odd thing to say, given that the presidency is in many ways the most imperial of our institutions (it is the single institution embodied by a single person). Yet at the same time it is the most democratic, as the presidency is the only office for which the people, as a whole, select a single, powerful leader.

In order to understand this office I look at three presidents who defined American greatness. The first is Abraham Lincoln, who saved the republic. The second is Franklin Roosevelt, who gave the United States the world's oceans. The third is Ronald Reagan, who undermined the Soviet Union and set the stage for empire. Each of them was a profoundly moral man . . . who was prepared to lie, violate the law, and betray principle in order to achieve those ends. They embodied the paradox of what I call the Machiavellian presidency, an institution that, at its best, reconciles duplicity and righteousness in order to redeem the promise of America.

I do not think being just is a simple thing, nor that power is simply the embodiment of good intentions. The theme of this book, applied to the regions of the world, is that justice comes from power, and power is only possible from a degree of ruthlessness most of us can't abide. The tragedy of political life is the conflict between the limit of good intentions and the necessity of power. At times this produces goodness. It did in the case of Lincoln, Roosevelt, and Reagan, but there is no assurance of this in the future. It requires greatness.

Geopolitics describes what happens to nations, but it says little about the kinds of regimes nations will have. I am convinced that unless we understand the nature of power, and master the art of ruling, we may not be able to choose the direction of our regime. Therefore, there is nothing contradictory in saying that the United States will dominate the next century yet may still lose the soul of its republic. I hope not, as I have children and now grandchildren—and I am not convinced that empire is worth the price of the republic. I am also certain that history does not care what I, or others, think.

This book, therefore, will look at the issues, opportunities, and inherent challenges of the next ten years. Surprise alliances will be formed, unexpected tensions will develop, and economic tides will rise and fall. Not surprisingly, how the United States (particularly the American president) approaches these events will guide the health, or deterioration, of the republic. An interesting decade lies ahead.

The Next Decade combines three themes. The first is the tension between the American empire and the American republic. The second is the character of the president needed to manage the unintended and unwanted empire while preserving the republic. The third is a forecast of the world in which we will be living during this decade.

As I write this preface to the paperback, about eight months after the hardcover was published, I am surprised only by the speed with which events have taken place, and the manner in which some events, which have loomed so large in the media and public mind, have already begun to fade.

Certainly the most important thing that has happened is the acceleration of the crisis of the European Union. Both in *The Next 100 Years* and in *The Next Decade,* I made the case that the European Union as an institution and Europe as a united ideal were untenable. It is not simply a matter of different cultures, although that is not a minor matter. The problem is a free trade zone with the world's second largest exporter—Germany—at its center, using the free trade zone to stabilize its own economy while undermining its partners' ability to develop economically. This problem, coupled with the bureaucracy in Brussels and a currency designed to bolster northern Europe's interests, made it difficult to imagine Europe surviving. In fact, it is not surviving. Certainly it will take a long time to die as an institution. But the reality of Europe that was imagined even a few years ago is gone. All that is left is the machinery of Europe and bitterness.

I spoke of China as a nation facing crisis. It is in that crisis. In order to keep businesses from going bankrupt and swelling the ranks of the unemployed, Chinese banks are lending failing enterprises money to repay their debts. The result is surging inflation that has made Chinese labor more expensive than Mexican. That means that the exports on which China depends to run its economy either become noncompetitive or profits are cut to the disappearing point. The economy grows but profit declines. This is what happened to Japan in 1990 and it is happening to China—and, as with Japan, the Western media is still celebrating China's success.

Russia has continued to grow in power as the only major nation not experiencing a financial crisis, while Turkey continues to increase its presence and influence in its region. The eastern Europeans have formed a Visegrad Battle Group consisting of Poland, the Czech Republic, Slovakia, and Hungary. It is a paper alliance at this point, far from an effective fighting force, but these countries are looking beyond NATO for their security.

What was not predicted in this book was the Arab Spring. I would argue that the Arab Spring never happened except in the fantasies of Westerners. No regime fell except for the Libyan and only because of NATO's intervention. The fall of Mubarak was not the fall of a regime but of a person. He was replaced by a military junta that continues the military regime created in the 1950s by Gamel Abdul Nasser. At this point, Syria's Assad has not fallen nor has any other regime. Bahrain's government remains in place, kept there by Saudi troops. The Arab Spring didn't happen. It just seemed about to and never quite jelled.

We must always remember that all unrest does not constitute revolutions; all revolutions are not successful; all successful revolutions do not create constitutional democracies. Certainly there were constitutional democrats in the crowds, but no matter how often they were interviewed by CNN and BBC, they did not constitute the whole of the crowd, many of whom were democratic but wanted to create Islamist regimes, not liberal ones. In the end, the region was swept by unrest, but what is most interesting is how little changed. The Arab world is the Arab world, and it does not yearn to be remade in the image of Europe and America. Nor was it.

The United States, as I argued, is in the best condition of any of the great powers. Unlike Europe, its economic problems are not causing it to shatter. Unlike China, its economic problems can be handled. This isn't to say that the economic problems of the United States have not been painful.

Nor should it be said that it has not created an institutional crisis or, more precisely, that the institutional crisis that has swept the world hasn't touched the United States. The single most important consequence of the global financial crisis was the delegitimation of the authority of the financial elite, who were seen as simultaneously corrupt and incompetent. The political elites intervened to stabilize the situation and, then failing to solve the problem, were themselves delegitimized.

The global crisis is that the publics of the major countries do not trust the political or financial elites. We can see this in Europe and China. We can also see this in the United States when movements on the left and right both challenge not so much the principles of the regime but the leadership. The Tea Party on the right and the Democratic left, in different ways and with different rhetoric, have both raised the question of whether the elites know what they are doing or are acting in the public interest.

This has deepened the crisis of the republic at a critical time. I have made the argument in this book that the empire threatens the republic. A crisis of confidence in the political elite at this point is particularly troublesome. Reconciling republic and empire in this decade is crucial. It won't wait. The empire is becoming an unmanageable burden to the republic. With the political elite increasingly distrusted, their ability to manage this extraordinarily difficult task approaches the impossible. Without public trust, it is impossible.

This is the crisis the United States faces. It is dealing with a fundamental contradiction in the regime and reality at a time when the leaders are held in low regard. This is a broad international phenomenon, but the crisis in the United States has implications for the world, because of the centrality of the United States to the international system. What happens in the United States does not stay in the United States.

I have become more pessimistic in the past months about solving the crisis. The kind of president we need has little to do with ideology and more to do with a willingness to wield power to moral ends. It is difficult to be president under current circumstances. But presidents change or they can be replaced. In either case, the key burden of managing the republic in a time of empire will fall to the president. That much has not changed in my mind. Certainly there is time, but there is precious little. A decade is but a blink in the eye of history.

THE NEXT DECADE

INTRODUCTION

REBALANCING AMERICA

A century is about events. A decade is about people.

I wrote *The Next 100 Years* to explore the impersonal forces that shape history in the long run, but human beings don't live in the long run. We live in the much shorter span in which our lives are shaped not so much by vast historical trends but by the specific decisions of specific individuals.

This book is about the short run of the next ten years: the specific realities to be faced, the specific decisions to be made, and the likely consequences of those decisions. Most people think that the longer the time frame, the more unpredictable the future. I take the opposite view. Individual actions are the hardest thing to predict. In the course of a century, so many individual decisions are made that no single one of them is ever critical. Each decision is lost in the torrent of judgments that make up a century. But in the shorter time frame of a decade, individual decisions made by individual people, particularly those with political power, can matter enormously. What I wrote in *The Next 100 Years* is the frame for understanding this decade. But it is only the frame.

Forecasting a century is the art of recognizing the impossible, then eliminating from consideration all the events that, at least logically, aren't going to happen. The reason is, as Sherlock Holmes put it, "When you have eliminated the impossible, whatever remains, *however improbable,* must be the truth."

It is always possible that a leader will do something unexpectedly foolish or brilliant, which is why forecasting is best left to the long run, the span over which individual decisions don't carry so much weight. But having forecast for the long run, you can reel back your scenario and try to see how it plays out in, say, a decade. What makes this time frame interesting is that it is sufficiently long for the larger, impersonal forces to be at play but short enough for the individual decisions of individual leaders to skew outcomes that otherwise might seem inevitable. A decade is the point at which history and statesmanship meet, and a span in which policies still matter.

I am not normally someone who gets involved in policy debates— I'm more interested in what *will* happen than in what I want to see happen. But within the span of a decade, events that may not matter in the long run may still affect us personally and deeply. They also can have real meaning in defining which path we take into the future. This book is therefore both a forecast and a discussion of the policies that ought to be followed.

We begin with the United States for the same reason that a study of 1910 would have to begin with Britain. Whatever the future might hold, the global system today pivots around the United States, just as Britain was the pivotal point in the years leading up to World War I. In *The Next 100 Years,* I wrote about the long-term power of the United States. In this book, I have to write about American weaknesses, which, I think, are not problems in the long run; time will take care of most of these. But because you and I don't live in the long run, for us these problems are very real. Most are rooted in structural imbalances that require solutions. Some are problems of leadership, because, as I said at the outset, a decade is about people.

This discussion of problems and people is particularly urgent at this moment. In the first decade after the United States became the sole global power, the world was, compared to other eras, relatively tranquil. In terms of genuine security issues for the United States, Baghdad and the Balkans were nuisances, not threats. The United States had no need for strategy in a world that appeared to have accepted American leadership without complaint. Ten years later, September 11 brought that illusion crashing to the ground. The world was more dangerous than we imagined, but the options seemed fewer as well. The United States did not craft a global strategy in response. Instead, it developed a narrowly focused politico-military strategy designed to defeat terrorism, almost to the exclusion of all else.

Now that decade is coming to an end as well, and the search is under way for an exit from Iraq, from Afghanistan, and indeed from the world that began when those hijacked airliners smashed into buildings in New York and Washington. The impulse of the United States is always to withdraw from the world, savoring the pleasures of a secure homeland protected by the buffer of wide oceans on either side. But the homeland is not secure, either from terrorists or from the ambitions of nation-states that see the United States as both dangerous and unpredictable.

Under both President Bush and President Obama, the United States has lost sight of the long-term strategy that served it well for most of the last century. Instead, recent presidents have gone off on ad hoc adventures. They have set unattainable goals because they have framed the issues incorrectly, as if they believed their own rhetoric. As a result, the United States has overextended its ability to project its power around the world, which has allowed even minor players to be the tail that wags the dog.

The overriding necessity for American policy in the decade to come is a return to the balanced, global strategy that the United States learned from the example of ancient Rome and from the Britain of a hundred years ago. These old-school imperialists didn't rule by main force. Instead, they maintained their dominance by setting regional players against each other and keeping these players in opposition to others who might also instigate resistance. They maintained the balance of power, using these opposing forces to cancel each other out while securing the broader interests of the empire. They also kept their client states bound together by economic interest and diplomacy, which is not to say the routine courtesies between nations but the subtle manipulation that causes neighbors and fellow clients to distrust each other more than they distrust the imperial powers. Direct intervention relying on the empire's own troops was a distant, last resort.

Adhering to this strategy, the United States intervened in World War I only when the standoff among European powers was failing, and only when it appeared that the Germans, with Russia collapsing in the east, might actually overwhelm the English and French in the west. When the fighting stopped, the United States helped forge a peace treaty that prevented France from dominating postwar Europe.

During the early days of World War II, the United States stayed out of direct engagement as long as it could, supporting the British in their efforts to fend off the Germans in the west while encouraging the Soviets to bleed the Germans in the east. Afterward, the United States devised a balance-of-power strategy to prevent the Soviet Union from dominating Western Europe, the Middle East, and ultimately China. Throughout the long span from the first appearance of the "Iron Curtain" to the end of the Cold War, this U.S. strategy of distraction and manipulation was rational, coherent, and effectively devious.

Following the collapse of the Soviet Union, however, the United States shifted from a strategy focused on trying to contain major powers to an unfocused attempt to contain potential regional hegemons when their behavior offended American sensibilities. In the period from 1991 to 2001, the United States invaded or intervened in five countries— Kuwait, Somalia, Haiti, Bosnia, and Yugoslavia—which was an extraordinary tempo of military operations. At times, American strategy seemed to be driven by humanitarian concerns, although the goal was not always clear. In what sense, for example, was the 1994 invasion of Haiti in the national interest?

But the United States had an enormous reservoir of power in the 1990s, which gave it ample room for maneuver, as well as room for indulging its ideological whims. When you are overwhelmingly dominant, you don't have to operate with a surgeon's precision. Nor did the United States, when dealing with potential regional hegemons, have to win, in the sense of defeating an enemy army and occupying its homeland. From a military point of view, U.S. incursions during the 1990s were spoiling attacks, the immediate goal being to plunge an aspiring regional power into chaos, forcing it to deal with regional and internal threats at a time and place of American choosing rather than allowing it to develop and confront the United States on the smaller nation's own schedule.

After September 11, 2001, a United States newly obsessed with terrorism became even more disoriented, losing sight of its long-term strategic principles altogether. As an alternative, it created a new but unattainable strategic goal, which was the elimination of the terrorist threat. The principal source of that threat, al Qaeda, had given itself an unlikely but not inconceivable objective, which was to re-create the Islamic caliphate, the theocracy that was established by Muhammad in the seventh century and that persisted in one form or another until the fall of the Ottoman Empire at the end of World War I. Al Qaeda's strategy was to overthrow Muslim governments that it regarded as insufficiently Islamic, which it sought to do by fomenting popular uprisings in those countries. From al Qaeda's point of view, the reason that the Islamic masses remained downtrodden was fear of their governments, which was in turn based on a sense that the United States, their governments' patron, could not be challenged. To free the masses from their intimidation, al Qaeda felt that it had to demonstrate that the United States was not as powerful as it appeared—that it was in fact vulnerable to even a small group of Muslims, provided that those Muslims were prepared to die.

In response to al Qaeda's assaults, the United States slammed into the Islamic world—particularly in Afghanistan and Iraq. The goal was to demonstrate U.S. capability and reach, but these efforts were once again spoiling attacks. Their purpose was not to defeat an army and occupy a territory but merely to disrupt al Qaeda and create chaos in the Muslim world. But creating chaos is a short-term tactic, not a long-term strategy. The United States demonstrated that it is possible to destroy terrorist organizations and mitigate terrorism, but it did not achieve the goal that it had articulated, which was to eliminate the threat altogether. Eliminating such a threat would require monitoring the private activities of more than a billion people spread across the globe. Even attempting such an effort would require overwhelming resources. And given that succeeding in such an effort is impossible, it is axiomatic that the United States would exhaust itself and run out of resources in the process, as has happened. Just because something like the elimination of terrorism is desirable doesn't mean that it is practical, or that the price to be paid is rational.

Recovering from the depletions and distractions of this effort will consume the United States over the next ten years. The first step—returning to a policy of maintaining regional balances of power—must begin in the main area of current U.S. military engagement, a theater stretching from the Mediterranean to the Hindu Kush. For most of the past half century there have been three native balances of power here: the Arab-Israeli, the Indo-Pakistani, and the Iranian-Iraqi. Owing largely to recent U.S. policy, those balances are unstable or no longer exist. The Israelis are no longer constrained by their neighbors and are now trying to create a new reality on the ground. The Pakistanis have been badly weakened by the war in Afghanistan, and they are no longer an effective counterbalance to India. And, most important, the Iraqi state has collapsed, leaving the Iranians as the most powerful military force in the Persian Gulf area.

Restoring balance to that region, and then to U.S. policy more generally, will require steps during the next decade that will be seen as controversial, to say the least. As I argue in the chapters that follow, the United States must quietly distance itself from Israel. It must strengthen (or at least put an end to weakening) Pakistan. And in the spirit of Roosevelt's entente with the USSR during World War II, as well as Nixon's entente with China in the 1970s, the United States will be required to make a distasteful accommodation with Iran, regardless of whether it attacks Iran's nuclear facilities. These steps will demand a more subtle exercise of power than we have seen on the part of recent presidents. The nature of that subtlety is a second major theme of the decade to come, and one that I will address further along.

While the Middle East is the starting point for America's return to balance, Eurasia as a whole will also require a rearrangement of relationships. For generations, keeping the technological sophistication of Europe separated from the natural resources and manpower of Russia has been one of the key aims of American foreign policy. In the early 1990s, when the United States stood supreme and Moscow lost control over not only the former Soviet Union but the Russian state as well, that goal was neglected. Almost immediately after September 11, 2001, the unbalanced commitment of U.S. forces to the Mediterranean-Himalayan theater created a window of opportunity for the Russian security apparatus to regain its influence. Under Putin, the Russians began to reassert themselves even prior to the war with Georgia, and they have accelerated the process of their reemergence since. Diverted and tied down in Iraq and Afghanistan, the United States has been unable to hold back Moscow's return to influence, or even to make credible threats that would inhibit Russian ambitions. As a result, the United States now faces a significant regional power with its own divergent agenda, which includes a play for influence in Europe.

The danger of Russia's reemergence and westward focus will become more obvious as we examine the other player in this second region of concern, the European Union. Once imagined as a supernation on the order of the United States, the EU began to show its structural weaknesses during the financial crisis of 2008, which led to the follow-on crisis of southern European economies (Italy, Spain, Portugal, and Greece). Once Germany, the EU's greatest economic engine, faced the prospect of underwriting the mistakes and excesses of its EU partners, it began to reexamine its priorities. The emerging conclusion is that Germany potentially shared a greater community of interest with Russia than it did with its European neighbors. However much Germany might benefit from economic alliances in Europe, it remains dependent on Russia for a large amount of its natural gas. Russia in turn needs technology, which Germany has in abundance. Similarly, Germany needs an infusion of manpower that isn't going to create social stresses by emigration to Germany, and one obvious solution is to establish German factories in Russia. Meanwhile, America's request for increased German help in Afghanistan and elsewhere has created friction with the United States and aligned German interests most closely with Russia.

All of which helps to explain why the United States' return to balance will require a significant effort over the next decade to block an accommodation between Germany and Russia. As we will see, the U.S. approach will include cultivating a new relationship with Poland, the geographic monkey wrench that can be thrown into the gears of a German-Russian entente.

China, of course, also demands attention. Even so, the current preoccupation with Chinese expansion will diminish as that country's economic miracle comes of age. China's economic performance will slow to that of a more mature economy—and, we might add, a more mature economy with over a billion people living in abject poverty. The focus of U.S. efforts will shift to the real power in northeast Asia: Japan, the third largest economy in the world and the nation with the most significant navy in the region.

As this brief overview already suggests, the next ten years will be enormously complex, with many moving parts and many unpredictable elements. The presidents in the decade to come will have to reconcile American traditions and moral principles with realities that most Americans find it more comfortable to avoid. This will require the execution of demanding maneuvers, including allying with enemies, while holding together a public that believes—and wants to believe—that foreign policy and values simply coincide. The president will have to pursue virtue as all of our great presidents have done: with suitable duplicity.

But all the cleverness in the world can't compensate for profound weakness. The United States possesses what I call "deep power," and deep power must be first and foremost balanced power. This means economic, military, and political power in appropriate and mutually supporting amounts. It is deep in a second sense, which is that it rests on a foundation of cultural and ethical norms that define how that power is to be used and that provides a framework for individual action. Europe, for example, has economic power, but it is militarily weak and rests on a very shallow foundation. There is little consensus in Europe politically, particularly about the framework of obligations imposed on its members.

Power that is both deeply rooted and well balanced is rare, and I will try to show that in the next decade, the United States is uniquely situated to consolidate and exercise both. More important, it will have little choice in the matter. There is an idea, both on the left and on the right, that the United States has the option of withdrawing from the complexities of managing global power. It's the belief that if the United States ceased to meddle in the affairs of the world, the world would no longer hate and fear it, and Americans could enjoy their pleasures without fear of attack. This belief is nostalgia for a time when the United States pursued its own interests at home and left the world to follow its own course.

There was indeed a time when Thomas Jefferson could warn against entangling alliances, but this was not a time when the United States annually produced 25 percent of the wealth of the world. That output alone entangles it in the affairs of the world. What the United States consumes and produces shapes the lives of people around the world. The economic policies pursued by the United States shape the economic realities of the world. The U.S. Navy's control of the seas guarantees the United States economic access to the world and gives it the potential power to deny that access to other countries. Even if the United States wanted to shrink its economy to a less intrusive size, it is not clear how that would be done, let alone that Americans would pay the price when the bill was presented.

But this does not mean that the United States is at ease with its power. Things have moved too far too fast. That is why bringing U.S. policy back into balance will also require bringing the United States to terms with its actual place in the world. We have already noted that the fall of the Soviet Union left the United States without a rival for global dominance. What needs to be faced squarely now is that whether we like it or not, and whether it was intentional or not, the United States emerged from the Cold War not only as the global hegemon but as a global empire.

The reality is that the American people have no desire for an empire. This is not to say that they don't want the benefits, both economic and strategic. It simply means that they don't want to pay the price. Economically, Americans want the growth potential of open markets but not the pains. Politically, they want to have enormous influence but not the resentment of the world. Militarily, they want to be protected from dangers but not to bear the burdens of a long-term strategy.

Empires are rarely planned or premeditated, and those that have been, such as Napoleon's and Hitler's, tend not to last. Those that endure grow organically, and their imperial status often goes unnoticed until it has become overwhelming. This was the case both for Rome and for Britain, yet they succeeded because once they achieved imperial status, they not only owned up to it, they learned to manage it.

Unlike the Roman or British Empire, the American structure of dominance is informal, but that makes it no less real. The United States controls the oceans, and its economy accounts for more than a quarter of everything produced in the world. If Americans adopt the iPod or a new food fad, factories and farms in China and Latin America reorganize to serve the new mandate. This is how the European powers governed China in the nineteenth century—never formally, but by shaping and exploiting it to the degree that the distinction between formal and informal hardly mattered.

A fact that the American people have trouble assimilating is that the size and power of the American empire is inherently disruptive and intrusive, which means that the United States can rarely take a step without threatening some nation or benefiting another. While such power confers enormous economic advantages, it naturally engenders hostility. The United States is a commercial republic, which means that it lives on trade. Its tremendous prosperity derives from its own assets and virtues, but it cannot maintain this prosperity and be isolated from the world. Therefore, if the United States intends to retain its size, wealth, and power, the only option is to learn how to manage its disruptive influence maturely.

Until the empire is recognized for what it is, it is difficult to have a coherent public discussion of its usefulness, its painfulness, and, above all, its inevitability. Unrivaled power is dangerous enough, but unrivaled power that is oblivious is like a rampaging elephant.

I will argue, then, that the next decade must be one in which the United States moves from willful ignorance of reality to its acceptance, however reluctant. With that acceptance will come the beginning of a more sophisticated foreign policy. There will be no proclamation of empire, only more effective management based on the underlying truth of the situation.

CHAPTER 1

THE UNINTENDED EMPIRE

The American president is the most important political leader in the world. The reason is simple: he governs a nation whose economic and military policies shape the lives of people in every country on every continent. The president can and does order invasions, embargos, and sanctions. The economic policies he shapes will resonate in billions of lives, perhaps over many generations. During the next decade, who the president is and what he (or she) chooses to do will often affect the lives of non-Americans more than the decisions of their own governments.

This was driven home to me on the night of the most recent U.S. presidential election, when I tried to phone one of my staff in Brussels and reached her at a bar filled with Belgians celebrating Barack Obama's victory. I later found that such Obama parties had taken place in dozens of cities around the world. People everywhere seemed to feel that the outcome of the American election mattered greatly to them, and many appeared personally moved by Obama's rise to power.

Before the end of Obama's first year in office, five Norwegian politicians awarded him the Nobel Peace Prize, to the consternation of many who thought that he had not yet done anything to earn it. But according to the committee's chair, Obama had immediately and dramatically changed the world's perception of the United States, and this change alone merited the prize. George W. Bush had been hated because he was seen as an imperialist bully. Obama was being celebrated because he signaled that he would not be an imperialist bully.

From the Nobel Prize committee to the bars of Singapore and São Paolo, what was being unintentionally acknowledged was the uniqueness of the American presidency itself, as well as a new reality that Americans are reluctant to admit. The new American regime mattered so much to the Norwegians and to the Belgians and to the Poles and to the Chileans and to the billions of other people around the globe because the American president is now in the sometimes awkward (and never explicitly stated) role of global emperor, a reality that the world—and the president—will struggle with in the decade to come.

THE AMERICAN EMPEROR

The American president's unique status and influence are not derived from conquest, design, or divine ordination but ipso facto are the result of the United States being the only global military power in the world. The U.S. economy is also more than three times the size of the next largest sovereign economy. These realities give the United States power that is disproportionate to its population, to its size, or, for that matter, to what many might consider just or prudent. But the United States didn't intend to become an empire. This unintentional arrangement was a consequence of events, few of them under American control.

Certainly there was talk of empire before this. Between Manifest Destiny and the Spanish American War, the nineteenth century was filled with visions of empire that were remarkably modest compared to what has emerged. The empire I am talking about has little to do with those earlier thoughts. Indeed, my argument is that the latest version emerged without planning or intention.

From World War II through the end of the Cold War, the United States inched toward this preeminence, but preeminence did not arrive until 1991, when the Soviet Union collapsed, leaving the U.S. alone as a colossus without a counterweight.

In 1796, Washington made his farewell address and announced this principle: "The great rule of conduct for us in regard to foreign nations is in extending our commercial relations, to have with them as little political connection as possible." The United States had the option of standing apart from the world at that time. It was a small country, geographically isolated. Today, no matter how much the rest of the world might wish us to be less intrusive or how tempting the prospect might seem to Americans, it is simply impossible for a nation whose economy is so vast to have commercial relations without political entanglements or consequences. Washington's anti-political impulse befitted the anti-imperialist founder of the republic. Ironically, the extraordinary success of that republic made this vision impossible.

The American economy is like a whirlpool, drawing everything into its vortex, with imperceptible eddies that can devastate small countries or enrich them. When the U.S. economy is doing well, it is the engine driving the whole machine; when it sputters, the entire machine can break down. There is no single economy that affects the world as deeply or ties it together as effectively.

When we look at the world from the standpoint of exports and imports, it is striking how many countries depend on the United States for 5 or even 10 percent of their Gross Domestic Product, a tremendous amount of interdependence. While there are bilateral economic relations and even multilateral ones that do not include the United States, there are none that are unaffected by the United States. Everyone watches and waits to see what the United States will do. Everyone tries to shape American behavior, at least a little bit, in order to gain some advantage or avoid some disadvantage.

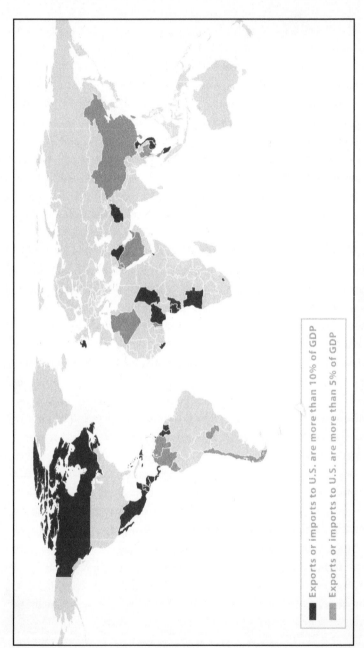

Major American Trade Relations

Historically, this degree of interdependence has bred friction and even war. In the nineteenth and early twentieth centuries, France and Germany feared each other's power, so each tried to shape the other's behavior. The result was that the two countries went to war with each other three times in seventy years. Prior to World War I, the English journalist (later a member of Parliament) Norman Angell wrote a widely read book called *The Great Illusion,* in which he demonstrated the high degree of economic interdependence in Europe and asserted that this made war impossible. Obviously, the two World Wars proved that that wasn't the case. Advocates for free trade continue to use this argument. Yet, as we will see, a high degree of global interdependence, with the United States at the center, actually increases—rather than diminishes—the danger of war.

That the world is no longer filled with relatively equal powers easily tempted into military adventures mitigates this danger somewhat. Certainly the dominance of American military power is such that no one country can hope to use main force to fundamentally redefine its relationship with the United States. At the same time, however, we can see that resistance to American power is substantial and that wars have been frequent since 1991.

While America's imperial power might degrade, power of this magnitude does not collapse quickly except through war. German, Japanese, French, and British power declined not because of debt but because of wars that devastated those countries' economies, producing debt as one of war's many by-products. The Great Depression, which swept the world in the 1920s and 1930s, had its roots in the devastation of the German economy as a result of World War I and the disruption of trade and financial relations that ultimately spread to encompass the world. Conversely, the great prosperity of the American alliance after 1950 resulted from the economic power that the United States built up—undamaged—during World War II.

Absent a major, devastating war, any realignment of international influence based on economics will be a process that takes generations, if it happens at all. China is said to be the coming power. Perhaps so. But the U.S. economy is 3.3 times larger than China's. China must sustain an extraordinarily high growth rate for a long time in order to close its gap with the United States. In 2009, the United States accounted for 22.5 percent of all foreign direct investment in the world, which, according to the United Nations Council on Trade and Development, makes it the world's single largest source of investment. China, by comparison, accounted for 4.4 percent.

The United States also may well be the largest borrower in the world, but that indebtedness does not reduce its ability to affect the international system. Whether it stops borrowing, increases borrowing, or decreases it, the American economy constantly shapes global markets. It is the power to shape that is important. Of course, it should also be remembered that every dollar the United States borrows, others lend. If the market is to be trusted, it is saying that lending to the United States, even at currently low interest rates, is a good move.

Many countries have impacts on other countries. What makes the United States an empire is the number of countries it affects, the intensity of the impact, and the number of people in those countries affected by these economic processes and decisions.

In recent years, for instance, Americans had a rising appetite for shrimp. This ripple in the U.S. market caused fish farmers in the Mekong Delta to adjust their production to meet the new demand. When the American economy declined in 2008, luxury foods like shrimp were the first to be cut back, a retrenchment that was felt as far away as those fish farms in the Mekong Delta. Following a similar pattern, the computer maker Dell built a large facility in Ireland, but when labor costs rose there, Dell shifted operations to Poland, even at a time when Ireland was under severe economic pressure. The United States is similarly shaped by other countries, as were Britain and Rome. But the United States is at the center of the web, not on the periphery, and its economy is augmented by its military. Add to that the technological advantage and we can see the structure of America's deep power.

Empires can be formal, with a clear structure of authority, but some can be more subtle and complex. The British controlled Egypt, but

Britain's formal power was less than clear. The United States has the global reach to shape the course of many other countries, but because it refuses to think of itself as an imperial power, it has not created a formal, rational structure for managing the power that it clearly has.

The fact that the United States has faced reverses in the Middle East in no way undermines the argument that it is an empire, albeit an immature one. Failure and empire are not incompatible, and in the course of imperial growth and expansion, disasters are not infrequent. Britain lost most of its North American colonies to rebellion a century before the empire reached its apex. The Romans faced civil wars in recurring cycles.

While the core of U.S. power is economic—battered though it might seem at the moment—standing behind that economic power is its military might. The purpose of the American military is to prevent any nation aggrieved by U.S. economic influence, or any coalition of such nations, from using force to redress the conditions that put it (or them) at a disadvantage. Like Rome's legions, American troops are deployed preemptively around the world, simply because the most efficient way to use military power is to disrupt emerging powers before they can become even marginally threatening.

The map below, in fact, substantially understates the American military presence. It does not, for instance, track U.S. Special Operations teams operating covertly in many regions, notably Africa. Nor does it include training missions, technical support, and similar functions. Some U.S. troops are fighting wars, some are interdicting drugs, some are protecting their host countries from potential attacks, and some are using their host countries as staging areas in case American troops are needed in another country nearby. In some cases these troops help support Americans who are involved in governing the country, directly or indirectly. In other cases, the troops are simply present, without controlling anything. Troops based in the United States are here not to protect the homeland as much as to be available for what the military calls power projection. This means that they are ready to serve anywhere the president sees fit to deploy them.

As befits a global empire, the United States aligns its economic sys-

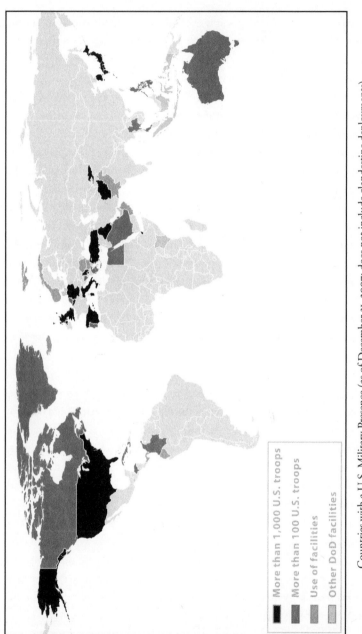

Countries with a U.S. Military Presence (as of December 31, 2007; does not include clandestine deployments)

Sources: Department of Defense, International Institute of Strategic Studies, STRATFOR

■ More than 1,000 U.S. troops

■ More than 100 U.S. troops

■ Use of facilities

■ Other DoD facilities

tem and its military system to stand as the guarantor of the global economy. The United States simultaneously provides technologies and other goods and services to buy, an enormous market into which to sell, and armed forces to keep the sea-lanes open. If need be, it moves in to police unruly areas, but it does this not for the benefit of other countries but for itself. Ultimately, the power of the American economy and the distribution of American military force make alignment with the United States a necessity for many countries. It is this necessity that binds countries to the United States more tightly than any formal imperial system could hope to accomplish.

Empires, the unintended consequence of power accumulated for ends far removed from dreams of empire, are usually recognized long after they have emerged. As they become self-aware, they use their momentum to consciously expand, adding an ideology of imperialism—think of Pax Romana or the British "white man's burden"—to empire's reality. An empire gets writers like Virgil and poets like Rudyard Kipling *after* it is well established, not before. And, as in both Rome and Britain, the celebrants of American empire coexist with those who are appalled by it and who yearn for the earlier, more authentic days.

Rome and Britain were trapped in the world of empire but learned to celebrate the trap. The United States is still at the point where it refuses to see the empire that it has become, and whenever it senses the trappings of empire, it is repelled. But the time has come to acknowledge that the president of the United States manages an empire of unprecedented power and influence, even while it may be informal and undocumented. Only then can we formulate policies over the next decade that will allow us to properly manage the world we find ourselves in charge of.

MANAGING THE IMPERIAL REALITY

Over the past twenty years, the United States has struggled to come to grips with the reverberations of being "last man standing" after the fall of the Soviet Union. The task of the president in the next decade is to move from being reactive to having a systematic method of managing the world that he dominates, a method that faces honestly and without flinching the realities of how the world operates. This means turning the American empire from undocumented disorder into an orderly system, a Pax Americana—not because this is the president's free choice, but precisely because he has no choice.

Bringing order to empire is a necessity because even though the United States is overwhelmingly powerful, it is far from omnipotent, and having singular power creates singular dangers. The United States was attacked on September 11, 2001, for example, precisely because of its unique power. The president's task is to manage that kind of power in a way that acknowledges the risks as well as the opportunities, then minimizes the risks and maximizes the benefits.

For those who are made squeamish by any talk of empire, much less talk of bringing order to imperial control, I would point out that the realities of geopolitics do not give presidents the luxury of exercising virtue in the way we think of it when applied to ordinary citizens. Two presidents who attempted to pursue virtue directly, Jimmy Carter and George W. Bush, failed spectacularly. Conversely, other presidents, such as Richard Nixon and John F. Kennedy, who were much more ruthless, failed because their actions were not directed at and unified by any overriding moral purpose.

In bringing order to empire, I propose that future presidents follow the example of three of our most strikingly effective leaders, men who managed to be utterly ruthless in executing a strategy that was nonetheless guided by moral principle. In these cases, moral ends did in fact justify means that were not only immoral but unconstitutional.

Abraham Lincoln preserved the Union and abolished slavery by initiating a concerted program of deception and by trampling on civil liberties. To maintain the loyalty of the border states, he never owned up to his intention to abolish slavery made clear in the great debates of 1858. Instead he dissembled, claiming that while he opposed the spread of slavery beyond the South, he had no intention of abolishing the right to own slaves in states where owning them was already legal.

But Lincoln did more than prevaricate. He suspended the right to habeas corpus throughout the country and authorized the arrest of pro-secession legislators in Maryland. He made no attempt to justify these actions, except to say that if Maryland and the other border states seceded, the war would be lost and the nation would be dismembered, leaving the Constitution meaningless.

Seventy-five years later, in the midst of another grave crisis for the nation, Franklin Roosevelt also did what needed to be done while lying to hide his actions from a public that was not yet ready to follow his lead. In the late 1930s, Congress and the public wanted to maintain strict neutrality as Europe prepared for war, but Roosevelt understood that the survival of democracy itself was at stake. He secretly arranged for the sale of arms to the French and made a commitment to Winston Churchill to use the U.S. Navy to protect merchant ships taking supplies to England—a clear violation of neutrality.

Like Lincoln, Roosevelt was motivated by moral purpose, which meant a moral vision for global strategy. He was offended by Nazi Germany, and he was dedicated to the concept of democracy. Yet to preserve American interests and institutions, he formed an alliance with Stalin's Soviet Union, a regime that in moral terms was every bit as depraved as the Nazis. At home he defied a Supreme Court ruling and authorized wiretapping without warrants as well as the interception and opening of mail. Yet his most egregious violation of civil liberties was to approve the detention and relocation of ethnic Japanese, regardless of their citizenship status. Roosevelt had no illusions about what he was doing. He was ruthlessly violating rules of decency in pursuit of moral necessity.

Ronald Reagan also pursued a ruthless path toward a moral purpose. His goal was destruction of what he called the evil empire of the Soviet Union, and he pursued it—in part by ramping up the arms race, which he knew the Soviets could not afford. He then went to elaborate and devious lengths to block Soviet support for national liberation movements in the Third World. He invaded Grenada in 1983 and supported insurgents fighting the Marxist government of Nicaragua. This led to the elaborate ruse of engaging Israel to sell arms to Iran in its war with Iraq and then funneling the profits to the Nicaraguan insurgents, as a way of bypassing a law specifically designed to prevent such intervention. We should also remember Reagan's active support for Muslim jihadists in Afghanistan fighting the Soviets. As with Roosevelt and Stalin, a future enemy can be useful to defeat a current one.

The decade ahead will not be a time of great moral crusades. Instead, it will be an era of process, a time in which the realities of the world as presented by facts on the ground will be incorporated more formally into our institutions.

During the past decade, the United States has waged a passionate crusade against terrorism. In the next decade, the need will be for less passion and for more meticulous adjustments in relations with countries such as Israel and Iran. The time also calls for the creation of alliance systems to include nations such as Poland and Turkey that have newly defined relations with the United States. This is the hard and detailed work of imperial strategy. Yet the president cannot afford the illusion that the world will simply accept the reality of overwhelming American hegemony, any more than he can afford to abandon the power. He can never forget that despite his quasi-imperial status, he is president of one country and not of the world.

That is why the one word he must never use is *empire*. The anti-imperial ethos of America's founding continues to undergird the country's political culture. Moreover, the pretense that power is distributed more evenly is useful, not just for other countries but for the United States as well. Even so, in the decade ahead, the informal reality of America's global empire must start to take on coherent form.

Because a president must not force the public to confront directly realities that it isn't ready to confront, he must become a master at managing illusions. Slavery could not have survived much beyond the 1860s, no matter how much the South wanted it to. World War II could not have been avoided, regardless of public leanings toward isolationism. Confrontation with the Soviet Union had to take place, even if the public was frightened by those crises. In each case, a strong president created a fabric of illusions to enable him to do what was necessary without causing a huge revolt from the public. In Reagan's case, when his weapons-dealing machinations came to light as "the Iran-contra affair," complete with congressional hearings and indictments and convictions for many of the participants, his well-maintained persona as a simpleminded fellow shielded his power and his image from the fallout. The goings-on in Israel, Iran, and Nicaragua were so complex that even his critics had trouble believing that he could have been responsible.

A GLOBAL STRATEGY OF REGIONS

America's fundamental interests are the physical security of the United States and a relatively untrammeled international economic system. As we will see when we turn to the current state of the world economy, this by no means implies a free trade regime in the sense that free-market ideologues might think of it. It simply means an international system that permits the vast American economy to interact with most, if not all, of the world. Whatever the regulatory regime might be, the United States needs to buy and sell, lend and borrow, be invested in and invest, with a global reach.

One quarter of the world's economy can't flourish in isolation, nor can the consequences of interaction be confined to pure economics. The American economy is built on technological and organizational innovation, up to and including what the economist Joseph A. Schumpeter called "creative destruction": the process by which the economy continually destroys and rebuilds itself, largely through the advance of disruptive technologies.

When American economic culture touches other countries, those affected have the choice of adapting or being submerged. Computers, for example, along with the companies organized around them, have had profoundly disruptive consequences on cultural life throughout the world, from Bangalore to Ireland. American culture is comfortable with this kind of flux, whereas other cultures may not be. China has taken on the additional burden of trying to adapt to a market economy while retaining the political institutions of a Communist state. Germany and France have struggled to limit the American impact, to insulate themselves from what they call "Anglo-Saxon economics." The Russians reeled from their first unbuffered exposure to this force in the 1990s and sought to find their balance in the following decade.

In response to the American whirlpool, the world's attitude, not surprisingly, is often sullen and resistant, as countries try to take advantage of or evade the consequences. President Obama sensed this resistance and capitalized on it. Domestically, he addressed the American need to be admired and liked, while overseas he addressed the need for the United States to be more conciliatory and less overbearing.

While Obama identified the problem and tried to manage it, resistance to imperial power remains a problem without a permanent solution. This is because ultimately it derives not from the policies of the United States but from the inherent nature of imperial power.

The United States has been in this position of near hegemonic power for only twenty years. The first decade of this imperial period was a giddy fantasy in which the end of the Cold War was assumed to mean the end of war itself—a delusion that surfaces at the end of every major conflict. The first years of the new century were the decade in which the American people discovered that this was still a dangerous planet and the American president led a frantic effort to produce an ad hoc response. The years from 2011 to 2021 will be the decade in which the United States begins to learn how to manage the world's hostility.

Presidents in the coming decade must craft a strategy that acknowledges that the threats that resurfaced in the past ten years were not an aberration. Al Qaeda and terrorism were one such threat, but it was actually not the most serious threat that the United States faced. The president can and should speak of foreseeing an era in which these threats don't exist, but he must not believe his own rhetoric. To the contrary, he must gradually ease the country away from the idea that threats to imperial power will ever subside, then lead it to an understanding that these threats are the price Americans pay for the wealth and power they hold.

All the same, he must plan and execute the strategy without necessarily admitting that it is there.

Facing no rival for global hegemony, the president must think of the world in terms of distinct regions, and in doing so set about creating regional balances of power, along with coalition partners and contingency plans for intervention. The strategic goal must be to prevent the emergence of any power that can challenge the United States in any given corner of the world.

Whereas Roosevelt and Reagan had the luxury of playing a single integrated global hand—vast but unitary—presidents in the decade ahead will be playing multiple hands at a highly fragmented table. The time when everything revolved around one or a few global threats is over. The balance of power in Europe is not intimately connected to that of Asia and is distinct from the balance of power that maintains the peace in Latin America. So even if the world isn't as dangerous to the United States as it was during World War II or the Cold War, it is far more complicated.

American foreign policy has already fragmented regionally, of course, as reflected in the series of regional commands under which our military forces are organized. Now it is necessary to openly recognize the same fragmentation in our strategic thinking and deal with it accordingly. We must recognize that there is no global alliance supporting the United States and that the U.S. has no special historical relationships with anyone. Another quote from Washington's farewell address is useful here: "The nation which indulges towards another a habitual hatred or a habitual fondness is in some degree a slave. It is a slave to its animosity or to its affection, either of which is sufficient to lead it astray from its duty and its interest." This means that NATO no longer has unique meaning for the United States outside of the European context and that Europe cannot be regarded as more important than any other part of the world. Nostalgia for "the special relationship" notwithstanding, the simple reality today is that Europe is not more important.

Even so, President Obama ran a campaign focused on the Europeans.

His travels before the 2008 election symbolized that what he meant by multilateralism was recommitting the United States to Europe, consulting Europe on U.S. actions abroad, and accepting Europe's cautions (now that they have lost their empires, Europeans always speak in terms of caution). Obama's gestures succeeded. The Europeans were wildly enthusiastic, and many Americans were pleased to be liked again. Of course, the enthusiasm dissipated rapidly as the Europeans discovered that Obama was an American president after all, pursuing American ends.

All of which brings us to the president's challenge in the decade ahead: to conduct a ruthless, unsentimental foreign policy in a nation that still has unreasonable fantasies of being loved, or at least of being left alone. He must play to the public's sentimentality while moving policy beyond it.

An unsentimental foreign policy means that in the coming decade, the president must identify with a clear and cold eye the most dangerous enemies, then create coalitions to manage them. This unsentimental approach means breaking free of the entire Cold War system of alliances and institutions, including NATO, the International Monetary Fund, and the United Nations. These Cold War relics are all insufficiently flexible to deal with the diversity of today's world, which redefined itself in 1991, making the old institutions obsolete. Some may have continuing value, but only in the context of new institutions that must emerge. These need to be regional, serving the strategic interests of the United States under the following three principles:

1. To the extent possible, to enable the balance of power in the world and in each region to consume energies and divert threats from the United States.
2. To create alliances in which the United States maneuvers other countries into bearing the major burden of confrontation or conflict, supporting these countries with economic benefits, military technology, and promises of military intervention if required.

3. To use military intervention only as a last resort, when the balance of power breaks down and allies can no longer cope with the problem.

At the height of the British Empire, Lord Palmerston said, "It is a narrow policy to suppose that this country or that is to be marked out as the eternal ally or the perpetual enemy of England. We have no eternal allies, and we have no perpetual enemies. Our interests are eternal and perpetual, and those interests it is our duty to follow." This is the kind of policy the president will need to institutionalize in the coming decade. Recognizing that the United States will generate resentment or hostility, he must harbor no illusions that he can simply persuade other nations to think better of us without surrendering interests that are essential to the United States. He must try to seduce these nations as much as possible with glittering promises, but in the end he must accept that efforts at seduction will eventually fail. Where he cannot fail is in his responsibility to guide the United States in a hostile world.

CHAPTER 2

REPUBLIC, EMPIRE, AND THE MACHIAVELLIAN PRESIDENT

The greatest challenge to managing an empire over the next decade will be the same challenge that Rome faced: having become an empire, how can the republic be preserved? The founders of the United States were anti-imperialists by moral conviction. They pledged their lives, fortunes, and sacred honor to defeat the British Empire and found a republic based on the principles of national self-determination and natural rights. An imperial relationship with other countries, whether intended or not, poses a challenge to those foundational principles.

If you believe that universal principles have meaning, it follows that an anti-imperial republic can't be an empire and retain its moral character. This has been an argument made in the United States as far back as the 1840s and the Mexican-American war. Today both ends of the political spectrum make the argument against foreign adventures. On the left, there is a long tradition of anti-imperialism. But if you look at some of the rhetoric emanating from the right, from libertarians as well as from some in the Tea Party, you see the same opposition to military involvement in other countries. The fear is linked to Dwight Eisenhower's warning to beware of the "military-industrial complex." If a career military officer and war hero such as Ike could voice this fear, you can see how deeply embedded it is in American political culture. I suspect that this will become a powerful strand in American politics over the next ten years, in a country where, across the political spectrum, the citizenry is weary of foreign involvement.

The fear of imperial ambition is completely justified. The Roman Republic was overwhelmed by empire. Empire created an ambition for money and power that devastated the republican virtues that were the greatest pride of Roman citizenship. Even if that pride wasn't fully justified, there is no question but that the Republic was destroyed not just by military rivalries that led to a coup d'état but by the vast amounts of money flowing into the imperial capital from citizens and foreigners trying to buy favor.

The same danger exists for the United States. American global power generates constant threats and ever greater temptations. It has been observed that ever since World War II, the United States has created a national security apparatus so shrouded in official secrecy that it cannot be easily overseen or even understood. This hugely expensive and cumbersome apparatus, along with the vast amounts of foreign economic activity—from immense trade to the foreign investments that drive global markets—creates a system that is not readily managed by democratic institutions and that is not always easily reconciled with American moral principles. It is not unimaginable that together these forces could render American democracy meaningless.

The problem is that like Rome in the time of Caesar, the United States has reached a point where it doesn't have a choice as to whether to have an empire or not. The vastness of the American economy, its entanglement in countries around the world, the power and worldwide presence of the American military, are in effect imperial in scope. Disentangling the United States from this global system is almost impossible, and if it were attempted, it would destabilize not only the American economy but the global system as well. When the price of anti-imperialism was understood, there would be scant support for it. Indeed, many foreign countries are less opposed to the American presence than they are to the way in which that presence is felt. They accept American power; they simply want it to serve their own national interests.

The dangers of imperial power are substantial, and these dangers will become increasingly contentious issues in American politics, just as they are already hotly debated around the world. In retrospect, the non-interventionism of the republic the founders created was rooted in the fact that the republic was weak, not that it was virtuous. The United States of thirteen former colonies could not engage in foreign entanglements without being crushed. The United States of 300 million people cannot avoid foreign entanglements.

Managing the unintended empire while retaining the virtues of the republic will be an important priority of the United States for a very long time, but certainly, in the wake of the jihadist wars, it will be a particularly intense challenge. Most of the discussion will be wishful thinking. There is no going back, and there are no neat solutions. The paradox is that the best chance of retaining the republic is not institutional but personal, and it will depend on a definition of virtue that violates our common notions of what virtue is. I don't look to the balance of power to save the republic, but to the cunning and wisdom of the president. The president certainly has a vast bureaucracy that he controls, and that controls him, but in the end it is the Lincolns, Roosevelts, and Reagans we remember, not bureaucrats or senators or justices. The reason is simple. Along with power, presidents exercise leadership. That leadership can be decisive, in the context of a decade or less.

Individual personalities would seem to be a thin reed on which to base a country's future. At the same time, the founders created the office of the president for a reason, and at the heart of that reason was leadership. The presidency is unique in that it is the only structure in which an institution and an individual are identical. Congress and the Supreme Court are aggregations of people who will rarely speak with a single voice. The presidency is the president alone, the only official elected by representatives of all the people. That is why we need to consider him as the primary agent for managing the relationship between empire and republic.

Let's begin by considering the character of presidents in general. Presidents differ from many other people in that they, by definition, take pleasure in power. They place its acquisition and use before other things, and they devote a good portion of their lives to its pursuit. A president's knowledge and instincts are so finely honed toward power that he understands it in ways that those of us who have never truly had it could not appreciate. The worst president is closer by nature to the best than either is to anyone who has not gone through what it requires to become president.

The degree and scope of the power that modern American presidents achieve inevitably make them see the world differently, even in comparison with other heads of state. No other leader must confront so much of the world in so many different ways. In our democracy, the president must achieve this position while pretending to be indistinguishable from his fellow citizens, a thought both impossible to imagine and frightening if true. The danger is that as the challenges of empire become greater and the potential threats more real, leaders will emerge who will need and demand a degree of power that slips beyond the constraints imposed by the Constitution.

It is both fortunate and ironic that in creating an anti-imperial government, the founders provided a possible road map for imperial leadership with republican constraints. They created the American presidency as an alternative both to dictatorship and to aristocracy, an executive that is weak at home but immensely powerful outside the United States. In domestic affairs, the Constitution dictates an executive that is hemmed in by an inherently unmanageable Congress and by a Supreme Court that is fairly inscrutable. The economy is in the hands of investors, managers, and consumers, as well as those of the Federal Reserve Bank (if not by the Constitution, then certainly by legislation and practice). The states hold substantial power, and much of civil society—religion, the press, pop culture, the arts—is beyond the president's control. This is exactly what the founders wanted: someone to preside over the country but not to rule it. Yet when the United States faces the world through its foreign policy, there is no more powerful individual than the occupant of the White House.

Article Two, Section Two, of the Constitution states, "The President shall be Commander in Chief of the Army and Navy of the United States, and of the Militia of the several States, when called into the actual Service of the United States." This is the only power given to the president that he does not share with Congress. Treaties, appointments, the budget, and the actual declaration of war require congressional approval, but the command of the military is the president's alone.

Yet over the years, the constitutional limitations that reined in the diplomatic prerogatives of earlier presidents have fallen by the wayside. Treaties require the approval of the Senate, but today treaties are rare and foreign policy is conducted with agreements and understandings, many arrived at secretly. Thus the conduct of foreign policy as a whole is now effectively in the hands of the president. Similarly, while Congress has declared war only five times, presidents have sent U.S. forces into conflicts around the world many more times than that. The reality of the American regime in the second decade of the twenty-first century is that the president's power on the world stage is almost beyond checks and balances, limited only by his skill in exercising that power.

When President Clinton decided to bomb Yugoslavia in 1999 and when President Reagan decided to invade Grenada in 1983, Congress could not stop them had it wished to. American presidents impose sanctions on nations and shape economic relations throughout the world. In practical terms, this means that an American president has the power to devastate a country that displeases him or reward a country that he favors. Legislation on war powers has been passed, but many presidents have claimed that they have the inherent right as commander in chief to wage war regardless of it. In practice, they have brought Congress along to support their policies. That is unlikely to change in the next decade.

It is in the exercise of foreign policy that the American president most resembles Machiavelli's prince, which isn't that surprising when you consider that the founders were students of modern political philosophy and that Machiavelli was its originator. Just as we must acknowledge the existence of an American empire, we must acknowledge the value of his insights and advice for our own situation. That the president's main concern is foreign policy and the exercise of power conforms to Machiavelli's teaching:

> A prince, therefore, must not have any other object or any other thought, nor must he adopt anything as his art but war, its institutions and its discipline; because that is the only art befitting one who commands. This discipline is of such efficacy that not only does it maintain those who were born princes but it enables men of private station on many occasions to rise to that position. On the other hand, it is evident that when princes have given more thought to delicate refinements than to military concerns, they have lost their state. The most important reason why you lose it is by neglecting this art, while the way to acquire it is to be well versed in this art.

The fundamental distinction in U.S. foreign policy, and in the exercise of power by U.S. presidents—the distinction discussed by Machiavelli—is between idealism and realism, a distinction embedded in the tradition of U.S. foreign policy. The United States was founded on the principle of national self-determination, which assumes a democratic process for selecting leaders, reflected in the Constitution. It was also built on principles of human freedom, enshrined in the Bill of Rights. Imperialism would seem to undermine the principle of self-determination, whether formally or informally. Moreover, the conduct of foreign policy supports regimes that are in the national interest but that don't practice or admire American principles of human rights. Reconciling American foreign policy with American principles is difficult, and represents a threat to the moral foundations of the regime.

The idealist position argues that the United States must act on the moral principles derived from the founders' elegantly stated intentions. The United States is seen as a moral project stemming from the Enlightenment ideals of John Locke and others, and the goal of American foreign policy should be to apply these moral principles to American actions and, more important, American ends. Following from this, the United States should support only those regimes that embrace American values, and it should oppose regimes that oppose those values.

The realist school argues that the United States is a nation like any other, and that as such it must protect its national interests. These interests include the security of the United States, the pursuit of its economic advantage, and support for regimes that are useful to those ends, regardless of those regimes' moral character. Under this theory, American foreign policy should be no more and no less moral than the policy of any other nation.

The idealists argue that to deny America's uniquely moral imperative not only betrays American ideals but betrays the entire vision of American history. The realists argue that we live in a dangerous world and that by focusing on moral goals we will divert attention from pursuit of our genuine interests, thereby endangering the very existence of the republic that is the embodiment of American ideals. It is important to bear in mind that idealism as a basis for American politics transcends ideologies. The left-wing variant is built around human rights and the prevention of war. The right-wing version is built around a neoconservative desire to spread American values and democracies. What these two visions have in common is the idea that American foreign policy should be primarily focused on moral principles.

In my view, the debate between realism and idealism fundamentally misstates the problem, and this misstatement will play a critical role in the next decade. Either it will be resolved or the imbalance within U.S. foreign policy will become ever more evident. The idealist argument constantly founders on a prior debate between the right of national self-determination and human rights. The American Revolution was built on both principles, but now, more than two centuries later, what do you do when a country such as Germany determines through constitutional processes to abrogate human rights? Which takes precedence, the right to national self-determination or human rights? What do you do with regimes that do not hold elections like those in the United States but that clearly embody the will of the people based on long-standing cultural practice? Saudi Arabia is a prime example. How can the United States espouse multiculturalism and then demand that other people select their leaders the way people do in Iowa?

The realist position is equally contradictory. It assumes that the national interest of a twenty-first-century empire is as obvious as that of a small eighteenth-century republic clinging to the eastern seaboard of North America. Small, weak nations have clear-cut definitions of the national interest—which is primarily to survive with as much safety and prosperity as possible. But for a country as safe and prosperous as the United States—and with an unprecedented imperial reach—the definition of the national interest is much more complicated. The realist theory assumes that there is less room for choice in the near term than there is, and that the danger is always equally great. The concept of realism cannot be argued with as an abstract proposition—who wants to be unrealistic? Coming up with a precise definition of what reality consists of is a much more complex matter. In the sixteenth century, Machiavelli wrote, "The main foundations of every state, new states as well as ancient or composite ones, are good laws and good arms. You cannot have good laws without good arms, and where there are good arms, good laws inevitably follow." This is a better definition of realism than the realists have given us.

I believe that the debate between realists and idealists is in fact a naive reading of the world that has held too much sway in recent decades. Ideals and reality are different sides of the same thing: power. Power as an end in itself is a monstrosity that does not achieve anything lasting and will inevitably deform the American regime. Ideals without power are simply words—they can come alive only when reinforced by the capacity to act. Reality is understanding how to wield power, but by itself it doesn't guide you toward the ends to which your power should be put. Realism devoid of an understanding of the ends of power is frequently another word for thugishness, which is ultimately unrealistic. Similarly, idealism is frequently another word for self-righteousness, a disease that can be corrected only by a profound understanding of power in its complete sense, while realism uncoupled from principle is frequently incompetence masquerading as tough-mindedness. Realism and idealism are not alternatives but necessary complements. Neither can serve as a principle for foreign policy by itself.

Idealism and realism resolve themselves into contests of power, and contests of power turn into war. To turn once again to Machiavelli: "War should be the only study of a prince. He should consider peace only as a breathing-time, which gives him leisure to contrive, and furnishes an ability to execute, military plans."

In the twentieth century, the United States was engaged in war 17 percent of the time—and these were not minor interventions but major wars, involving hundreds of thousands of men. In the twenty-first century, we have been engaged in war almost 100 percent of the time. The founders made the president commander in chief for a reason: they had read Machiavelli carefully and they knew that, as he wrote, "there is no avoiding war; it can only be postponed to the advantage of others."

The greatest virtue a president can have is to understand power. Presidents are not philosophers, and the exercise of power is an applied, not an abstract, art. Trying to be virtuous will bring not only the president to grief but the country as well. During war, understanding power means that crushing the enemy quickly and thoroughly is kinder than either extending the war through scruples or losing the war through sentimentality. This is why conventional virtue, the virtue of what we might call the good person, is unacceptable in a president. Again as Machiavelli put it, "The fact is that a man who wants to act virtuously in every way necessarily comes to grief among so many who are not virtuous."

Machiavelli introduces a new definition of virtue, which instead of personal goodness consists of being cunning. For princes, virtue is the ability to overcome fortune. The world is what it is, and as such, it is unpredictable and fickle, and the prince must use his powers to overcome the surprises the world will present. His task is to protect the republic from a world full of people who are not virtuous in any conventional sense.

Presidents may run for office on ideological platforms and promised policies, but their presidency is actually defined by the encounter between fortune and virtue, between the improbable and the unexpected—the thing that neither their ideology nor their proposals prepared them for—and their response. The president's job is to anticipate what will happen, minimize the unpredictability, then respond to the unexpected with cunning and power.

From Machiavelli's point of view, ideology is trivial and character is everything. The president's virtue, his insight, his quickness of mind, his cunning, his ruthlessness, and his understanding of the consequences are what matters. Ultimately, his legacy will be determined by his instincts, which in turn reflect his character.

The great presidents never forget the principles of the republic and seek to preserve and enhance them—in the long run—without undermining the needs of the moment. Bad presidents simply do what is expedient, heedless of principles. But the worst presidents are those who adhere to principles regardless of what the fortunes of the moment demand.

The United States cannot make its way in the world by shunning nations with different values and regimes that are brutal, all the while carrying out exclusively noble actions. The pursuit of moral ends requires a willingness to sup with the devil.

I began this chapter by speaking of the tension between the American republic and empire in the decade ahead. Whatever moral scruples we might have about being an empire, this is the role history has cast us in. If the danger in becoming an empire is that we lose the republic, certainly the realist view of foreign policy would take us there, if not intentionally, then simply through indifference to moral issues. At the same time, idealists would bring down the republic by endangering the nation, not through intent but through hostility or indifference to power. Of course, the fall of the republic won't occur in the next decade. But the decisions made during the next decade will profoundly affect the long-term outcome.

Over the next decade, the president won't have the luxury of ignoring either ideals or reality. Instead he must choose the uncomfortable synthesis of the two that Machiavelli recommended. The president must focus not only on the accumulation and use of power but on its limits. A good regime backed by power and leaders who understand the virtue both of the regime and of power is what is required. This is not a neat ideological package that explains and reduces everything to simplistic formulas. Rather, it is an existential stance toward politics that affirms moral truths in politics without becoming their simpleminded prisoner, and that uses power without worshipping it.

In preventing the unintended empire from destroying the republic, the critical factor will not be the balance of power among the branches of government, but rather a president who is committed to that constitutional balance, yet willing to wield power in his own right. In order to do this, the president must grasp the insufficiency of both the idealist and the realist positions. The idealists, whether of the neoconservative or the liberal flavor, don't understand that it is necessary to master the nature of power in order to act according to moral principles. The realists don't understand the futility of power without a moral core.

Machiavelli writes that "the one who adapts his policy to the times prospers, and likewise that the one whose policy clashes with the demands of the times does not." Morality in foreign policy might be eternal, but it must also be applied to the times. Applying it to the next decade will be particularly difficult, as the next decade poses the challenge of the unintended empire.

CHAPTER 3

THE FINANCIAL CRISIS
AND THE RESURGENT STATE

Two global events frame the next decade: President Bush's response to September 11 and the financial panic of 2008. Understanding what happened and why in both cases amplifies our sense of what it means to be an empire and what its price is, especially when we consider how these interrelated events, which began as domestic American concerns, came to engulf the entire world. Let's begin with the financial crisis.

Every business cycle ends in a crash, and one sector usually leads the way. The Clinton boom ended in 2000, when the dot-coms crashed; the Reagan boom of the 1980s ended in spectacular fashion with the collapse of the savings-and-loans. From this perspective, there was nothing at all extraordinary about what happened in 2008.

The reason for such booms and busts is fairly simple. As the economy grows, it generates money, more than the economy can readily consume. When there is a surplus of money chasing assets such as homes, stocks, or bonds, prices rise and interest rates fall. Eventually prices reach irra-

tional levels, and then they collapse. Money becomes scarce, and inefficient businesses are forced to shut down. Efficient businesses survive,
and the cycle starts again. This has been repeated over and over since
modern capitalism arose.

Sometimes the state interferes with this cycle by keeping money
cheap in order to avoid the crash and the recession that inevitably follows. Money is, after all, an artifice invented by the state. The Federal
Reserve Bank can print as much money as it wants, and it can purchase
government debt with it. That's what the Federal Reserve did in the
aftermath of September 11. The Bush administration didn't want to raise
taxes to pay for the war on terror, and the Fed cooperated by financing
the war by, essentially, lending money to the government. The result was
that no one felt the war's economic impact—at least, not right away.

Bush's reasons were derived both from geopolitics and from partisan
domestic politics. He was at war with the jihadists, and he did not want
to raise taxes to pay for his military interventions. Instead, he wanted the
total revenue from taxes to rise by way of a stimulated economy. The theory was that the combination of military spending, tax cuts, and low
interest rates would allow the economy to surge, increasing tax revenues
enough to pay for the war. If this supply-side gambit didn't work, Bush
reasoned, he would still have the benefit of not undermining political
support through tax hikes before the 2004 elections. He also assumed
that he could deal with the economic imbalances after the election, as
the war wound down. His problem was that the war didn't wind down,
and he grossly underestimated how long and intense it would become.
As a result, he and the Fed never got around to cooling off the economy,
and the war and this economic policy continue to define his presidency.

Another element that led to the collapse of 2008 was the cheap
money pouring into one particular segment of the economy, the residential housing market. In part this was an economic calculation. Housing
prices tend to rise over time, which gives real estate the appearance of a
conservative investment. Government programs also encouraged individuals to buy homes, and during this era that encouragement extended

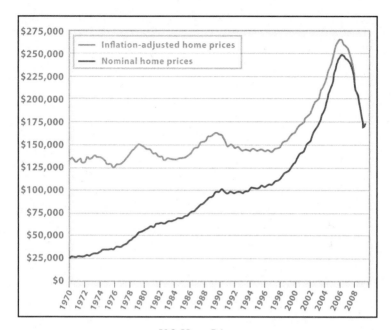

U.S. Home Prices

to a wider segment of the population than ever before. The perception of safety, combined with government policy, brought extraordinary amounts of money into the market, along with speculators and millions of low-income buyers who in ordinary times never would have qualified for the mortgages they took on.

The price of homes had risen for the past generation, but as this chart above shows, that story of steady growth is a bit deceptive. If you adjust home prices for inflation, they have fluctuated in a narrow band between 1970 and 2000. But mortgages don't rise with inflation. So if you borrowed $20,000 to buy a $25,000 house in 1970, by 2000 that house would be worth around $125,000 and you'd have paid off your mortgage. But $125,000 was not much more than $25,000 in real terms. You felt richer because the numbers were higher and because you had paid off your debt, but the truth was that home ownership was not a great way to create actual gains. On the other hand, the record showed that you were not likely to lose money either, and that gave lenders confidence. If worse came to worst, they could always seize the house and sell it, thus getting their money back.

With cheap money enabling more people to buy houses, demand rose, which meant that housing prices took off like a rocket in 2001, then accelerated further after 2004. Lenders kept looking for more and more borrowers for their cheap money, which meant lending to people who were less and less likely to repay these now "subprime" loans. The climax came with the invention of the five-year variable-rate mortgage, which enabled people to buy houses for monthly payments that were frequently lower than rent on an apartment. These rates exploded after five years, but if a buyer could not meet the new payments and lost the house, at least he would have enjoyed some good years and was simply back where he started. If housing prices stayed steady, he could refinance, so all in all, he didn't seem to be taking much of a risk.

Nor did the lenders appear to be risking much, especially given that they made their money on closing costs and other transaction fees, then sold the mortgages (and passed along the risk) to secondary investors in what became known as bundles. In packaging these loans for the secondary market, lenders emphasized the lifetime income stream, which made the subprime loans appear to be the perfect conservative investment.

Everyone was making money and no one could get hurt—it was the oldest story in the book. And most people didn't care or didn't want to believe that the bubble could burst.

However, reality began to intrude. New homeowners who never would have qualified for an ordinary loan in ordinary times began to default, and as properties came on the market from forced sale or foreclosure, prices that had been counted on to keep going up began to fall. During the run-up, small investors had bought multiple houses, fixed them up a bit, and resold them for a quick profit. But as boom turned to bust and speculators were unable to "flip" the houses at profit, they rushed to unload them at whatever price they could, which drove prices further down. By 2007, the mild decline that had begun in 2005 became a rout. In truth, all that happened was that prices returned to the highest level within their prior historic range; the froth was disappearing, but the basic value was still there. Nonetheless, many of the people who had put money into these houses were devastated.

With the collapse of the housing market, the mortgages that had been bundled and sold to investors no longer had a clear value. Because these investors had believed that prices would never fall, they had never looked at what was actually inside their bundles. The more aggressive investors in bundled mortgages, investment banks such as Bear Stearns and Lehman Brothers, had leveraged their positions many times over, and by the time the loan payments were due, the value of the underlying assets was so murky that no one would buy them, or even refinance the loans. Unable to cover their bets, these big players went bankrupt. And since many of the people who had bought these supposedly conservative investments, including the commercial paper issued by the banks, were in other countries, the entire global system went down.

The story of the collapse often focuses on the United States, but the damage was truly worldwide. Residents of eastern Europe—Poland, Hungary, Romania, and other countries—who in normal times had never been able to afford a house had bought in. Austrian and Italian banks in particular, backed with European and Arab money, had wanted to provide mortgages, but interest rates in eastern Europe were high. So the banks offered these new, eager, and unsophisticated buyers loans at much lower rates, only denominated in euros, Swiss francs, and even yen.

The problem was that these homeowners weren't paid in these currencies but in zlotys or forints. A Polish homeowner essentially paid for his mortgage by first buying yen, then paying the bank. The fewer yen a zloty bought, the more zlotys the homeowner had to spend and the more expensive his monthly payment became. If these zlotys rose against the yen or the Swiss franc, there were no problems. But if the zlotys fell against the yen or the Swiss franc, there were huge problems. Every month, more and more eastern Europeans were buying Euros and other currencies. As the financial crisis deepened, there was a flight to safety;

and eastern European currencies plunged. Homeowners were squeezed and broken.

Major expansions always end in financial irrationality, and this irrationality was global. If the Americans went to the limit with subprime mortgages, the Europeans went a step further by enticing homeowners to gamble on global currency markets.

There is a constant refrain that we have not seen such a catastrophic economic event since the Great Depression. That is triply untrue, because similar collapses have happened three other times since World War II. This is a crucial fact in understanding the next decade, because if the financial crisis could be compared only to the Great Depression, then my argument about American power might be difficult to make. But if this kind of crisis has been relatively common since World War II, then its significance declines, and it is more difficult to argue that the 2008 panic represents a huge blow to the United States.

The fact is that such events are common. In the 1970s, for instance, there was a significant threat to the municipal bond market. Bonds issued by states and local governments are especially attractive because they are not subject to federal tax. Such bonds are also considered all but risk-free, the assumption being that government entities will never default on their debts so long as they have the power to tax. In the 1970s, however, New York City couldn't meet debt payments and couldn't or wouldn't raise taxes. If New York defaulted, the entire financing system for state and local government would devolve into chaos, so the federal government bailed out New York, making it clear that Washington was prepared to guarantee the market.

During that same period there was a surge of investment in the Third World, primarily to fund the development of natural resources such as oil and metals. Mineral prices were rising along with everything else in the 1970s, and investors assumed that because minerals are finite and irreplaceable, the prices would never fall. Investors also assumed that loans to the Third World governments that usually controlled these resources were safe, given the perception that sovereign countries never defaulted on debt.

In the mid-1980s, the belief in rising prices and stable governments, like most comfortable assumptions, turned out to be misguided. Mineral and energy prices plunged, and the extraction industries predicated on high prices collapsed. The money invested—much of it injected as loans—was lost. Third World countries, forced to choose between defaulting and raising taxes (which would further impoverish their citizens and trigger uprisings), opted to default, which threatened to swamp the global financial system. This prompted a U.S.-led multinational bailout of Third World debt. Under George Bush, Sr., Secretary of the Treasury Nicholas Brady created a system of guarantees, issuing what were called "Brady bonds" to create stability.

And then came the savings-and-loan crisis. Savings-and-loan institutions, which had been created to take consumer deposits and generate home loans—think Jimmy Stewart in *It's a Wonderful Life*—were given the right to invest in other assets, which led them into the commercial real estate market. This appeared to be only a small step beyond their traditional residential market, and the expansion carried the same "conventional wisdom" guarantee that prices would never fall. In a growing economy, or so it was thought, the price of commercial real estate, from office buildings to malls, could only go up.

Once again, the unimaginable happened. Commercial real estate prices dropped, and many of the loans made by the S and Ls went into default. The size of the problem was vast and cut two ways. First, individual depositor money was at risk on a large scale. Second, the failure of an entire segment of the financial industry, which had resold its commercial mortgages into the broader market, was poised for catastrophe.

The federal government intervened by taking control of failed S and Ls—meaning most S and Ls—and assuming their liabilities. Mortgages in default were foreclosed, and the underlying property was taken over by a newly created institution called the Resolution Trust Corporation. Rather than try to sell all this real estate at once, thereby destroying the market for the next decade, the RTC, backed by federal guarantees that potentially could have risen to about $650 billion, took control of the real estate of failed savings-and-loans.

The crisis of 2008 was based on the same desire for low risk, and on the same assumption that a certain class of assets was indeed low-risk because its price couldn't fall. It was met with a similar federal government intervention to bail out the system, and, just as before, everyone thought it was the end of capitalism. What is important to note is the consistent pattern, including the overstatement of the consequences. To some extent, this is a psychological phenomenon. With pain comes panic, and the management of panic is a question of leadership. Consider how it was managed in the past.

Both Franklin Roosevelt and Ronald Reagan came to power amid economic crises. Roosevelt, of course, faced the Great Depression. Reagan faced the stagflation that overtook the economy in the 1970s—high unemployment combined with high inflation and high interest rates. The economic problems both presidents encountered were part of global economic dislocations, and both posed a profound crisis of confidence in the United States. The crisis in the 1930s prompted Roosevelt's famous line, "We have nothing to fear but fear itself."

Roosevelt and Reagan both understood the psychological element in financial crises. The anticipation of economic hardship causes people to rein in their buying in order to protect themselves. The more they cut back, the worse the economic problems become. As an economic crisis deepens, it calls into question the integrity and leadership of elites, which can create political instability and destabilize society itself. That social uncertainty can in turn make it impossible for a country to act decisively in the world. Roosevelt faced the rise of fascism; Reagan came to power facing what was generally believed to be the growing power of the Soviet Union. Neither could afford the destabilizing consequences of a severe economic crisis, yet neither knew with any certainty how to solve the problem through economic policy. Both attacked the psychology of the problem, trying to create the sense that, most of all, something was being done.

In retrospect, Roosevelt's frantic one hundred days of legislation had little effect on the Depression, which was ended by World War II rather than by his economic policies. Reagan also promised actions, although in the end the solution rested not with the president but with the Federal Reserve. Nonetheless, describing the times as being "Morning in America," a phrase that was part of his 1984 campaign, Reagan, like Roosevelt before him, tried to change the expectations of the public, stabilizing the political situation and buying time for the economy to heal without weakening the state.

Both Roosevelt and Reagan understood that the real threat of an economic crisis would be its political impact, with the misery that piled up wrecking the entire system. They understood that their job as leader was not to solve the problem—the president really has little control over the economy—but to convince the public not only that he has a plan but that he is altogether confident of that plan's success, and that only a cynic or someone indifferent to the public's well-being would dare to question him on the details. This is not an easy thing to pull off; it takes a master politician, which is to say a master of illusion. Roosevelt certainly saved the country from serious instability and, in spite of the lack of recovery, positioned it to fight World War II. Reagan saved the country from the sense of malaise that the Carter administration was known for and set the stage for the reversal of fortunes with the Soviets.

Roosevelt and Reagan did one other thing that was in their power to deal with the crisis. They shifted the boundary between public and private, state and the market. Roosevelt dramatically increased the power of the federal government. Reagan decreased it. The problem they were addressing wasn't the economic crisis itself, but a fundamental political crisis. In the 1929 depression, the financial elite had lost the confidence of the public. They appeared not so much corrupt as incompetent. Under Hoover, they were permitted to play out their hand, but then the situation got worse. Roosevelt intervened, shifting some of the power that had been in the hands of the financial elite to the political elite. Had he not done so, the sense that all the country's elites had failed might have prevailed, a sentiment that led to fascism in places such as Italy and Germany.

The reverse happened under Reagan. In the 1980s, the political elite was perceived to be behind the economic crisis, and the public blamed the structure of "big government" left behind by Roosevelt. Reagan shifted the balance between the state and the market back the other way, weakening the state to strengthen the market.

Part of rebuilding confidence has to do with understanding which part of the elite—political, corporate, financial, media—is to be held responsible for the crisis. By essentially putting one set of elites or another into receivership, transferring their authority in many ways to other elites, Reagan and Roosevelt gave the public the sense that the president was acting decisively and taking power away from those who had failed. This eased the sense that everyone was helpless, and indeed cleared the way for at least some reforms that didn't hurt, might have helped, and certainly were needed symbolically. In the end, the crises worked out both because of the underlying power of the United States and because of the resilience of the modern state and corporation, which cannot live apart, yet have trouble living together.

Neither Bush nor Obama was able to manage the national psyche as Roosevelt and Reagan had. Bush lost control of the war and was blind-sided by the financial crisis. He fell behind the curve after Iraq and never caught up. Obama created expectations he could not fulfill, then failed to create the illusion that he was fulfilling them. But of course Reagan ran into similar problems at first. The issue that is unknown but that will affect the next decade deeply is whether Obama can recover and lead. Can he understand that when Roosevelt spoke about fearing fear, he meant that the president's job is to appear to be effective whether or not he is? If Obama doesn't learn that, the nation will survive. Presidents come and go, but this is a fragile time, with the legitimacy of the presidency and the country itself caught between the demands of republic and empire.

When we talk about shifting the boundaries between corporate and political elites and between the state and the market, this inevitably raises ideological issues. For the left, strengthening the corporate elite and the market threatens democracy and equality. For the right, strengthening the political elite and the state threatens individual freedom and property rights. It is an interesting debate to watch, save that the problem is not moral or philosophical but simply practical. The great distinction that prompts such heated ideological debate just isn't there.

The modern free market is an invention of the state, and its rules are not naturally ordained but simply the outcome of political arrangements. The reason I say this is that the practical foundation of the modern economy is the corporation, and the corporation is a contrivance made possible by the modern state. The corporation is an extraordinary invention. It creates an entity that the law says is liable for the debts of a business. The individuals who own the business, whether a sole proprietorship or a huge publicly held entity, are not held liable for those debts personally. Their exposure can be no greater than their initial investment. In this way, the law and the state shift the risk from the debtors to the creditors. If the business fails, the creditors are left holding the bag. Nothing like this existed before the birth of "chartered companies" in the seventeenth century. Before that time, if you owned a business, you were liable for all of it. Without this innovation, there would be no stock market as we know it, no investment in start-ups, little entrepreneurship.

But this apportionment of risk is a political decision. There is nothing natural in the idea that the boundaries of individual risk are drawn where they are. Indeed, over time, these boundaries shift. The corporation exists only because the law created it. The political decision to create corporations also means that corporate law, not the law of nature, defines the precise boundaries of risk and liability. There may theoretically be some sort of natural market; but a market dominated by limited liability corporations, from the Fortune 500 to the local plumber, is inherently political.

Since 1933 and the New Deal, the issue of corporate risk has been bound up with the issue of social stability. The structure of risk has been built around the social requirements. During the Roosevelt administration, the boundaries of state control expanded. Under Reagan, they contracted.

What the 2008 crisis did around the world was redefine the boundaries between corporations and the state, increasing state power and the power of politicians, reducing market autonomy and the power of the financial elite. This had minimal impact on China and Russia, where the system was already tilted toward the state. It had some effect on Europe, where state power has always been greater than in the United States. It had substantial effect on the United States, where the market and the financial elite had dominated since Reagan. It also kicked off a political brawl between left and right over whether this shift was justified. In the United States in particular, the boundaries are always shifting and the argument is always couched in moral terms. In spite of variations, the strengthening of the state will be one of the defining characteristics of the next decade globally.

Along with helping define the boundary between state and corporate control, presidents and other politicians manage the appearance of things, largely by manipulating fear and hope. What made Roosevelt and Reagan great was not only that they readjusted the boundary of state and market to suit the needs of their historic era, but that they created the atmosphere in which this appeared to be not just a technical operation but a moral necessity. Whether they believed this or not is less important than the fact that they caused others to believe, and through that belief enabled the technical realignment to take place.

The most significant effect of the crisis of 2008 on the next decade will be geopolitical and political, not economic. The financial crisis of 2008 drove home the importance of national sovereignty. A country that did not control its own financial system or currency was deeply vulnerable to the actions of other countries. This awareness made entities such as the European Union no longer seem as benign as they had been. In the next decade, the trend will turn away from limiting economic sovereignty and toward increasing economic nationalism.

A similar effect will take place on the political level. An enormous struggle that we can see in China, Russia, Europe, the United States, and elsewhere has broken out between economic and political elites. Because the failure of the market and the financial elite cost the latter credibility, the first round clearly went to the state and political elites. In some countries, this shift is going to last for a long while. In the United States, the truce that has existed since the Reagan years has broken down and the battle will continue to rage. *Rage* is the proper word, since that has been the tone of the debate. But American politics have always been operatic, with visions of doom a constant undertone. Still, the world finds political uncertainty on such fundamental issues in the United States more than a little unsettling.

Oddly enough, it is on the economic level that the pain of 2008 will have the least enduring effects. It is absurd to compare this downturn to the Great Depression. The GDP fell by almost 50 percent during the Depression. Between 2007 and 2009, the GDP fell by only 4.1 percent. This is not even the worst recession since World War II. That honor goes to the recessions of the 1970s and early 1980s, when we saw the triple hit: unemployment and inflation over 10 percent and interest rates on mortgages over 20 percent.

While the current economic crisis is nothing like that, it is still painful, and Americans have a low tolerance for economic pain. There are even bigger issues on the horizon, beyond this decade, when demographics shift, labor becomes scarce, and the immigration issue will become the dominant matter facing the United States. But that is still a ways off, and it will not be affecting the coming decade. This decade will not be an exuberant one, and it will strain both individual lives and the political system. But it will not change the fundamental world order much, and the United States will remain the dominant power. Ironically, one measure of U.S. dominance is how much a miscalculation by the American financial elite can impact the world, and how much pain American mistakes can inflict on everyone else.

CHAPTER 4

FINDING THE BALANCE OF POWER

The attack by al Qaeda on September 11 forced the United States into a response that escalated into a two-theater war, lesser combat in a host of other countries, and the threat of war with Iran. It defined the past decade, and managing it will be the focus of at least the first part of the decade to come.

The United States obviously wants to destroy al Qaeda and other jihadist groups in order to protect the homeland from attack. At the same time, the other major American interest in this context is the protection of the Arabian Peninsula and its oil—oil that the United States does not want to see in the hands of a single regional power. For as long as the United States has had influence in the region, it has preferred to see Arabian oil in the hands of the Saudi royal family and other sheikhdoms that were relatively dependent on the United States. That will continue to be a strategic imperative.

The corollary that frames U.S. options is that only two countries in the region have been potentially large and powerful enough to dominate the Arabian Peninsula: Iran and Iraq. Rather than occupy Arabia to protect the flow of oil, the United States has followed the classic strategy of empire, encouraging the rivalry between Iran and Iraq, playing off one against the other to balance and thus effectively neutralize the power of each. This strategy preceded the fall of the shah of Iran in 1979, when the United States encouraged a conflict between Iran and Iraq, then negotiated a settlement between them that maintained the tension.

After the fall of the shah, the Iraqi government of Saddam Hussein, largely secular but ethnically Sunni, attacked the Islamist and largely Shiite nation of Iran. Throughout the 1980s, the United States shifted its weight between the sides, trying to prolong the war by making sure that neither side collapsed. About two years after the war, which Iraq won by a narrow margin, Saddam tried to claim the Arabian Peninsula, beginning with invading Kuwait. At this point the United States applied overwhelming force, but only long enough to evict, not invade, Iraq. The United States once again made certain that the regional balance of power maintained itself, thereby protecting the flow of oil from the Arabian Peninsula—America's core interest—without the need for an American occupation.

This was the status quo when Osama bin Laden tried to redefine the geopolitical reality of the Middle East and South Asia on September 11, 2001. With the attacks on New York and Washington he inflicted pain and suffering, but the most profound effect of his action was to entice an American president to abandon America's successful, long-standing strategy. In effect, Bin Laden succeeded in getting an American president to take the bait.

In the long term, Bin Laden's goal was to re-create the caliphate, the centralized rule of Islam that had been instituted in the seventh century and that had dominated the Middle East until the fall of the Ottoman Empire. Bin Laden understood that even to begin to achieve this return to religious geopolitical unity, nation-states in the Islamic world would have to undergo revolutions to unseat their current governments, then replace them with Islamist regimes that shared his vision and beliefs. In 2001, the only nation-state that shared his vision fully was Afghanistan. Isolated and backward, it could serve as a base of operations, but only temporarily. It might be a springboard to more important nations like Pakistan, Saudi Arabia, and Egypt, but it was too isolated and primitive ever to be more than that.

Bin Laden's analysis was that many in the Muslim world shared his beliefs in some sense, but that given the realities of power, their support would only be tepid and insufficient to his ends. To begin moving his project forward, he had to trigger an uprising in at least one and preferably several of the more important Islamic countries. Doing that was impossible as long as the Muslim masses viewed their governments as overwhelmingly powerful and immovable fixtures.

As Bin Laden saw it, this problem was primarily one of perception, because the governments in the region were in fact weaker than they appeared. The apparent military and economic power of Pakistan, Saudi Arabia, and Egypt derived from the relationship of these countries with the Christian world (as he thought of it), and particularly with the leading Christian power, the United States. But Bin Laden surmised that even with their borrowed power, these governments were still vulnerable. His task was to demonstrate this weakness to the Muslim masses, then set in motion a series of uprisings that would transform the politics of the Islamic world. He failed in this, but his followers have continued this strategy, and their attempts to reshape the politics of the Islamic world, which have been under way since the nineteenth century, will continue to be a significant geopolitical theme of the decade to come.

The short-term goal of the September 11 attacks was to accelerate this process by attacking prominent American targets at the heart of the imperial power structure. Bin Laden's hope was that by exposing the vulnerability of even the United States, he could diminish Muslim perceptions that their own governments were invulnerable.

The attacks of September 11 were only marginally about the United States, and the exact nature of the American response to Bin Laden's gambit mattered little, because any response could be used to his advantage. If the Americans did nothing, this would confirm their weakness. If the Americans responded aggressively, this would confirm that they were indeed the enemies of Islam.

But while the attacks were aimed primarily at the Muslim psyche, the psychological impact on Americans turned out to be hugely important. The unexpectedness of the attacks, the fact that they were mounted using a fixture of everyday life—commercial airliners—and the fact that casualties were substantial created a sense of panic. How many other teams were in place? Where would al Qaeda strike next? Did al Qaeda possess weapons of mass destruction? Even more than in the wake of Pearl Harbor, Americans emerged from the shock of September 11 with a sense of personal dread. The possibility that they and their loved ones might be killed next was very real to them. This was a pervasive and profound sense of unease that the government had to address by appearing to take decisive action.

The psychological alarms that went off among the American people served to compound the strategic problem facing the U.S. government. Al Qaeda by itself—unless it did possess weapons of mass destruction—did not pose a genuine strategic threat. It could not shatter the United States. However, if the disruption it initiated had the desired effect in the Islamic world and regimes that were linked to the United States started to fall, ultimately that would have a huge impact on American strategy. If the Egyptian government were overthrown, for example, the position of Israel would change and an American anchor in the region would be threatened. If the Saudi government was endangered, the flow of oil from the region might be interrupted. The strategic danger was not the destruction of America's population centers, economic infrastructure, or military might, but simply al Qaeda's potential political success in the region—and that quite apart from Bin Laden's distant dream of the caliphate.

The United States as well as al Qaeda identified the strategic battle-field clearly: the hearts and minds of Muslims. But for the president it was American hearts and minds that first needed to be calmed and reassured that actions were being taken to protect the homeland. The FBI moved aggressively to track down anyone even remotely suspected of being associated with al Qaeda, and security was revamped at airports, but neither effort was particularly effective at the time. In many ways, the United States continues to operate under the doctrine of putting enormous resources into security measures of limited effectiveness in order to calm the American public's legitimate fears. Reconciling resources with operational reality and public perception will be a critical task for the next decade.

The assault on America's sense of well-being also demanded that al Qaeda's leaders be captured or killed. In strategic terms this was a questionable priority, but a president must satisfy not only the desire for reassurance but also the desire for revenge. Here the challenge was compounded by the fact that al Qaeda is a sparse network spread out around the globe, operating without a central headquarters or a conventional chain of command. Al Qaeda encourages sympathizers to strike out on their own and innovate. So while it is possible to carry out acts of retribution against these terrorists, it is impossible to actually destroy al Qaeda, because it isn't an organization in any conventional sense. Because there is no infrastructure and no chain of command, there is no real head to be decapitated.

What did make strategic sense was a minimal infusion of force to disrupt al Qaeda's planning, training, and limited command capabilities. Al Qaeda considered itself safe while operating out of Afghanistan, a landlocked country with no ports of entry. Bin Laden and his colleagues had some familiarity with American operations, both from observing Operation Desert Storm in 1991 and from training with Americans in Afghanistan during the Soviet-Afghan war of the 1980s. Desert Storm in particular had showed al Qaeda that even when ports were available, Americans planned obsessively, and planning took time. With winter approaching, al Qaeda's rational estimate was that even if the United States chose to go looking for them in Afghanistan, no action was possible before the spring. The Pakistani port of Karachi would be essential for an invasion, and negotiations for its use might delay an assault even longer.

The Bush administration, however, calculated that it couldn't wait until spring. The president really did want to decapitate or at least disrupt al Qaeda, but politically he had to respond to demands for an immediate and highly visible response. The attacks had shaken confidence in America's defenses, and the president had to rebuild that confidence while also building a political base for what could be an extended war. He could ill afford a crisis in confidence about American prosperity at this juncture, so it was in this atmosphere that the war on terror began to affect economic decisions as well. If it took six months to launch American counteraction, the already tenuous political situation would deteriorate, and the president would lose support for the effort even before it was launched. Bush's decision to go ahead was one of those individual judgments that can and do affect the lives of millions over the span of a decade, and certainly the fallout from that decision will continue to color much of the decade to come.

There was also a legitimate strategic reason for haste: the United States wanted to make certain that regimes in the Middle East didn't fall, or even begin to recalculate their interests. While the United States might have been perceived as a great power, it also was seen as a power that was unprepared to risk a great deal in the region. Ronald Reagan's decision to withdraw from Beirut after the bombing of the Marine barracks, George H. W. Bush's decision not to go on to Baghdad after liberating Kuwait, and Bill Clinton's decision to withdraw from Somalia, followed by his rather anemic response to pre-9/11 al Qaeda attacks, all created an image of a country unwilling to take risks and suffer losses. Meanwhile, Muslim governments saw the very real possibility of being toppled by political unrest fomented by al Qaeda's capable and ruthless covert force, particularly if they collaborated with the United States.

These governments were not about to become jihadists, but neither were they prepared to expose themselves on behalf of the United States. They expected the United States to continue its policy of limited risk taking, so for them, cooperation with the U.S. appeared to pose serious risks with few advantages. The Americans demanded intelligence sharing on al Qaeda, for instance, but these governments, which did not expect the United States to stand by them for the long haul, were reluctant to participate. The longer the United States failed to act, the lower the Muslim countries' propensity to assist.

Al Qaeda miscalculated by focusing too much on the consequences of the attack for the Islamic world and not enough on the political and strategic pressures September 11 created for Bush. There was no doubt that the United States would act aggressively, and for the reasons cited above, sooner rather than later. The target had to be al Qaeda, which meant that the area of operations had to be Afghanistan.

In mid-September 2001, the United States sent in CIA operatives to make deals with local Afghan warlords. At the same time, the United States dispatched Special Operations Forces and paramilitary CIA units to fight alongside anti-Taliban Afghans and to target American air strikes on Taliban positions. In particular, the United States made a deal with the Northern Alliance, a Russian-backed group of anti-Taliban organizations. Having been defeated by the Taliban in their civil war in the 1990s, the Northern Alliance now welcomed the opportunity to strike back, and the Russians had no objection. Other warlords were simply bought. The United States also had the active cooperation of Iran.

Afghanistan provided the illusion of an invasion, but what really happened was the resumption of a civil war, backed by American air power. The fighting that began a month after September 11 was done primarily by Afghans, supported by air strikes from carriers and bombers based in the Persian Gulf and the Indian Ocean. But rather than massing in front of the major cities and becoming targets to be bombed by B-52s, the Taliban, in classic insurgent fashion, dispersed, then regrouped later to resume the battle.

As a result, the Taliban was never actually defeated, but the United States did achieve three of its goals. First, it reassured the American public that it was able to protect them by mounting military action anywhere in the world. This wasn't altogether true, but it was true enough to be comforting. Second, it signaled to the Islamic world that the United States was absolutely committed to the conflict. More sophisticated than the American public, Muslim leaders noted that the major American contribution was air power, while the heavy lifting was done by the Afghans. This was not definitive evidence of American commitment; it was, however, better than no action. Third, the action inflicted damage on al Qaeda. Bin Laden and others escaped, but their command-and-control structure was disrupted, which forced the leaders to become fugitives. As a result, they became increasingly isolated and largely irrelevant.

Afghanistan was in some ways a sleight of hand, but it achieved what could be achieved. The United States had launched a disruptive spoiling attack—a classic American maneuver. The Bush administration installed and protected a government, knowing that most of Afghanistan was outside its reach and that creating a democracy there was not in the cards. Nine years later, Afghanistan is still far from resolved, and it will certainly be the problem that has to be solved in order to move ahead in the next decade.

From al Qaeda's point of view, however, U.S. actions in Afghanistan and elsewhere in the Middle East served as clear evidence for Muslims that the United States was their enemy. The jihadists waited for uprisings and toppled regimes—an upheaval that never came. The regimes survived, partly because the Islamic street, as it was called, feared that the security apparatus of their regimes was still brutally effective, and partly because these regimes continued to hedge their bets. They read the U.S. spoiling attack for what it was and held back their own commitment. Both Saudi Arabia's and Pakistan's intelligence sharing remained limited, as neither wanted to commit itself to the United States without clear signs of how far the U.S. was prepared to go. As it became clearer that there would be no uprisings, al Qaeda became more aggressive in the region.

THE IRAQ GAMBIT

The next venture in the U.S. war on terror was the assault on Iraq in 2003. It is easy to argue today that the invasion was an unqualified mistake, but it is important to recall the context in which the decision to invade was made. In February 2002, the Saudis ordered American forces off their soil. The Pakistanis, in spite of heavy pressure from both India and the United States, made only modest gestures of commitment in support of the American effort. The general perception was that the United States had done what it was going to do in Afghanistan and was now hoping that other nations would carry the burden for it, both in intelligence and in operations.

Without the full cooperation of the Saudis and Pakistanis, the United States had limited options. It could conduct an intelligence war against al Qaeda, as the Israelis had done with Black September in Europe in the 1970s; but without contributing partners in the region, the U.S. intelligence capability against al Qaeda was extremely constrained.

A second option was for the United States to move into a purely defensive mode, relying on Homeland Security while hoping that the Afghan operation had disrupted al Qaeda's command structure enough to prevent new attacks. Theoretically, the FBI could round up sleeper cells while the borders were protected from infiltration and airports secured against terrorists. Attractive on paper, this plan was impossible in practice. The FBI could never guarantee that there were no more sleeper cells in the country, and points of entry into the United States could never be completely secured. Any illusion of safety this effort gave the American public, and any support it might buy the president for a job well done, would last only until the next terrorist attack, the timing and nature of which were completely unknown. When such an attack came, the question of America's willingness to assert itself and take risks in the Muslim world would surface again, with no clear answer. After Afghanistan, what?

The Bush administration tried to craft a strategy that forced the Saudis and Pakistanis to be more aggressive in intelligence gathering and sharing and that placed the United States in a dominant position in the Middle East, from which it could project power.

These were the underlying reasons for the invasion of Iraq. The military action had the immediate result of creating a new strategic reality. It intimidated Saudi Arabia in particular, placing U.S. armor a few days' drive from Saudi oil fields. It also gave the United States control of the most strategic country in the region, Iraq, which borders on Kuwait,

Saudi Arabia, Jordan, Syria, Turkey, and Iran. So controlling Iraq achieved the short-term goals of the war on terror, but it violated the principle that the United States does not become a permanent player in any region. The Bush administration had wagered that it could sacrifice this part of U.S. strategy—maintaining regional balances of power through surrogates while holding U.S. forces in reserve—in return for other benefits. It was a bad choice on a menu of worse choices, a point that has to be remembered when we consider the nature of imperial power: it may feel compelled to act even when all options are flawed.

Obtaining those benefits, however, required the United States to succeed not just in invading but in pacifying Iraq. The invasion succeeded, without a doubt, and the Saudis markedly increased their cooperation on intelligence. But dominating the most strategic country in the region turned out to be impossible. U.S. forces, having rolled into Baghdad with ease, found themselves quickly tied down in an insurgency that required them to focus all their force inward, when the intent had been to use Iraq as a base from which to project force outward.

This failure of the occupation transformed the war. Iraq became an end in itself, and the ultimate goal became not the creation of a new strategic reality in the region but simply the withdrawal of U.S. forces within a reasonable time frame. The best hope was to leave behind a neutral government; at worst, the end result of the invasion would be chaos.

Iraq became decoupled from America's broader strategy and became a case study in the relationship among morality, strategy, and leadership. From a purely moral point of view, eliminating the Saddam Hussein regime could hardly have been faulted. He was a monster and his regime was monstrous. But that was not the moral imperative to which Bush had committed his presidency. His stated moral imperative was to wage a war on terror, and the occupation of Iraq made sense to the American people only to the extent that it served that goal.

In deciding to invade in 2003, George W. Bush placed his moral obsession above the fundamental principle of American strategy: maintaining a balance in each region without committing substantial numbers of troops. There are many regions, and if the United States began deploying occupation forces in each of these, the burden would quickly outstrip American capacity. Moreover, U.S. forces had supplanted Iraq's own forces as the counterweight to Iran, now the largest indigenous power in the region. If at some point the United States simply withdrew from Iraq, Iran would by default dominate the entire Persian Gulf. Whatever the invasion contributed to the war against al Qaeda, the strategic costs of Iraq became too high.

For the invasion of Iraq to be aligned with America's long-standing strategic principles, U.S. forces would have had to occupy Iraq quickly and efficiently and without significant resistance. Then the United States would have had to rapidly construct a viable regime in Baghdad, complete with a substantial military force, to take over the role of balancing its historical enemy, Iran. If this could have been done in, say, five years, Bush would have achieved both his moral and strategic goals. He would have delivered the necessary shock to the Muslim world, intimidated the Saudis, and been able to use Iraq's strategic location to pressure countries in the region. The United States could have then withdrawn, leaving regional players to balance each other once more.

The Bush strategy failed because the premise was faulty: there was resistance that could not be readily suppressed. The greatest intelligence mistake of the war did not concern weapons of mass destruction but rather the failure to understand that insurgency had long been Saddam Hussein's default plan for dealing with an invasion. It also involved a failure to understand that by trying to destroy Saddam's Sunni-dominated Baathist Party, the United States effectively drove the Sunnis out of government and turned power over to their religious and cultural rivals, the Shiites. Terrified of a Shiite government (which, incidentally, would have some affinity with the Shiite majority that dominated Iran), the Sunnis in Iraq were put in a position where they had nothing to lose and embraced random shootings and roadside bombs.

But Bush's miscalculation ran deeper. He counted on the support of the Shiites in opposing the Sunni establishment, but discounted the degree to which the Iraqi Shiites were intertwined with the heavily Shiite Iranians. The Iranians had no interest in seeing Iraq resurrected under a pro-American government that would once again threaten Iran, so the United States wound up trapped from two directions. The Sunnis went to war against the occupation, and the Shiites, influenced by Iran, did everything they could to avoid the kind of cooperation that would turn them into an American dependency.

Bush violated strategic principles, hoping to return to the main path later, but he got trapped in the local realities, which he could not manage. As the situation deteriorated, his credibility with the American public declined. He could have survived the fact that his initial justification for the war, the existence of weapons of mass destruction, proved untrue. But he could not survive being trapped in a multisided war with no end in sight.

There were other errors that undermined this president's ability to lead. His second justification for the invasion was the need to create a democratic Iraq. This did not resonate with the American public, which saw no pressing reason for such an effort. This nation-building motivation was in fact a lie. As we noted in the case of Lincoln, Roosevelt, and Reagan, great presidents often have to lie to serve their greater moral purpose. But Bush failed to convince because his clearly stated moral imperative—defeating terrorism—had diverged from strategic reality to such an extent that his entire foreign policy appeared convoluted and chaotic, which made him appear incompetent. There were too many separate explanations, too many cases of special pleading. The failure to align moral objectives with strategic goals, and both with a coherent myth for popular consumption, crushed him.

In 2007, too late to save his presidency, Bush instituted the surge. This effort had less to do with military strategy than it did with using military force to set the stage for a negotiated settlement with the Sunnis. Once that was put in place, the Shiites, afraid of an American-backed Sunni force, became somewhat more cooperative, and the violence died down.

With Iraq no longer an effective counterweight, the balance of power with Iran broke down completely. An American withdrawal of forces would leave Iran the dominant force in the region, with no local power to block it—a prospect that completely unnerved the Arabian powers, as well as Israel and the United States. It is this imbalance that sets the stage for the regional problems that will continue to face the American president in the decade to come.

As the second decade of the twenty-first century began, the dual problem facing the United States in this region was withdrawing its forces without leaving Iran unchecked by a countervailing power. Given that there were no other candidates for the job of blocking Iranian ambitions, it appeared that the United States could not withdraw from Iraq until it had created a government in Baghdad strong enough to restore balance.

The Iranians had clearly welcomed the invasion of Iraq. Long before September 11, they had done everything possible to induce the United States to step in and eliminate Saddam Hussein. Indeed, much of the intelligence forecasting that American troops would not encounter resistance had come from Iranian sources.

Once American boots were on the ground, Iran began to threaten U.S. interests in Iraq directly by becoming deeply involved with various Shiite factions, then by supplying weapons to the Sunnis to keep the conflict going. Iran had also supported Taliban forces in western Afghanistan, as well as Hezbollah in Lebanon.

The Iranians had expected the United States to create an Iraqi government that marginalized the Sunnis and emerged as primarily Shiite. They anticipated that once the United States withdrew, such a government would become an Iranian satellite. They expected the Americans to lean on Iran's Shiite allies to govern Iraq, but the United States threw them a curve by attempting to govern Iraq directly through various institutions and individuals. Nonetheless, given the protracted difficulty of forming a government and the eventual withdrawal of the Americans, the outcome is likely still to leave Iran in a favorable position.

But these factors are exactly what has proved so dangerous to the government in Tehran. Trapped between trying to govern a rebellious country directly and turning over responsibility to a government penetrated by Iranian agents and sympathizers and then withdrawing, the United States had to consider a more radical possibility: an attack that would overthrow Iranian president Mahmoud Ahmadinejad and the regime that his presidency was based on.

With its 70 million people inside mountainous borders, Iran is by virtue of topography an effective fortress. Given that the terrain makes a direct invasion impossible, the Americans have tried multiple times to generate a revolution similar to the ones that toppled governments in the former Soviet Union. Over the years, these attempts have always failed. But after the failures in Iraq, and to the extent that the United States could neither revive the balance of power nor leave Iran the dominant power in the Persian Gulf region, it would be natural enough for the Americans to consider some kind of attack to oust the Iranian government. The fact that this regime is split between old clerics who came to power with Ayatollah Khomeini and younger, nonclerical leaders such as Ahmadinejad adds to Iranian worries. But the leaders' primary concern is that they have seen other U.S.-sponsored uprisings succeed, particularly in the former Soviet Union, and they cannot take the chance that the United States won't get lucky again.

The Iranians noted the manner in which North Korea had managed a similar problem in the 1990s, when its government feared that the collapse of Soviet communism would lead to its own collapse. Trying to portray themselves as more dangerous and psychologically unstable than they were, the Koreans launched a nuclear weapons program. To convince people that they might actually use those weapons, they made statements that appeared quite mad. As a result, everyone feared a regime collapse that might lead to unpredictable results. Thus the North Koreans managed to create a situation in which powers such as the United States, China, Russia, Japan, and South Korea tried to coax them to the table with aid. The North Koreans were so successful that they had the great powers negotiating to entice them to negotiate. It was an extraordinary performance.

Playing to America's nuclear phobia, the Iranians have been working on nuclear technology for a decade, a program that has included crafting themselves in the image of North Korea, as unpredictable and dangerous. Like the North Koreans, they managed to maneuver themselves into a position where the permanent members of the UN Security Council, plus Germany, were trying to negotiate with them over the issue of whether or not they would negotiate.

The collapse of Iraq had left the United States in an extremely difficult situation with limited options. An air strike against Iranian nuclear targets would most likely spur a patriotic resurgence that would only strengthen the regime. And Iran had substantial counters, including the ability to further destabilize Iraq and to some extent Afghanistan. Iran could also unleash Hezbollah, a far more capable terrorist organization than al Qaeda. Or it could mine the Strait of Hormuz, creating economic chaos by blocking the flow of oil from the Persian Gulf.

Thus the violation of America's long-standing policy of regional balances and limited engagement led to a geopolitical worst-case scenario. Iran was now the dominant native power in the Persian Gulf, and only the United States had the means to counterbalance it, which would further violate America's basic strategic principles. Moreover, the unbalanced focus on this one region left the United States weak in other parts of the world, trapped off-balance, with no clear counter in sight.

This is the defining geopolitical problem that President Obama inherited and that he and all other presidents of the next decade will have to deal with. Iran has become the pivot on which the Middle East will turn. In many ways, it was always the pivot. But before the United States could deal with Iran, it had to do something definitive about Islamic terror. It devoted its resources to wars it saw as directed against terrorism, which effectively insulated Iran from the threat of American intervention and even enhanced its position in the region.

The economic and geopolitical events of the past decade were intertwined. They created a crisis of confidence in the American public as well as drawing American strategic thinking into a series of short-term, tactical solutions. The Iran question is tied up with fears that rising oil prices will crush the economic recovery, as well as with the impact of action on the jihadist war. September 11 and the events of 2008 have combined to create a trap for American strategic thinking. As the United States moves forward into the next decade, it must escape the trap. The economic problem will resolve itself in time. The geopolitical challenge of terrorism requires decisions.

CHAPTER 5

THE TERROR TRAP

President George W. Bush called his response to the al Qaeda attacks of September 11 the Global War on Terror. If he had called the response a war on radical Islam, he would have alienated allies in the Islamic world that the United States badly needed. If he had called it a war on al Qaeda, he would have precluded attacking terrorists who were not part of that specific group. Bush tried to finesse this problem with a semantic sleight of hand, but this left him open to political and strategic confusion.

President Obama dropped the term *war on terror*, and rightly so. Terrorism is not an enemy but a type of warfare that may or may not be adopted by an enemy. Imagine if, after Pearl Harbor, an attack that relied on aircraft carriers, President Roosevelt had declared a global war on naval aviation. By focusing on terrorism instead of al Qaeda or radical Islam, Bush elevated a specific kind of assault to a position that shaped American global strategy, which left the United States strategically off-balance.

Obama may have clarified the nomenclature, but he left in place a significant portion of the imbalance, which is an obsession with the threat of terrorist attacks. As we consider presidential options in the coming decade, it appears imperative that we clear up just how much of a threat terrorism actually presents and what that threat means for U.S. policy.

According to the Prussian military theorist Carl von Clausewitz, war is a continuation of politics by other means. Victory in World War II did not consist of compelling Japan to stop using aircraft carriers. Victory meant destroying Japan's ability to wage war, then imposing American will—a political end. If a president is to lead a nation into war, he must crisply designate both the enemy and the end being sought. If terror was the enemy after September 11, then everyone who could use terror was the enemy, which is an awfully long list. If for political reasons a president cannot clearly identify who is to be fought and why, then he must carefully reexamine whether he can win, and thus whether or not he should engage. If the cost of naming the enemy is diplomatically or politically unacceptable, then the war is not likely to go well.

Despite Bush's decision to focus the war on terrorism, the Islamic world knew that the real enemy being targeted was radical Islam. This was the ground that al Qaeda had sprung from, and Bush was not going to fool anyone into thinking otherwise. When he could not truthfully and coherently explain his reason for invading Iraq, the strategy began to unravel.

Bush's semantic and strategic confusion intensified when his war on terror expanded to include the effort to unseat the Iraqi government. Saddam Hussein, targeted by that effort, was a secular militarist rather than a religious Islamist, and he was no friend of al Qaeda. He had not been involved in al Qaeda terrorism prior to the invasion of Iraq, but he and al Qaeda did share a common enemy: the United States. For this reason, Bush felt that he could not discount the danger of an alliance of convenience between the state of Iraq and the stateless radicals, al Qaeda. His solution was to make a preemptive attack. Bush and his advisers reasoned that destroying Saddam's regime and occupying Iraq would deny al Qaeda a potential base while gaining the United States a strategic base of operations of its own.

Nonetheless, inasmuch as the larger strategy had been identified as a war on terror and inasmuch as Saddam had not recently engaged in terrorism, the invasion of Iraq appeared unjustified. If the war had been more clearly focused on al Qaeda as the enemy, then the invasion would have appeared much more plausible, because a war against a specific group would have included hostility toward that group's allies and even potential allies, which Saddam certainly was.

In a democracy, the foundation of public support is a clear picture of the enemy's threat and of your own purpose in confronting that threat. Such clarity not only mobilizes the public, it provides a coherent framework for communicating with that public. Truman's presidency never recovered from his use of the term *police action* to refer to the Korean War, a conflict in which more than thirty thousand Americans died. Roosevelt's war against Germany, Japan, and Italy, on the other hand, survived endless subterfuges, attacks on the innocent, and alliances with the truly evil, because Roosevelt made it clear who the enemy was and why we had to fight and defeat it.

THE SIGNIFICANCE OF TERROR

Terrorism is an act of violence whose primary purpose is to create fear and, through that, a political result. The bombing of London by Germany in World War II was a terror attack, in that the goal was not to cripple the British ability to wage war, but to generate a psychological and political atmosphere that might split the public from the government and force the government into negotiations. Palestinian terrorism in the 1970s and 1980s, from assassination to hijacking aircraft, was designed to draw attention to their cause and maximize the appearance of Palestinian power. As I've tried to show, al Qaeda's terrorism was also designed for a political end. The issue is simple: how much effort should be devoted to stopping terror and its consequences compared to other strategic tasks?

Terrorism is normally undertaken in lieu of more effective action. Had the Germans been able to destroy the British navy or the Palestinians been able to destroy the Israeli army, they would have done so. It would have been a more efficient and direct route to their ends. Terrorism derives from weakness, focusing on the psyche in order to make the terrorist appear more powerful than he is. The terrorist's goal is to be treated as a significant threat when in fact he isn't one. As the name implies, the terrorist is creating a state of mind. His ultimate goal is to be taken as an enormous, indeed singular threat. This creates the foundation for the political process the terrorist wants to initiate. Some merely want to be taken seriously. Al Qaeda wanted to convince the Islamic world that it was so powerful it was the most important thing on American minds.

Al Qaeda in fact achieved that goal.

By declaring a war on terror, the United States signaled that it regarded this single threat as transcending all others. Protecting the United States against terrorist acts became the central thrust of American global strategy, consuming enormous energy and resources. But terrorism as practiced by al Qaeda does not represent a strategic danger to the United States. It can and at times will kill perhaps thousands of Americans, and it will cause pain and generate fear. But terrorism in and of itself cannot destroy the material basis of the American republic.

Because terrorism—even including nuclear terrorism—does not represent an existential threat to the United States, a foreign policy focused singularly on terrorism is fundamentally unbalanced. The lack of balance consists of devoting all available resources to one threat among many while failing to control other threats that are of equal or greater significance and danger. This is not an argument to ignore terrorism, but rather an argument that terrorism needs to be considered within the context of national strategy. This is where George W. Bush got trapped, and his successors run the risk of falling into the same snare.

Like Lincoln, Roosevelt, and Reagan, Bush had to manage the psy-

chology of the country while pursuing his strategic end, but two phe-
nomena proved to be his undoing. First, the more successful he was at
blocking al Qaeda, the more the psychological trauma faded. Some of
the public moved from demanding the most extreme measures to being
shocked at the measures being taken. Bush should have anticipated this,
but by regarding the war on terror as an end in itself, he lost his sense of
its place in the broader strategic and political context. Second, he was
not able to shift his focus in keeping with the change in public opinion,
because he did not understand the purpose of his own global war on terror. That purpose was not to defeat terrorism but to satisfy the psychological needs of the public. Yet Bush continued at full bore long after the
country no longer felt at risk.

In being fixated on terrorism as a freestanding strategic goal, Bush
devoted huge resources to battles he couldn't win and to theaters that
were not obviously connected to terrorism. In fighting a Global War on
Terror, he not only lost perspective, he forgot to manage the full range of
other U.S. strategic interests. He was so obsessed with the Islamic world,
for example, that he didn't devote the attention and resources necessary
to deal with the reemergence of Russia.

The issue therefore is how to transition from a complete focus on terrorism and the Islamic world to a more balanced strategy. Part of the
problem is public opinion. Dealing with the Islamic world is a passionate subject in the United States, one that divides the country. Many
regard the Islamic world as not only the prime issue but the only issue on
the American agenda. It is the president's job to align with public opinion and to tack with it while quietly pursuing his own moral and strategic ends. The problem that President Obama and other presidents will
face in the next decade is to place terrorism and al Qaeda in perspective
while redefining American interests in the Islamic world. This needs to
be done in such a way that the public doesn't turn on the president, particularly when the inevitable terrorist attacks do occur. He must satisfy
public opinion both when it is terrified and outraged by attacks and
when it turns complacent about terrorism and is shocked at the things
that have been done to battle it. Above all, the president must deal with

the Islamic world as it is, without allowing public passion to influence his ultimate intentions.

This is not an argument for complacency. For example, even though the likelihood is small, the consequences of an attack with weapons of mass destruction would be enormous. Appropriate resources must be devoted to the threat. That does indeed mean war, covert or overt, and war potentially involves costs and commitments that run the risk of outstripping the threat. The president's task is to align threat, consequences, and effort with other challenges, and shape them into a coherent strategy. The United States has many threats and interests and cannot respond to only one. Fear alone cannot drive strategy.

The president must, as we have said, always soothe the nerves of the public, and must always show his commitment to stopping terrorism. At the same time, he must resist the temptation to try the impossible or undertake actions that have disproportionate costs relative to effect. He can lie to the public, but he must never lie to himself. Above all, he must understand the real threats to the country and act against those.

Apart from the killings at Fort Hood in 2009, September 11 was the only successful attack in the United States during ten years of war. Those coordinated attacks on New York and Washington were the result of a multiyear, intercontinental operation that cost al Qaeda nineteen of its most committed and capable operatives. Two major office buildings were destroyed in New York, and in Washington the Pentagon suffered extensive damage. Three thousand Americans were killed. But for a nation of 300 million people, the material consequences of the attack were in fact minimal.

This is not meant to trivialize the deaths or to dismiss the horror that Americans experienced on that day. My point is merely to emphasize that while you and I are allowed the luxury of our pain, a president isn't. A president must take into account how his citizens feel and he must manage them and lead them, but he must not succumb to personal feelings. His job is to maintain a ruthless sense of proportion while keeping the coldness of his calculation to himself. If he succumbs to sentiment, he will make decisions that run counter to the long-term interests of his country. A president has to accept casualties and move on. When the Japanese attacked Pearl Harbor, Roosevelt called for vengeance but privately decided to focus on Germany and not Japan. He understood that a president could not allow himself to craft strategy out of emotion.

The purpose of war, according to von Clausewitz, is to impose your will on another nation by rendering that other nation incapable of resisting. The primary means for doing this is to destroy the nation's military, or to undermine the population's will to resist. Instilling terror can destroy an army; for example, the Mongols paralyzed their enemies with the knowledge of their relentless and ruthless cruelty. The Greek city-states would fight their wars to the bitter end, spurred on by fear of the slavery that awaited them if they were conquered. So the net effect of terror is hard to predict.

During World War II, neither the Germans nor the British made any bones about the purpose of what the British called "nighttime area bombing." The targeting of civilians was a tactic designed to generate terror among the public, in the hope that the civilians would at the very least become less effective in running the wartime economy, and at the extreme possibly rise up against their own regimes. In Japan, the Americans pursued the same ends by using incendiary devices, taking advantage of the fact that most Japanese buildings were made of wood. In three days of conventional bombing over Tokyo, U.S. air forces killed 100,000 Japanese civilians, more than were killed at Hiroshima. Yet until the introduction of the atomic bomb, the terror strategy failed, just as it had failed in both Germany and Britain. Rather than destroying faith in the government, the bombing of civilian areas rallied the public to support the war effort. The attacks inspired outrage while making it easy for the targeted governments to portray the consequences of defeat as being too horrible even to contemplate. If the enemy was willing to go to such lengths to divert resources during a war simply to kill civilians, imagine what they would do when the war was over. Terror made it easy to demonize the enemy and made surrender unthinkable.

In conventional warfare, terror is delivered by massed force. But terror also can be delivered through a covert operation by a very small number of individuals: a commando attack. These operations were once generally confined to assassinations, but after the invention of high explosives—and force multipliers for high explosives, such as airliners—commando terrorism focused on civilian targets with the goal of producing casualties as an end in itself.

It is important here to distinguish carefully between commandos whose goals are military and those whose targets are civilian and whose purpose is terror. The French Resistance in 1944 attacked German transport facilities in an attempt to undermine their invader's ability to wage war directly. The terror commando's goal, however, is not to harm the enemy's military but to undermine enemy morale by generating a sense of vulnerability. Sometimes the audience isn't even the target country but public opinion elsewhere, as with the attacks of September 11.

By generating fear, helplessness, and rage, terrorism transforms public opinion, which then demands that the government provide protection from terrorists and punish such people for their actions. The more effective the terrorist attack is, the more frightened the population is, and the more compelled the government is to respond aggressively and visibly. Once again, in the face of terror, the president must convince the public that he shares their sentiments while taking actions that appear to satisfy their cravings both for security and for revenge.

One such largely symbolic action taken since September 11 has been the attempt to bolster the airport security system. Despite billions of dollars and untold measures of passenger frustration, a terrorist with training can still devise any number of ways to get explosives or other devices through the system. Some terrorists might be deterred, and the system will find others. But while increased airport security can decrease the threat, it cannot stop it.

There is simply no security system that is both granular enough to detect terrorists reliably and efficient enough to allow the air transport system to function. El Al, Israel's airline, is frequently held up as an example, but El Al has thirty-five planes. According to the Bureau of Transportation Statistics, the combined American air fleet has nearly eight thousand planes and over twenty-six thousand takeoffs per day.

The Transportation Security Administration says it screened 1.8 million passengers per day on average in 2009. These are staggering numbers.

What the limitations of airport screening tell us is that if al Qaeda failed to strike the United States again during the first decade of the twenty-first century, it was not because of security precautions per se. It is even doubtful that the people who design the airport security system expect it to work. Their real objective is to calm the public by ostentatiously demonstrating that steps are being taken. The greater the ostentation and inconvenience, the more comforting the system appears.

But the increasing sophistication of explosives makes it possible to kill dozens of people with a device carried by an individual, hundreds of people with a device hidden in a car or truck, and thousands of people with an aircraft that acts as an explosive. The world is awash in such explosives, and the borders of the continental United States are about nine thousand miles long. The United States is also a trading country, and ships and planes and trucks arrive daily. Any one of those conveyances could contain people and explosives prepared to kill other people. It is also true that among 300 million Americans, there could be any number of homegrown terrorists preparing to strike at any time.

For these reasons, true homeland security in a country like the United States is impossible, and the task will remain impossible in the next decade. There are no silver bullets. Eliminating Islamist terrorism is similarly impossible. It is possible to reduce the threat, but the greater the reduction we hope to achieve, the greater the cost. Given unlimited possibilities and limited resources, it is safe to say that there will continue to be terrorist attacks on the United States, regardless of the efforts being made.

The president of the United States must know this with crystal clarity, and he must always act on the basis of what he knows, but he must never admit these limits to the public. He must constantly demonstrate that he is doing all he can to destroy the enemy and to protect the homeland, and he must always convey a sense that the elimination of Islamist terrorism is possible, all the while knowing that it is not.

As we embark on the policy decisions of the next decade, the larger point is that turning all American resources to an end that is unobtainable, against a threat that can and will have to be endured, is not only pointless but something that can create windows of opportunity for other enemies and other assaults.

While terrorism can kill Americans and can create a profound sense of insecurity, the obsessive desire to destroy terrorism can undermine—as it already has undermined—the United States strategically. This is an important point for the leaders of the next decade to consider. This is why even though thousands of Americans might be killed by terrorists—myself and my loved ones among them—terrorism should not be elevated to the status of an issue towering above all others. At all times, strategy must remain proportional to the threat.

TERROR AND WEAPONS OF MASS DESTRUCTION

Another unpleasant reality that will loom over the next ten years, which needs to be considered separately, is weapons of mass destruction. The existence of such weapons will occasionally prompt severe responses from the presidents who lead us. The damage that a nuclear device might do would dwarf that of conventional terrorism. Whereas conventional terrorism is rarely strategic, weapons of mass destruction can have a profound effect on the material condition of the country.

To turn our attention back to Bush, there was in fact more to his response to September 11 than simply stopping conventional terrorism. After that day, the Bush administration received intelligence that a nuclear device—a Soviet-era suitcase bomb, to be specific—had been stolen and might be in the hands of al Qaeda. Thus the specter that haunted the administration in the closing months of 2001 was that at any moment an American city might be destroyed by a nuclear weapon.

It was this threat that defined the Bush administration's initial efforts. The president and vice president were never in the same city at the same time, and all intelligence and security services were directed to find the weapon. It would appear that they never found it, or it may never have existed. After years of mishandling, it may have malfunctioned, or it may have been intercepted and the government chose not to reveal its existence.

Regardless, weapons of mass destruction, particularly nuclear devices, represent a class of threat that cannot be tolerated. It would take many nuclear weapons to actually destroy the infrastructure and population of the United States, but a single attack by a nuclear weapon could destabilize public morale to such an extent that it would paralyze the country for an extended period of time.

In a small terrorist attack in which dozens die, like the suicide bombings in Israel, the probability that any one individual out of a population of 300 million will be a victim is small. The probability of dying from an ordinary accident or from disease in the next year is far higher than that of being killed in a suicide bombing. The events of September 11 distorted the perception of danger for a while, and people avoided flying, and perhaps avoided crowded places and landmark buildings. But as time passed, the sense of being subject to attack declined. The danger was on most people's minds when they went to the airport, and perhaps when they entered the Sears Tower or the Empire State Building or the Capitol. But over time, the perceived risk of being in the wrong place at the wrong time was assimilated into the general background noise. As this happened, for many people the demand that all steps be taken to guard against terror turned to dismay at what they regarded as excesses, inconveniences, and intrusions.

With weapons of mass destruction, the probabilities and the persistence of fear are different. Assume that an American city were destroyed by a nuclear device. Once a WMD attack had destroyed one city, the number of targets a terrorist might want to hit next would be relatively small, but for anyone living in one of the major cities, there would be the immediate, reasonable fear that the enemy had more such weapons and that at any instant they might strike again.

From a terrorist's perspective, wasting a nuclear weapon on Spokane, Washington, or Bangor, Maine, makes no sense. It is the major cities that are the centers of political, economic, and social life. For them to be evacuated by frightened citizens would bring not only chaos but abandonment of entire economic and communications systems while millions of refugees fled to nowhere in particular. This response to the fear of mass annihilation from a completely random threat would be the ultimate objective of terrorism using WMDs.

Terrorists of many stripes—Palestinian, European, Japanese—have been operating since the late 1960s, and most of these groups would have jumped at the chance to inflict the kind of damage a weapon of mass destruction can engender. Many of these groups have been technically far more sophisticated than al Qaeda. So why has there never been an effective attack with a weapon of mass destruction?

The simple answer is that while constructing and deploying a WMD is easy to imagine, it is very difficult to execute. Existing weapons are relatively few, heavily guarded, difficult to move, and likely to kill the terrorist well before the terrorist gets a chance to kill anyone else. There have been many reports of Soviet-era nuclear weapons, and biological and chemical weapons, being available on the black market, but most of the offers were made by intelligence agencies trying to lure terrorists into a trap. If you were a terrorist offered a suitcase nuke by a former Soviet colonel, how could you possibly tell whether what you were looking at was the real thing or just a box stuffed with wires and blinking lights? The same uncertainty would have to hold for chemical or biological weapons as well. Intelligence services don't have to know who is selling real WMDs in order to scare away the customers, and the allure of acquiring these weapons contracted considerably when the number of intelligence officers offering them for sale as entrapment outnumbered legitimate offers by one hundred to one.

There is, of course, the option of making such a weapon yourself, and every year some undergraduate posts a diagram of how to build a nuclear device. Between that sketch and success are the following steps: acquiring the fissile material, along with all the necessary circuitry and casings; acquiring the machinery needed to machine the fissile material to the precise tolerances needed in order to detonate it; engaging the experts who could actually do these things once you had the material and the equipment; finding a very secure facility where these experts could work and live, and so on. The chances of being detected are compounded at each stage of this torturous process. Even if you could acquire the highly guarded fissile material, the machines needed for producing a nuclear weapon are highly specialized, and their manufacturers are few and far between. When a private individual shows up with his American Express card to order one of these machines, the chances that he will be detected are very good indeed.

With biological and chemical weapons, you add to these same risks the likelihood that the only person you'll kill will be yourself and your immediate accomplices. Chemical and biological weapons carry an extra layer of complexity in that they have to be dispersed. When a Japanese group released sarin, an extremely deadly nerve gas, in a Tokyo subway, the contamination remained localized and only a few people were killed, not the substantial numbers the terrorists had hoped for. People always speak of how a speck of this or that could wipe out an entire city. Certainly—but first you have to figure out how to spread it around.

Only one country ever produced a nuclear weapon from scratch, and that was the United States. The British got their nukes in compensation for their contribution to the American research effort. The French also acquired the technology from the Americans, which they then regifted to Israel. The Russians stole the knowledge from the Americans, then transferred it to both the Chinese and the Indians. The Chinese gave the technology to the Pakistanis. The point is, the development of these weapons through an independent research program is enormously difficult, which is why Iran is still struggling and North Korea has never gotten it quite right.

Just as the financial crisis has created a domestic imbalance in the United States, September 11 has generated a strategic imbalance. This will have to be addressed in the next decade, and difficult decisions will have to be made. A strategy designed to prevent regional hegemons from threatening American interests is a balance-of-power strategy. It requires an American presence in multiple regions. The next decade, therefore, will be about redefining American strategy so that it can pursue these interests. That will mean moving beyond the war on terror and redefining interests throughout each region as well as the world. A good place to begin thinking about this is Israel.

CHAPTER 6

REDEFINING POLICY:
THE CASE OF ISRAEL

The United States faces no more complex international relationship than the one it maintains with Israel, nor one more poorly understood, most of all by the Americans and the Israelis. U.S.-Israeli relations would appear to poison U.S.-Islamic relations and complicate the termination of warfare in the Middle East. In addition, there are some who believe that Israel exercises control over U.S. foreign policy, a view not confined to Islamic fundamentalists. The complex reality, as well as the even more complex perception of the tie that binds the United States and Israel, will continue to be a fundamental issue for the United States' global strategy over the next decade.

U.S.-Israeli relations are also a case study for the debate between realists and idealists in foreign policy. America's close relations with Israel are based both on national interest and on the moral belief that the United States must support regimes similar to itself. This latter idea has, of course, become an intense philosophical battleground. On the idealist side are those who focus on the kind of regime Israel has: an island of democracy in a sea of autocrats. But there are also those who argue that because of its treatment of the Palestinians, Israel has forfeited any moral claims. On the realist side are those who argue that Israel gets in the way of better relations with the Arabs, and those who argue that they are allies in the war against terrorism.

If there is any place where finding a coherent path that incorporates both strategic and moral interests is more difficult, I can't think of one. But to truly understand this complex state of affairs, we must go back in history.

Given the antiquity of the Middle East, it is fortunate that understanding its contemporary political geography requires going back only as far as the thirteenth century. This was the time when the Byzantine Empire was fading and control of the areas bordering the Black Sea and the eastern Mediterranean shifted to the Ottoman Turks. By 1453 the Turks had conquered Constantinople, and by the sixteenth century they were in command of most of the territory that had once fallen to Alexander the Great. Most of North Africa, Greece, and the Balkans, as well as the area along the eastern shore of the Mediterranean, was under Ottoman control from the time of Columbus to the twentieth century.

All this came to an end when the Ottomans, who had allied with Germany, were defeated in World War I. To the victors went the spoils, which included the extensive Ottoman province known as Syria. A secret wartime deal between the British and the French, the Sykes-Picot agreement, had divided this territory between the two allies on a line running roughly from Mount Hermon due west to the sea. The area to the north was to be placed under French control; the area to the south was to be placed under the control of the British. Further divisions gave rise not only to the modern country of Syria but to Lebanon, Jordan, and Israel as well.

The French had sought to be an influence in this region since the days of Napoleon. They had also made a commitment to defend the Arab Christians in the area against the majority Muslim population. During a civil war that raged in the region in the 1860s, the French had allied with factions that had forged ties with France. Paris wanted to maintain that alliance, so in the 1920s, when the French were at last in control, they turned the predominantly Maronite (Christian) region of Syria into a separate country, naming it after the dominant topographical characteristic, Mount Lebanon. As a state, then, Lebanon had no prior reality. Its main unifying feature was that its people felt an affinity with France.

The British area to the south was divided along similarly arbitrary lines. During World War I, the Muslim clan that ruled the western Hejaz region of the Arabian Peninsula, the Hashemites, had supported the British. In return, the British promised to install this group as rulers of Arabia after the war. But London made commitments to other tribes as well. Based in Kuwait, a rival clan, the Saud, had launched a war against the Turks in 1900, trying to take control of the eastern and central parts of the Arabian Peninsula. In a struggle that broke out shortly after World War I, the Sauds defeated the Hashemites, so the British gave Arabia to them—hence today's Saudi Arabia. The Hashemites received the consolation prize of Iraq, where they ruled until 1958, when they were overthrown in a military coup.

The Hashemites left in Arabia were moved to an area to the north along the eastern bank of the Jordan River. Centered on the town of Amman and lacking any other obvious identity, this new protectorate became known as Trans-Jordan, as in "the other side of the Jordan River." After the British withdrew in 1948, Trans-Jordan became contemporary Jordan, a country that, like Lebanon and Saudi Arabia, had never existed before.

West of the Jordan River and south of Mount Hermon was yet another region that had once been an administrative district of Ottoman Syria. Most of it had been called Filistin, undoubtedly after the Philistines, whose hero Goliath had fought David thousands of years before. The British took the term *Filistin,* ran it through some ancient Greek, and came up with Palestine as the name for this new region. Its capital was Jerusalem, and its residents were thereafter called Palestinians.

None of these remnants was a nation in the sense of having a common history or identity except for Syria itself, which could claim a lineage going back to biblical times. Lebanon, Jordan, and Palestine were

French and British inventions, created for their political convenience. Their national history went back only as far as Mr. Sykes and Monsieur Picot and some British double-dealing in Arabia.

Which is not to say that the inhabitants did not have a historical connection to the land they lived on. If not their homeland, the territory was certainly a home, but even here there was complexity. Under Ottoman rule, the ownership of the land, particularly in Palestine, had been semifeudal, with absentee landlords collecting rent from the *felaheen,* or peasants, who actually tilled the soil.

Enter the Jews. Members of the European Diaspora had been moving into this region since the 1880s, joining relatively small Jewish communities that had existed there (and in most other Arab regions) for centuries. This immigration was part of the Zionist movement, which—motivated by the European idea of the nation-state—sought to create a Jewish homeland in the region the Jews had last controlled in biblical times.

The Jews came in small numbers, settling on land purchased with funds raised by Jews in Europe. Frequently this land was bought from the absentee landlords, who sold it out from under their Arab tenants. From the Jewish point of view, this was a legitimate acquisition of land. From the tenants' point of view, it was a direct assault on their livelihood, as well as an eviction from land their families had farmed for generations. As more Jews arrived, the acquisition of land, the title to which was frequently dubious anyway, became less scrupulous and even more intrusive.

While the Arabs generally (but not universally) saw the Jews as alien invaders, they did not agree on something perhaps more important: to whom did the residents of Palestine owe national allegiance?

The Syrians regarded Palestine the way they regarded Lebanon and Jordan—as an integral part of Syria. They opposed an independent Palestine, just as they opposed the existence of an independent Jewish state, for the same reason they opposed Lebanese and Jordanian independence: for them, the Sykes-Picot agreement was a violation of Syria's long-standing territorial integrity.

The Hashemites, formerly from the Arabian Peninsula, had even greater problems with the Palestinians. The Hashemites were, after all, an Arabian tribe transplanted on the east bank of the Jordan. After the British left in 1948, they became rulers by default of what is today the West Bank. While sharing Arab ethnicity and the Muslim faith with the Palestinians who were native to the area, these transplants were profoundly different in culture and history. In fact, the two groups were quite hostile to each other. The Hashemite (now Jordanian) view was that Palestine was legally theirs, at least the part left after Israel gained independence. Indeed, from the time that the Jews became more numerous and powerful in Palestine, the Hashemite rulers of Jordan saw these new emigrants from eastern Europe and elsewhere as allies against the native Palestinians.

To the southwest of Israel were the Egyptians, who at various points had also been dominated by the French and the British, as well as by the Ottomans. In 1956 they experienced a military coup that brought Gamal Abdel Nasser to power. Nasser opposed the existence of Israel, but he had a very different vision of the Palestinians. Nasser's dream was the creation of a single Arab nation, a United Arab Republic, which he succeeded in establishing very briefly with the Syrians. For him, all of the countries of the Arab world were illegitimate products of imperialism and all should join together as one, under the leadership of the largest and most powerful Arab country, Egypt. Viewed in that context, there was no such thing as Palestine, and the Palestinians were simply Arabs occupying a certain ill-defined piece of land.

All the Arab states within the region, then, save the Jordanians, wanted the destruction of Israel, but none supported, or even discussed, an independent Palestine. The Gaza strip, occupied by Egypt during the 1948 Israeli War of Independence, was administered as part of Egypt for the next twenty years. The West Bank remained a part of Jordan. The Syrians wanted all of Jordan and Palestine returned to them, along with Lebanon. This was complicated enough, but then the Six Day War of 1967 shuffled the deck once more.

In 1967, Egypt expelled UN peacekeeping forces from the Sinai Peninsula and remilitarized it. They also blockaded the Straits of Tiran and the Bab el Mandeb, cutting off the port of Eilat from the Red Sea. In response, the Israelis attacked not only the Egyptians but also the Jordanian West Bank, which had shelled Jerusalem, and the Golan Heights in Syria, which had shelled Israeli settlements.

Israel's success, including the occupation of Jordan west of the river, transformed the entire region. Suddenly a large population of unwilling Palestinian Arabs was under the rule of an Israeli state. Israel's initial intent seems to have been to trade the conquered areas for a permanent peace agreement with its neighbors. However, at a meeting held in Khartoum after the 1967 war, the Arab states replied with the famous "three no's": no negotiation, no recognition, no peace. At this point the Israeli occupation of these formerly Palestinian areas became permanent.

It was also at this point that the Palestinians first came to be viewed as a separate nation. The Egyptians had sponsored a group known as the Palestine Liberation Organization and installed a young man named Yasir Arafat to lead it. Nasser still clung to the idea of an Arab federation, but no other nations chose to accept his leadership. Nasser wasn't prepared to submit to anyone else, which left the PLO and its constituent organizations, such as al-Fatah, by default the sole advocates for a Palestinian state.

The Jordanians were happy to have the Palestinians living in Israeli territory, as an Israeli problem. They were also happy to recognize the PLO as representing the Palestinian people, and just as happy that the Israelis didn't allow the Palestinians to be independent. The Syrians supported their own organizations, such as the Popular Front for the Liberation of Palestine, which advocated that Israel should be destroyed and that the Palestinians should be incorporated into Syria. So the recognition of Palestinian nationalism by the Arabs was neither universal nor friendly. Indeed, Arab support for the Palestinians seemed to increase in proportion to the distance the Arabs were from Palestine.

It should be obvious from this summary that the moral argument that rages about the rights of Israel, which any American president must deal with, is enormously complex. Beyond the substantial displacement of populations that occurred with the creation of modern Israel, the immigration of European Jews did not constitute the destruction of a Palestinian nation, because no such nation had ever existed. The Palestinian national identity in fact emerged only out of resistance to Israeli occupation after 1967. And the hostility toward Palestinian national claims was as intense from Arabs as it was from Jews. Israeli foreign policy was shaped by these realities and took advantage of them in order to impose the current political order on the region. But whatever was the case in the past, there is certainly today a self-aware Palestinian nation, and that is part of what must inform U.S. policy going forward.

Apart from dealing with this incredibly convoluted history, which weighs on any moral judgment, U.S. policy in this region must accommodate two other basic facts. First, whatever the Israelis' historical claim, from a twentieth-century perspective, the Jews were settlers from another continent who displaced the natives. Then again, it is difficult for Americans, who displaced their own native population even more thoroughly, to make a moral case against Israel for usurping Palestinian land and mistreating the indigenous people.

A more powerful moral argument is the one that Roosevelt made in support of France and England against Nazi Germany: Israel (excluding the West Bank and Gaza) is a democratic country, and the United States is the "arsenal of democracy." This means that the United States has a special relationship with democratic states, as well as obligations that transcend geopolitics. Therefore, the United States must support democratic Israel exclusive of other moral or even geopolitical considerations.

Realists would disagree. They would argue that the moral claims of any side can have no hold on the United States, and that the United States must shape its policies to its national interest. However, as I have argued, pursuing a national interest without reference to a moral purpose leaves the national interest shallow and incomplete. More important, defining the national interest in the region on its own terms is extraordinarily difficult. The moral compass must be there, but it points in many directions. The pursuit of the national interest is less obvious than it might appear.

Morality rooted in historical claims can be shaped to suit, and is by all sides. A simple moral judgment doesn't deal with the realities on the ground, and simply arriving at a coherent moral position is breathtakingly difficult. As for the realist position, it is extraordinarily difficult to extract what that might be. So the question is, how do we frame a realistic foreign policy that will serve the moral purpose and national interest in the decade to come? To find the answer, we need to consider the history of the relationship between Israel and the United States.

THE UNITED STATES AND ISRAEL

The United States recognized Israeli independence in 1948, but the two countries were hardly allies in any sense of the term. While the United States always recognized Israel's right to exist, that fact never really drove U.S. policy. The primary American interest in 1948, when Israel came into being, was the containment of the Soviet Union, and the American focus was primarily on Turkey and Greece. Greece had an internal Communist insurgency. Both Greece and Turkey had an external Soviet threat as well. For the United States, Turkey was the key to the region. It was only a narrow strait in Turkey, the Bosporus, that blocked the Soviet fleet in the Black Sea from entering the Mediterranean Sea in force. If that strait fell into Soviet hands, the Soviets would be able to challenge American power and threaten southern Europe.

The major impediment to the U.S. strategy of containment in the Middle East was that the British and French were trying to reestablish the influence in the region that they had held before World War II. Seeking to develop closer ties in the Arab world, the Soviets could and did exploit hostility to the Europeans' machinations. Things came to a head in 1956, after Nasser took power and nationalized the Suez Canal.

Neither the British nor the French (who were fighting to suppress an anticolonial revolt in Algeria and who were striving to reclaim their influence in Lebanon and Syria) wanted Egypt to control the canal. Neither did Israel. In 1956, the three nations hatched a plot for an Israeli invasion of Egypt, but with a twist. After Israel reached the canal, British and French forces would intervene, seizing the canal to secure it from the Israeli invasion and potential conflict with Egypt. It was one of those ideas that must have made sense when sketched on a cocktail napkin after a few drinks.

In the American view, the adventure was not only doomed to failure but would drive Egypt into the Soviet camp, giving them a strong and strategic ally. Since anything that might increase Soviet power was unacceptable to the United States, the Eisenhower administration intervened against the Suez scheme, forcing British and French withdrawal and Israel back to the 1948 lines. In the late 1950s, there was no love lost between Israel and the United States.

The strategic problem for Israel was that its national security requirements always outstripped its industrial and military base. In other words, given the challenges it faced from Egypt and Syria, and potentially from Jordan, not to mention the Soviet Union, it could not produce the weapons it needed in order to protect itself. To ensure a steady source of weapons, it needed a major foreign patron.

Israel's first patron was the Soviet Union, which saw Israel as an anti-British power that might become an ally. The USSR supplied weapons to Israel through Czechoslovakia, but this relationship crumbled quickly. Then France, still fighting in Algeria, replaced the Soviets as Israel's benefactor. The Arab countries supported the Algerian rebels, and thus it was in France's interest to have a strong Israel standing alongside France in opposition. So the French supplied the Israelis with aircraft, tanks, and the basic technology for their nuclear weapons.

At this time the United States still saw Israel as of marginal importance to its broader strategic goals in the area. After the Suez crisis, however, the United States began to reconsider its strategic relationships. The Americans had intervened on behalf of Egypt in Suez, but the Egyptians migrated into the Soviet camp regardless. The French and British had left behind a series of regimes, in Syria and Iraq in particular, that were inherently unstable and highly susceptible to the Nasserite doctrine of militarily driven Arab nationalism. Syria had begun moving into the

Soviet camp as early as 1956, but in 1963 a left-wing military coup sealed that position. A similar coup occurred that same year in Iraq.

By the 1960s, American support for the Arabs had begun to look like an increasingly questionable enterprise. Despite the fact that the only assistance the United States was providing Israel was food, the Arab world had turned resolutely anti-American. The Soviets were prepared to fund projects the United States wouldn't fund, and the Soviet model was more attractive to Arab socialists. The United States remained fairly aloof for a while, content to let France maintain the relationship with Tel Aviv. But when the United States began supplying antiaircraft systems to anti-Soviet regimes in the region, Israel was included on the gift list.

In 1967, Charles de Gaulle ended the Algerian war and sought to resume France's prior relationship with the Arab world, and he did not want Israel attacking its neighbors. When the Israelis disregarded his demands and launched the Six Day War, they lost access to French weapons. Israel's victory over its Arab neighbors in the 1967 conflict generated pro-Israeli support in the United States, which was bogged down in Vietnam; the Israelis seemed to provide a model of swift and decisive warfare that revitalized the American spirit. The Israelis capitalized on that feeling to aggressively woo the United States.

Struggling with the Vietnam War and public opinion, Lyndon Johnson saw American public infatuation with Israeli military successes as useful in two ways. First, the generation for support of any war might strengthen support for the Vietnam War. Second, the Israeli victory had strengthened an already powerful Soviet hand in Egypt and Syria, making Israel a useful ally. A strategic basis for the U.S.-Israeli relationship emerged. The Soviets had penetrated Syria and Iraq in the mid-1960s and were already building up the military of both countries. The Soviets' strategy for dealing with their encirclement by U.S. allies was to try to leapfrog them, recruiting their own allies to their rear and then trying to increase the political and military pressure on them. Turkey, which had always been at the center of U.S. strategic thinking, was the key for the Soviets, as it was for the Americans. The coups in Syria and Iraq—well before 1967—had intensified the strategic problem for the United States. Turkey was now sandwiched between a powerful Soviet Union to the north and two Soviet clients to the south. If the Soviets placed their own forces in Iraq and Syria, Turkey could find itself in trouble, and with it would go the entire American strategy of Soviet containment.

The Israelis now represented a strategic asset, allowing the United States to play leapfrog in return. In order to tie down Iraqi forces, the United States armed Iran, important in its own right because it shared a border with the Soviets. Israel did not share a border with the Soviets, but it did border Syria, and a pro-American Israel served to tie down the Syrians while making a Soviet deployment into Syria more complex and risky. In addition, Israel stood in opposition to Egypt. The Soviets were not only arming the Egyptians, they were using the port of Alexandria as a naval base, which could develop into a threat to the U.S. Sixth Fleet in the Mediterranean.

Contrary to widespread belief, the Egyptians and Syrians did not become pro-Soviet because of U.S. support for Israel. In fact, it was the other way around. The Egyptian shift and the Syrian coup happened before America replaced France as Israel's source of weapons, a development that in fact happened in response to Egyptian and Syrian policies. Once Egypt and Syria aligned with the Soviets, arming the Israelis became a low-cost solution for restricting Egyptian and Syrian forces while forcing the Soviets on the defensive in those countries. This helped secure the Mediterranean for the United States and relieved pressure on Turkey. It was at this point, and for strategic—not moral—reasons, that the United States began supplying a great deal of aid to Israel.

The U.S. strategy worked. The Egyptians expelled the Soviets in 1973. They signed a peace treaty with Israel in 1978. While the Syrians remained pro-Soviet, the expulsion of Soviet forces from Egypt blunted the Soviet threat in the Mediterranean. However, another threat had emerged in the meantime: Palestinian terrorism.

The PLO had been crafted by Nasser as part of his extended struggle with the monarchies of the Arabian Peninsula, an effort to topple the royal houses and integrate them into his United Arab Republic. Soviet intelligence, wanting to weaken the United States by contributing to instability in Arabia, trained and deployed PLO operatives. The situation became critical in September 1970, when Yasir Arafat engineered an uprising against the Hashemite rulers of Jordan, key allies of the United States and covert allies of Israel. At the same time, Syria moved armor south into Jordan, clearly intending to use the chaos to reassert Syrian authority. The Israeli air force intervened to block the Syrians, while the United States flew in Pakistani troops to support Jordanian forces to put down the uprising. About ten thousand Palestinians were killed in the fighting, and Arafat fled to Lebanon.

This conflict was the origin of the group known as Black September, which, among other things, carried out the massacre of Israeli athletes at the Munich Olympics in 1972. Black September was the covert arm of Arafat's Fatah movement, but what made it particularly important was that it also served Soviet interests in Europe. During the 1970s, the Soviets had organized a destabilization campaign, mobilizing terrorist groups in France, Italy, and Germany, among others, and supporting organizations such as the Irish Republican Army.

The Palestinians became a major force in this "terrorist international," a development that served to further bind the United States and Israel together. To prevent the destabilization of NATO, the United States wanted to shut down the Soviet-sponsored terrorist organizations, whose members were being trained in Libya and North Korea. For their part, the Israelis wanted to destroy the Palestinians' covert capability. The CIA and Mossad, Israel's foreign intelligence agency, cooperated intensely for the next twenty years to suppress the terrorist movement, which did not weaken until the mid-1980s, when the Soviets shifted to a more conciliatory policy toward the West. During this time, the CIA and Mossad also cooperated in securing the Arabian Peninsula against covert Soviet and PLO operations.

The collapse of the Soviet Union—and indeed, the shift in policy that took place after Leonid Brezhnev's death—changed this dynamic dramatically. Turkey was no longer at risk. Egypt was a decaying, weak nation of no threat to Israel. It was also quite hostile to Hamas. Formed in 1987, Hamas was a derivative of the Muslim Brotherhood that had threatened the regime of Egyptian president Hosni Mubarak. Syria was isolated and focused on Lebanon. Jordan was in many ways now a protectorate of Israel. The threat from the secular, socialist Palestinian movement that had made up the PLO and that had supported the terrorist movements in Europe had diminished greatly. U.S. aid to Israel stayed steady while Israel's economy surged. In 1974, when the aid began to flow in substantial amounts, it represented about 21 percent of the Israeli gross domestic product. Today it represents about 1.4 percent, according to the Congressional Research Office.

Once again, it is vital to understand that U.S.-Israeli cooperation did not generate anti-Americanism in the Arab world but resulted from it. The interests that tied Israel and the United States together from 1967 to 1991 were clear and substantial. Equally important to understand is the fact that since 1991, the basis of the relationship has been much less clear. The current state of play makes it necessary to ask precisely what the United States needs from Israel and what, for that matter, Israel needs from the United States. As we consider American foreign policy over the next ten years, it is also vital to ask exactly how a close tie with Israel serves U.S. national interests.

As for the moral issue of rights between the Israelis and the Palestinians, the historical record is chaotic. To argue that the Jews have no right in Palestine is a defensible position only if you are prepared to assert that Europeans have no right to be in America or Australia. At the same time, there is an obvious gulf between the right of Israel to exist and the right of Israel to occupy the home territory of large numbers of Palestinians who don't want to be occupied. On the other hand, how can you demand that Israel surrender control when large numbers of Palestinians won't acknowledge Israel's right to exist? The moral argument becomes dizzying and cannot be a foundation for a foreign policy on either side. Supporting Israel because we support democracies is a far more persuasive argument, but even that must be embedded in the question of national interest. And it must be remembered that the United States has been inconsistent in applying this principle, to say the least.

CONTEMPORARY ISRAEL

The Israel of today is strategically secure. It has become the dominant power among the bordering states by creating a regional balance of power among its neighbors that is based on mutual hostility as well as dependence by some of them on Israel.

By far the most important element of this system is Egypt, which once represented the greatest strategic threat to Israel. The Egyptians' decision in the 1970s that continued hostility toward Israel and alignment with the Soviet Union were not in their interests led to a peace treaty in which the Sinai became a demilitarized zone. This kept Egyptian and Israeli forces from impinging on each other. Without a threat from Egypt's military, Israel was secure, because Syria by itself did not represent an unmanageable threat.

The peace between Egypt and Israel always appears to be tenuous, but it is actually built on profoundly powerful geopolitical forces. Egypt cannot defeat Israel, for reasons that are geographical as well as technological. To defeat Israel, Egypt would have to create a logistical system through the Sinai that could support hundreds of thousands of troops, a system that would be hard to build and difficult to defend.

The Israelis cannot defeat Egypt, nor could they stand a prolonged war of attrition. To win they would have to win swiftly, because Israel has a small standing army and must draw manpower from its civilian reserves, which is unsustainable over an extended period. Even in 1967, when victory came within days, the manpower requirements for the battle paralyzed the Israeli economy. Even if Israel could defeat the Egyptian army, it could not occupy Egypt's heartland, the Nile River basin. This region is home to more than 70 million people, and the Israeli army simply does not have the resources even to begin to control it.

Because of this stalemate, Egypt and Israel would risk much and gain little by fighting each other. In addition, both governments are now battling the same Islamic forces. The Egyptian regime today still derives from Gamal Abdel Nasser's secular, socialist, and militarist revolution. It was never Islamic and was always challenged by devout Muslims, particularly those organized around the Muslim Brotherhood, the Sunni organization that is the strongest force in opposition to established regimes throughout the Arab world. The Egyptians repressed this group. They fear that a success by Hamas might threaten the stability of their regime. Therefore, whatever grumbling they might do about Israeli Palestinian policy, they share Israel's hostility to Hamas and work actively to contain Hamas in Gaza.

Israel's accord with Egypt is actually the most important relationship it has. So long as Egypt remains aligned with Israel, Israel's national security is assured, because no other combination of neighbors can threaten it. Even if the secular Nasserite regime fell, it would be a generation before Egypt could be a threat, and then only if it gained the patronage of a major power.

Nor does Israel face a threat from Jordan, even though the Jordan River line is the most vulnerable area that Israel faces. It is several hundred miles long, and the distance between that line and the Tel Aviv–Jerusalem corridor is less than fifty miles. However, the Jordanian military and intelligence forces guard this frontier for Israel, a peculiar circumstance that exists for two reasons.

First, the Jordanian-Palestinian hostility is a threat to the Hashemite regime, and the Israelis serve essential Jordanian national security interests by suppressing the Palestinians. Second, the Jordanians are much too few and much too easily defeated by the Israelis to pose a threat. The only time that the Jordan River line could become a threat would be if some foreign country (Iraq or Iran, most likely) were to send its military to deploy along that line. Since desert separates the Jordan River from these countries, deploying and supplying forces would be difficult. But more than that, such a deployment would mean the end of the Hashemite kingdom of Jordan, which would do everything it could to prevent a significant deployment and would be backed by the Israelis. Israel and Jordan are in this way joined at the hip.

That leaves Syria, which by itself poses no threat to Israel. Its forces are smaller than Israel's fully mobilized ones, and the areas in which it could attack are too narrow to exploit effectively. But far more important, Syria is a country that is oriented toward the west, and therefore toward Lebanon, which it not only regards as its own but is where its ruling elite, the Alawites, have close historic ties.

Lebanon is the interface between the northern Arab world and the Mediterranean. Beirut's banks and real estate, as well as the Bekaa Valley's smuggling and drug trade, are of far more practical interest to the Syrians than any belief that all of Ottoman Syria belongs to them. Their practical interests are in dominating and integrating Lebanon informally into their national economy.

Following the 1978 Camp David Accords between Egypt and Israel, and faced with hostility from Iraq, the Syrians found themselves isolated in the region. They were also hostile to Arafat's Fatah movement, going so far as to invade Lebanon in 1975 to fight the Palestinians. Nevertheless, they saw themselves at risk. The Iranian revolution in 1979 created a new relationship, however distant, and one that allowed the Syrians to increase their strength in Lebanon, using Iran's ideological and financial resources. In the 1980s, following Israel's own invasion of Lebanon, an anti-Israeli Shiite militia was formed, called Hezbollah. In part, Hezbollah is simply a part of the Lebanese political constellation. In part, it is a force designed to fight Israel. But in return for receiving a free hand in Lebanon from Israel, Syria guaranteed to restrain Hezbollah actions against Israel. This agreement broke down in 2006, when the United States forced Syrian uniformed forces out of Lebanon, as punishment for supporting jihadists in Iraq. As a result Syria renounced any promise it had made to Israel.

The deeper the detail, the more dizzyingly complex and ambiguous this region becomes, so a summary of the strategic relationships is in order. Israel is at peace with Egypt and Jordan, a far from fragile peace based on substantial mutual interests. With Egypt and Jordan aligned with Israel, Syria is weak and isolated and poses no threat. Hezbollah is a threat, but not one with the weight of fundamentally threatening Israel.

The primary threat to Israel comes from inside its boundaries, from the occupied and hostile Palestinians. But while their primary weapon, terrorism, can be painful, terrorism cannot ultimately destroy the Israelis. Even when Hezbollah and other external forces are added, the State of Israel is not at risk, partly because the resources those forces can bring to bear are inadequate, and partly because Syria, fearing Israeli retaliation, limits what these groups can do.

Indeed, Israel's problems have been lessened by the split among the Palestinians. Fatah, Arafat's organization, was until the 1990s the main force within the Palestinian community. Like the Nasserite movement it came from, it was secular and socialist, not Islamist. During the 1990s, Hamas, an Islamic Palestinian movement, arose, which has split the Palestinians, essentially creating a civil war. Fatah controls the West Bank; Hamas controls Gaza. The Israelis, playing the balance-of-power game within the Palestinian community as well as in the region, are now friendly and supportive of Fatah and hostile to Hamas. The two groups are as likely to fight each other as they are to fight Israel.

The danger of terrorism for the Israelis, beyond the personal tragedies it engenders, is that it can shift Israeli policy away from strategic issues and toward simple management of the threat. The killing of Israelis by suicide bombers is never going to be acceptable, and no Israeli government can survive if it dismisses the concern. But the balance of power makes Israel secure from threats by nation-states, and the threat of terrorism within the occupied territories is secondary.

The problem for Israel remains the same as it was in biblical times. Israel has always been able to control Egypt and whatever powers were to the east and north. It was only the distant great powers, such as Babylon, Persia, Alexandrian Greece, and Rome, that were able to overwhelm the ancient kingdom of the Jews. These empires were the competitors that Israel didn't have the weight to manage and sometimes engaged with catastrophically by overestimating its strength or underestimating the need for diplomatic subtlety.

Terrorism puts Israel in the same position today. The threat of this violence is not that it will undermine the regime but that it will cause the regime to act in ways that will cause a major power to focus on Israel.

Nothing good can come from Israel's showing up too brightly on the global radar screen.

From the Israeli point of view, Palestinian unhappiness or unrest or even terrorism can be lived with. What Israel cannot accommodate is the intervention of a major power spurred on by Israeli actions against the Palestinians. Great powers—imperial powers—can afford to spend a small fraction of their vast resources on issues that satisfy marginal interests or that merely assuage public opinion. That small fraction can dwarf the resources of a country like Israel, which is why Israel must maintain its regional arrangements and prudently manage the Palestinians and their terrorism.

The only such imperial power today is the United States. As such, it has varied global interests, some of which it has neglected during a time of preoccupation with terrorism and radical Islam. The United States must uncouple its foreign policy from this focus on terrorism and realign with countries that do not see terrorism as the singular problem of the world, and that do not regard Israeli occupation of territory with large numbers of Palestinians as being in their interests.

At the same time, there are numerous regional powers, such as Russia and Europe, that can have enormous impacts on Israel, and Israel cannot afford to be indifferent to their interests. Unless Israel reevaluates its own view of terrorism and the Palestinians, it may find itself isolated from many of its traditional allies, including the United States. This would not destroy Israel but would be a precondition for its destruction.

As we've seen, U.S. support for Israel was not the main driver of Muslim hostility to the United States, and no evolution of events in Israel directly affects core American interests. Accordingly, the United States would gain little by breaking with Israel, or by forcing the Israelis to change their policies toward the Palestinians. In fact, the net effect of an estrangement between the United States and Israel would be panic among Israel's neighbors. As mentioned earlier, support for the Palestinians increases the farther away you get from them, and that support in the Arab world is largely rhetorical.

Apart from skirmishes in Lebanon, Israel maintains a stable balance of power and does it without American assistance. Jordan and Egypt actually depend on Israel in many ways, as do other Arab countries. The Israelis are not going to be overwhelmed by the Palestinians, and thus the complex regional balance of power in the eastern Mediterranean will stay in place regardless of what the United States does or doesn't do. All of which leads to the conclusion that as far as the Israeli-Palestinian conflict goes, we should let sleeping dogs lie.

The best option for the American president is to marginalize the conflict as a concern without actually doing anything to signify a shift. The United States should quietly adopt a policy of disengagement from Israel, which would appear to mean simply accepting the current imbalance of power. Yet in the longer term, its purpose would be to reestablish the balance of power, containing Israel within its framework, without endangering Israel's existence. It would, however, compel Israel to reconsider what its national interests are.

Publicly distancing the United States from Israel would not only appear to open opportunities for Syria and Egypt, it would also present domestic political problems within the United States. The Jewish vote is small, but Jewish political influence is outsized because of carefully organized and funded lobbying efforts. Add to this mix Christian conservatives who regard Israel's interests as theologically important and the president faces a powerful bloc that he doesn't want to antagonize. For these reasons the president should continue sending envoys to build road maps for peace, and he should continue to condemn all sides for whatever outrages they commit. He should continue to make speeches supporting Israel, but he must have no ambitions for a "lasting peace," because any effort toward achieving that goal could in fact destabilize the region.

The things the United States needed from Israel in the past no longer exist. The United States does not need Israel to deal with pro-Soviet regimes in Egypt and Syria while the U.S. is occupied elsewhere. Israel is, however, valued for sharing intelligence and for acting as a base for supplies to support U.S. fighting in the region. Israel is not faced with the likelihood of major conventional war anytime soon. It does not need vast and sudden deliveries of tanks or planes, as it did in 1973. Nor does it need the financial assistance the United States has provided since 1974. Israel's economy is robust and growing.

For Israel, foreign aid means far less than close ties with U.S. hedge funds do. Israel is quite capable of handling itself financially. What the foreign aid signifies to Israel, which has no formal treaty with the United States, is a public commitment by the United States to Israel. Israel uses that as a card both in the region and to comfort Israeli public opinion. What the United States once got in return for that aid was a stable partner in the region, which could not manage without the money. Now the United States has a partner regardless of the aid. On the negative side of the ledger, the aid provides grounds for Islamicist arguments that the United States is the source of all their problems, including ruthless behavior on the part of the Israelis. Given that the aid is marginal in importance, that price is too high. Giving up this commitment to aid would actually help Israel by eliminating a prime argument of the anti-Israeli lobby in the United States.

Of course, this is all window dressing for the core policy of simply allowing the balance of power to be reestablished. Israel was of great value to the United States during the second part of the Cold War. After the Cold War, the benefits to the United States of the relationship have declined while the costs have risen. The equation does not call for a break in relations with Israel. It calls for a recalibration based on current realities. Israel does not need foreign aid and is not in strategic danger from conventional forces. There is a mutual need for intelligence sharing and weapons development, but that is by definition a fairly quiet development.

There is no moral challenge here. No democratic ally is being abandoned, and Israel's survival is not at issue. At the same time, while settlement in the West Bank may be a fundamental national interest to Israel, it is not of interest to the United States. These are two sovereign nations, which means that both get to define the relationship. And every relationship has to be viewed in terms of its value to the broadest sense of the national interest. What the United States needed from Israel thirty-five years ago is not what it needs today.

From the Israeli side, the primary pressure to reach an agreement with the Palestinians comes from concerns that they will find themselves alienated from the United States and particularly Europe over their treatment of the Palestinians. Economic relations are important to Israel, but so are cultural ties. But the Israelis have internal pressures. Given the Palestinian disarray, the idea of reaching a settlement with a Palestinian state that is unable or unwilling to control terrorist attacks from its territory has limited support. Any settlement would require concessions to the Palestinians that the Israelis would not want to make and that, given the weakness of the Palestinians, they are not inclined to make.

The Arab-Israeli balance of power is out of kilter. Egypt and Jordan have opted out of the balance, and Israel is free to create realities on the ground. It is not in the interest of the United States for Israel, or any country, to have freedom of action in the region. As I have said, the balance of power must be the governing principle of the United States. The United States must reshape the regional balance of power partly by moving closer to Arab states, partly by drawing back from Israel. This does not pose an existential threat to Israel, which would pose a moral challenge. Israel is in no danger of falling and does not depend on the United States to survive. That was in the past. It is not the case in the next decade. The United States needs distance. It will take it. There will be domestic political resistance. There will also be domestic political support. This is not an abandonment of Israel, but relations between two nations can't be frozen in an outdated mode.

The complicating factor in this analysis is the rest of the Islamic world, particularly Iran and Turkey. The former threatens to become a nuclear power, and the latter will become a powerful force in the region, shifting away from close ties with Israel. Having begun with a narrow focus on Israel, we need to switch to a broader lens. And that is how, as a case study, the balance of power of an empire works.

CHAPTER 7

STRATEGIC REVERSAL:
THE UNITED STATES,
IRAN, AND THE MIDDLE EAST

Beyond the special case of Israel, the area between the eastern Mediterranean and the Hindu Kush remains the current focus of U.S. policy. As we've noted, the United States has three principal interests there: to maintain a regional balance of power; to make certain that the flow of oil is not interrupted; and to defeat the Islamist groups centered there that threaten the United States. Any step the United States takes to address any one of these objectives must take into account the other two, which significantly increases the degree of difficulty for achieving even one.

Adding to this challenge is that of maintaining the balance of power in three regions of the area: the Arabs and the Israelis, the Indians and the Pakistanis, and the Iraqis and the Iranians. Each of these balances is in disarray, but the most crucial one, that between the Iranians and the Iraqis, collapsed completely with the disintegration of the Iraqi state and military after the U.S. invasion of 2003. The distortion of the India-Pakistan balance is not far behind, as the war in Afghanistan continues to destabilize Pakistan.

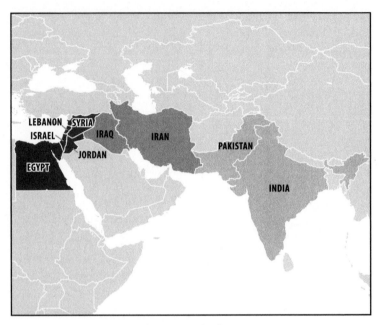

Three Regional Balances

As we saw in the last chapter, the weakness of the Arab side has created a situation in which the Israelis no longer have to concern themselves with their opponents' reactions. In the decades ahead, the Israelis
will try to take advantage of this to create new realities on the ground,
while the United States, in keeping with its search for strategic balance,
will try to limit Israeli moves.

The Indo-Pakistani balance is being destabilized in Afghanistan, a
complex war zone where American troops are pursuing two competing
goals, at least as stated officially. The first is to prevent al Qaeda from
using Afghanistan as a base of operations; the second is to create a stable
democratic government. But denying terrorists a haven in Afghanistan
achieves little, because groups following al Qaeda's principles (al Qaeda
prime, the group built around Osama bin Laden, is no longer fully functioning) can grow anywhere, from Yemen to Cleveland. This is an especially significant factor when the attempt to disrupt al Qaeda requires

destabilizing the country, training the incipient Afghanistan army, managing the police force of Afghan recruits, and intruding into Afghan politics. There is no way to effectively stabilize a country in which you have to play such an intrusive role.

Unscrambling this complexity begins with recognizing that the United States has no vital interest in the kind of government Afghanistan develops, and that once again the president cannot allow counterterrorism to be a primary force in shaping national strategy.

But the more fundamental recognition necessary for ensuring balance over the next ten years is that Afghanistan and Pakistan are in fact one entity, both sharing various ethnic groups and tribes, with the political border between them meaning very little. The combined population of these two countries is over 200 million people, and the United States, with only about 100,000 troops in the region, is never going to be able to impose its will directly and establish order to its liking.

Moreover, the primary strategic issue is not actually Afghanistan but Pakistan, and the truly significant balance of power in the region is actually that between Pakistan and India. Ever since independence, these two countries partitioned from the same portion of the British Empire have maintained uneasy and sometimes violent relations. Both are nuclear powers, and they are obsessed with each other. While India is the stronger, Pakistan has the more defensible terrain, although its heartland is more exposed to India. Still, the two have been kept in static opposition—which is just where the United States wants them.

Obviously, the challenges inherent in maintaining this complex balance over the next ten years are enormous. To the extent that Pakistan disintegrates under U.S. pressure to help fight al Qaeda and to cooperate with U.S. forces in Afghanistan, the standoff with India will fail, leaving India the preeminent power in the region. The war in Afghanistan must inevitably spread to Pakistan, triggering internal struggles that can potentially weaken the Pakistani state. This is not certain, but it is too possible to dismiss. With no significant enemies other than the Chinese, who are sequestered on the other side of the Himalayas, India would be free to use its resources to try to dominate the Indian Ocean basin, and it would very likely increase its navy to do so. A triumphant India would obliterate the balance the United States so greatly desires, and thus the issue of India is actually far more salient than the issues of terrorism or nation-building in Afghanistan.

That is why over the next ten years the primary American strategy in this region must be to help create a strong and viable Pakistan. The most significant step in that direction would be to relieve pressure on Pakistan by ending the war in Afghanistan. The specific ideology of the Pakistani government doesn't really matter, and the United States can't impose its views on Pakistan anyway.

Strengthening Pakistan will not only help restore the balance with India, it will restore Pakistan as a foil for Afghanistan as well. In both these Muslim countries there are many diverging groups and interests, and the United States cannot manage their internal arrangements. It can, however, follow the same strategy that was selected after the fall of the Soviet Union: it can allow the natural balance that existed prior to the U.S. invasion of Afghanistan to return, to the extent possible. The United States can then spend its resources helping to build a strong Pakistani army to hold the situation together.

Jihadist forces in Pakistan and Afghanistan will probably reemerge, but they are just as likely to do so with the United States bogged down in Afghanistan as with the U.S. gone. The war simply has no impact on this dynamic. There is a slight chance that a Pakistani military, with the incentive of U.S. support, might be somewhat more successful in suppressing the terrorists, but this is uncertain and ultimately unimportant. Once again, the key objective going forward is maintaining the Indo-Pakistani balance of power.

As in the case of stepping back from Israel, the president will not be able to express his strategy for dealing with Afghanistan, Pakistan, and India openly. Certainly there will be no way for the United States to appear triumphant, and the Afghan war will be resolved much as Vietnam was, through a negotiated peace agreement that allows the insurgent forces—in this case the Taliban—to take control. A stronger Pakistani army will have no interest in crushing the Taliban but will settle for controlling it. The Pakistani state will survive, which will balance India, thus allowing the United States to focus on other balance points within the region.

THE REGION'S HEARTLAND: IRAN AND IRAQ

The balance of power between Iran and Iraq remained intact until 2003, when the United States invasion destroyed both Iraq's government and army. Since then the primary force that has kept the Iranians in check has been the United States. But the United States has announced that it intends to withdraw its forces from Iraq, which, given the state of the Iraqi government and military, will leave Iran the dominant power in the Persian Gulf. This poses a fundamental challenge both for American strategy and the extremely complex region. Consider the alliances that might occur absent the United States.

Iraq's population is about 30 million. Saudi Arabia's population is about 27 million. The entire Arabian Peninsula's population is about 70 million, but that is divided among multiple nations, particularly between Saudi Arabia and Yemen. The latter has about one third of this population, and is far away from the vulnerable Saudi Arabian oil fields. In contrast, Iran alone has a population of 70 million. Turkey has a population of about 70 million. In the broadest sense, these figures and how these populations combine into potential alliances will define the geopolitical reality of the Persian Gulf region going forward. Saudi Arabia's population—and wealth—combined with Iraq's population can counterbalance either Iran or Turkey, but not both. During the Iran-Iraq war of the 1980s, it was Saudi Arabia's support for Iraq that led to whatever success that country enjoyed.

While Turkey is a rising power with a large population, it is still a limited power, unable to project its influence as far as the Persian Gulf. It can press Iraq and Iran in the north, diverting their attention from the gulf, but it can't directly intervene to protect the Arabian oil fields. Moreover, the stability of Iraq, such as it is, is very much in Iran's hands.

Iran might not be able to impose a pro-Iranian regime in Baghdad, but it has the power to destabilize Baghdad at will.

With Iraq essentially neutralized, its 30 million people fighting each other rather than counterbalancing anyone, Iran is for the first time in centuries free from significant external threat from its neighbors. The Iranian-Turkish border is extremely mountainous, making offensive military operations there difficult. To the north, Iran is buffered from Russian power by Armenia, Azerbaijan, and Georgia, and in the northeast by Turkmenistan. To the east lie Afghanistan and Pakistan, both in chaos. If the United States withdraws from Iraq, Iran will be free from an immediate threat from that enormous power as well. Thus Iran is, at least for the time being, in an extraordinary position, secure from overland incursions and free to explore to the southwest.

With Iraq in shambles, the nations of the Arabian Peninsula could not resist Iran even if they acted in concert. Bear in mind that nuclear weapons are not relevant to this reality. Iran would still be the dominant Persian Gulf power even if its nuclear weapons were destroyed. Indeed, a strike solely on Iran's nuclear facilities could prove highly counterproductive, causing Iran to respond in unpleasant ways. While Iran cannot impose its own government on Iraq, it could, if provoked, block any other government from emerging by creating chaos there, even while U.S. forces are still on the ground, trapped in a new round of internal warfare but with a smaller number of troops available.

Iran's ultimate response to a strike on its nuclear facilities would be to try to block the Strait of Hormuz, where about 45 percent of the world's exported seaborne oil flows through a narrow channel. Iran has antiship missiles and, more important, mines. If Iran mined the strait and the United States could not clear that waterway to a reasonable degree of confidence, the supply line could be closed. This would cause oil prices to spike dramatically and would certainly abort the global economic recovery.

Any isolated attack on Iran's nuclear facilities—the kind of attack that Israel might undertake by itself—would be self-defeating, making Iran more dangerous than ever. The only way to neutralize those facili-

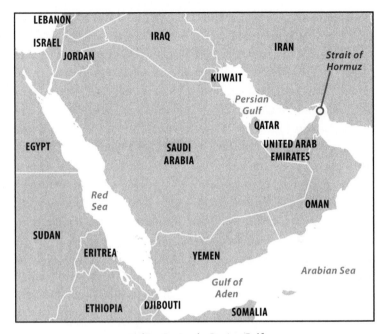

Arabian Peninsula, Persian Gulf

ties without incurring collateral damage is to attack Iran's naval capability as well, and to use air power to diminish Iran's conventional capability. Such an attack would take months (if it were to target Iran's army), and its effectiveness, like that of all air warfare, is uncertain.

For the United States to achieve its strategic goals in the region, it must find a way to counterbalance Iran without maintaining its current deployment (already reduced to 50,000 troops) in Iraq and without actually increasing the military power devoted to the region. A major air campaign against Iran is not a desirable prospect; nor can the United States count on the reemergence of Iraqi power as a counterweight, because Iran would never allow it. The United States has to withdraw from Iraq in order to manage its other strategic interests. But coupled with this withdrawal, it must think radical thoughts.

In the next decade, the most desirable option with Iran is going to be delivered through a move that now seems inconceivable. It is the option chosen by Roosevelt and Nixon when they faced seemingly impossible strategic situations: the creation of alliances with countries that had previously been regarded as strategic and moral threats. Roosevelt allied the United States with Stalinist Russia, and Nixon aligned with Maoist China, each to block a third power that was seen as more dangerous. In both cases, there was intense ideological rivalry between the new ally and the United States, one that many regarded as extreme and utterly inflexible. Nevertheless, when the United States faced unacceptable alternatives, strategic interest overcame moral revulsion on both sides. The alternative for Roosevelt was a German victory in World War II. For Nixon, it was the Soviets using American weakness caused by the Vietnam War to change the global balance of power.

Conditions on the ground put the United States in a similar position today vis-à-vis Iran. These countries despise each other. Neither can easily destroy the other, and, truth be told, they have some interests in common. In simple terms, the American president, in order to achieve his strategic goals, must seek accommodation with Iran.

The seemingly impossible strategic situation driving the United States to this gesture is, as we've discussed, the need to maintain the flow of oil through the Strait of Hormuz, and to achieve this at a time when the country must reduce the forces devoted to this part of the world.

The principal reason that Iran might accede to a deal is that it sees the United States as dangerous and unpredictable. Indeed, in less than ten years, Iran has found itself with American troops on both its eastern and western borders. Iran's primary strategic interest is regime survival. It must avoid a crushing U.S. intervention while guaranteeing that Iraq never again becomes a threat. Meanwhile, Iran must increase its authority within the Muslim world against the Sunni Muslims who rival and sometimes threaten it.

In trying to imagine a U.S.-Iranian detente, consider the overlaps in these countries' goals. The United States is in a war against some—but not all—Sunnis, and these Sunnis are also the enemies of Shiite Iran. Iran does not want U.S. troops along its eastern and western borders. (In point of fact, the United States does not want to be there either.) Just as the United States wants to see oil continue to flow freely through Hormuz, Iran wants to profit from that flow, not interrupt it. Finally, the Iranians understand that the United States alone poses the greatest threat to their security: solve the American problem and regime survival is assured. The United States understands, or should, that resurrecting the Iraqi counterweight to Iran is simply not an option in the short term. Unless the United States wants to make a huge, long-term commitment of ground forces in Iraq, which it clearly does not, the obvious solution to its problem in the region is to make an accommodation with Iran.

The major threat that might arise from this strategy of accommodation would be that Iran oversteps its bounds and attempts to occupy the oil-producing countries in the Persian Gulf directly. Given the logistical limitations of the Iranian army, this would be difficult. Also given that it would bring a rapid American intervention, such aggressive action on the part of the Iranians would be pointless and self-defeating. Iran is already the dominant power in the region, and the United States has no need to block indirect Iranian influence over its neighbors. Aspects of Iran's influence would range from financial participation in regional projects to significant influence over OPEC quotas to a degree of influence in the internal policies of the Arabian countries. Merely by showing a modicum of restraint, Iranians could gain unquestioned preeminence, and economic advantage, while seeing their oil find its way to the market. They could also see substantial investment begin to flow into their economy once more.

Even with an understanding with the United States, Iranian domination of the region would have limits. Iran would enjoy a sphere of influence dependent on its alignment with the United States on other issues, which means not crossing any line that would trigger direct U.S. intervention. Over time, the growth of Iranian power within the limits of such clear understandings would benefit both the United States and Iran. Like the arrangements with Stalin and Mao, this U.S.-Iranian alliance would be distasteful yet necessary, but also temporary.

The great losers in this alliance, of course, would be the Sunnis in the

Arabian Peninsula, including the House of Saud. Without Iraq, they are incapable of defending themselves, and as long as the oil flows and no single power directly controls the entire region, the United States has no long-term interest in their economic and political well-being. Thus a U.S.-Iranian entente would also redefine the historic relationship of the United States with the Saudis. The Saudis will have to look at the United States as a guarantor of its interests while trying to reach some political accommodation with Iran. The geopolitical dynamic of the Persian Gulf would be transformed for everyone.

The Israelis too would be threatened, although not as much as the Saudis and other principalities on the Persian Gulf. Over the years, Iran's anti-Israeli rhetoric has been extreme, but its actions have been cautious. Iran has played a waiting game, using rhetoric to cover inaction. In the end, the Israelis would be trapped by the American decision. Israel lacks the conventional capability for the kind of extensive air campaign needed to destroy the Iranian nuclear program. Certainly it lacks the military might to shape the geopolitical alignments of the Persian Gulf region. Moreover, an Iran presented with its dream of a secure western border and domination of the Persian Gulf could become quite conciliatory. Compared to such opportunities, Israel for them is a minor, distant, and symbolic issue.

Until now, the Israelis still had the potential option of striking Iran unilaterally, in hopes of generating an Iranian response in the Strait of Hormuz, thereby drawing the United States into the conflict. Should the Americans and Iranians move toward an understanding, Israel would no longer have such sway over U.S. policy. An Israeli strike might trigger an entirely unwelcome American response rather than the chain reaction that Israel once could have hoped for.

The greatest shock of a U.S.-Iranian entente would be political, on both sides. During World War II, the U.S.-Soviet agreement shocked Americans deeply (Soviets less so, because they had already absorbed Stalin's prewar nonaggression pact with Hitler). The Nixon-Mao entente, seen as utterly unthinkable at the time, shocked all sides. Once it happened, however, it turned out to be utterly thinkable, even manageable.

When Roosevelt made his arrangement with Stalin, he was politically vulnerable to his right wing, the more extreme elements of which already regarded him as a socialist favorably inclined to the Soviets. Nixon, as a right-wing opponent of communism, had an easier time. President Obama will be in Roosevelt's position, without the overwhelming threat of a comparatively much greater evil—that is, Nazi Germany.

President Obama's political standing would be enhanced by an air strike more than by a cynical deal. An accommodation with Iran will be particularly difficult for him because it will be seen as an example of weakness rather than of ruthlessness and cunning. Iranian president Ahmadinejad will have a much easier time selling such an arrangement to his people. But set against the options—a nuclear Iran, extended air strikes with all attendant consequences, the long-term, multidivisional, highly undesirable presence of American forces in Iraq—this alliance seems perfectly reasonable.

Nixon and China showed that major diplomatic shifts can take place quite suddenly. There is often a long period of back-channel negotiations, followed by a breakthrough driven either by changing circumstances or by skillful negotiations.

The current president will need considerable political craft to position the alliance as an aid to the war on al Qaeda, making it clear that Shiite-dominated Iran is as hostile to the Sunnis as it is to Americans. He will be opposed by two powerful lobbies in this, the Saudis and the Israelis. Israel will be outraged by the maneuver, but the Saudis will be terrified, which is one of the maneuver's great advantages, increasing American traction over its policies. The Israelis can in many ways be handled more easily, simply because the Israeli military and intelligence services have long seen the Iranians as occasional allies against Arab threats, even as the Iranians were supporting Hezbollah against Israel. They have had a complex relationship over the last thirty years. The Saudis will condemn this move, but the pressure it places on the Arab world would be attractive to Israel. Even so, the American Jewish community is not as sophisticated or cynical as Israel in these matters, and its members will be vocal. Even more difficult to manage will be the Saudi lobby, backed as it is by American companies that do business in the kingdom.

There will be several advantages to the United States. First, without fundamentally threatening Israeli interests, the move will demonstrate that the United States is not controlled by Israel. Second, it will put a generally unpopular country, Saudi Arabia—a state that has been accustomed to having its way in Washington—on notice that the United States has other options. For their part, the Saudis have nowhere to go, and they will cling to whatever guarantees the United States provides them in the face of an American-Iranian entente.

Recalling thirty years of hostilities with Iran, the American public will be outraged. The president will have to frame his maneuver by offering rhetoric about protecting the homeland against the greater threat. He will of course use China as an example of successful reconciliation with the irreconcilable.

The president will have to deal with the swirling public battles of foreign lobbies and make the case for the entente. But he will ultimately have to maintain his moral bearings, remembering that in the end, Iran is not America's friend any more than Stalin and Mao were.

If ever there was a need for secret understandings secretly arrived at, this is it, and much of this arrangement will remain unspoken. Neither country will want to incur the internal political damage from excessive public meetings and handshakes. But in the end, the United States needs to exit from the trap it is in, and Iran has to avoid a real confrontation with the United States.

Iran is an inherently defensive country. It is not strong enough to be either the foundation of American policy in the region or the real long-term issue. Its population is concentrated in the mountains that ring its borders, while much of the center of the country is minimally or completely uninhabitable. Iran can project power under certain special conditions, such as those that obtain at the moment, but in the long run it is either a victim of outside powers or isolated.

An alliance with the United States will temporarily give Iran the upper hand in relations with the Arabs, but within a matter of years the United States will have to reassert a balance of power. Pakistan is unable to extend its influence westward. Israel is much too small and distant to counterbalance Iran. The Arabian Peninsula is too fragmented, and the duplicity of the United States in encouraging it to increase its arms is too obvious to be an alternative counterweight. A more realistic alternative is to encourage Russia to extend its influence to the Iranian border. This might happen anyway, but as we will see, that would produce major problems elsewhere.

The only country capable of being a counterbalance to Iran and a potential long-term power in the region is Turkey, and it will achieve that status within the next ten years regardless of what the United States does. Turkey has the seventeenth largest economy in the world and the largest in the Middle East. It has the strongest army in the region and, aside from the Russians and possibly the British, probably the strongest army in Europe. Like most countries in the Muslim world, it is currently divided between secularists and Islamists within its own borders. But their struggle is far more restrained than what is going on in other parts of the Muslim world.

Iranian domination of the Arabian Peninsula is not in Turkey's interest because Turkey has its own appetite for the region's oil, reducing its dependency on Russian oil. Also, Turkey does not want Iran to become more powerful than itself. And while Iran has a small Kurdish population, southeastern Turkey is home to an extremely large number of Kurds, a fact that Iran can exploit. Regional and global powers have been using support for the Kurds to put pressure on or destabilize Iraq, Turkey, and Iran. It is an old game and a constant vulnerability.

In the course of the next decade the Iranians will have to divert major resources in order to deal with Turkey. Meanwhile, the Arab world will be looking for a champion against Shiite Iran, and despite the bitter history of Turkish power in the Arab world during the Ottoman Empire, Sunni Turkey is the best bet.

In the next ten years, the United States must make certain that Turkey does not become hostile to American interests and that Iran and Turkey do not form an alliance for the domination and division of the Arab world. The more Turkey and Iran fear the United States, the greater the likelihood that this will happen. The Iranians will be assuaged in the short run by their entente with the Americans, but they will be fully aware that this is an alliance of convenience, not a long-term friendship. It is the Turks who are open to a longer-term alignment with the United States, and Turkey can be valuable to the United States in other places, particularly in the Balkans and the Caucasus, where it serves as a block to Russian aspirations.

As long as the United States maintains the basic terms of its agreement with Iran, Iran will represent a threat to Turkey. Whatever the inclinations of the Turks, they will have to protect themselves, and to do that, they must work to undermine Iranian power in the Arabian Peninsula and the Arab countries to the north of the peninsula—Iraq, Syria, and Lebanon. They will engage in this not only to limit Iran but also to improve their access to the oil to their south, both because they will need that oil and because they will want to profit from it.

As Turkey and Iran compete in the next decade, Israel and Pakistan will be concerned with local balances of power. In the long run, Turkey cannot be contained by Iran. Turkey is by far the more dynamic country economically, and therefore it can support a more sophisticated military. More important, whereas Iran has geographically limited regional options, Turkey reaches into the Caucasus, the Balkans, Central Asia, and ultimately the Mediterranean and North Africa, which provides opportunities and allies denied the Iranians. Iran has never been a significant naval power since antiquity, and because of the location of its ports, it can never really be one in the future. Turkey, in contrast, has frequently been the dominant power in the Mediterranean and will be so again. Over the next decade we will see the beginning of Turkey's rise to dominance in the region. It is interesting to note that while we can't think of the century without Turkey playing an extremely important role, this decade will be one of preparation. Turkey will have to come to terms with its domestic conflicts and grow its economy. The cautious foreign policy Turkey has followed recently will continue. It is not going to plunge into conflicts and therefore will influence but not define the region. The United States must take a long-term view of Turkey and avoid pressure that could undermine its development.

As a solution to the complex problems of the Middle East, the American president must choose a temporary understanding with Iran that gives Iran what it wants, that gives the United States room to withdraw, and that is also a foundation for the relationship of mutual hostility to the Sunni fundamentalists. In other words, the president must put the Arabian Peninsula inside the Iranians' sphere of influence while limiting their direct controls, and while putting the Saudis, among others, at an enormous disadvantage.

This strategy would confront the reality of Iranian power and try to shape it. Whether it is shaped or not, the longer-term solution to the balance of power in the region will be the rise of Turkey. A powerful Turkey would counterbalance Iran and Israel, while stabilizing the Arabian Peninsula. In due course the Turks will begin to react by challenging the Iranians, and thus the central balance of power will be resurrected, stabilizing the region. This will create a new regional balance of power. But that is not for this decade.

I am arguing that this is a preferred policy option given the circumstances. But I am also arguing that this is the most logical outcome. The alternatives are unacceptable to both sides; there is too much risk. And when the alternatives are undesirable, what remains—however preposterous it appears—is the most likely outcome.

To see how that would affect wider circles of power and their balance, we turn to the next concern, the balance between Europe and Russia.

CHAPTER 8

THE RETURN OF RUSSIA

The collapse of the Soviet Union appeared to signal Russia's demise as an international player, but news of that death was premature. A nation so large, so filled with resources, and so strategically located doesn't simply dissolve into the air. In the 1990s, the USSR's fall nonetheless shattered the vast empire assembled by the czars and held together by the Communists, leaving Moscow in control of a fraction of what it held in 1989. Muscovy alone (and Siberia), the region that had been the kernel of the empire, remained in Russian hands. As long as that core remained, however, the game wasn't over. The Russian Federation, sorely weakened, still survived, and it will play an increasingly significant role in the next decade.

While Russia suffered breakaway regions and an economy in shambles, the United States emerged as the sole remaining global power, able to dominate the planet in a casual, almost indolent fashion. But the Soviet collapse gave the United States only a limited time frame in which to drive a stake into the heart of its old rival, ensuring that it stayed down. The United States could have applied stress to the Russian system by supporting secessionist movements or by increasing economic pressure. Such moves might very well have caused the entire Russian Federation to crumble, enabling its former junior partners to absorb what was left and form a new balance of power in Eurasia.

At the time, however, the effort did not seem worth the risk, mostly because Russia appeared unlikely to emerge from its chaos for generations. Destroying what was left of Russian power did not even appear to be necessary, because the United States could create the regional balance of power it wanted simply by expanding NATO and the alliance system eastward.

But the United States was also deeply concerned about the future of the Soviet nuclear arsenal, which was even more massive than the American one. Further chaos in the region would have made the weapons vulnerable to terrorists and black marketers, among other risks. The United States wanted nuclear weapons within the former Soviet Union to be under the control of one state that could be watched and shaped, and that state was Russia, not Ukraine or Belarus or all the rest. Thus while the Russian nuclear arsenal had not preserved the Soviet Union, it did save the Russian Federation—at least from U.S. intervention.

During the 1990s the non-Russian members of the former Soviet Union, countries such as Kazakhstan and Ukraine, were desperate to be organized. By rapidly and aggressively integrating them into NATO, the United States could have increased the strength and cohesiveness of these encircling nations to bottle up Russia and the former Soviet republics as well, and Russia would have been helpless to stop the process.

Yet while the United States had plans to do exactly this, it did not move quickly enough. Only eastern Europe and the Baltic states were absorbed into NATO, a significant strategic shift that becomes more significant when you consider this fact: when the Soviet Union still controlled East Germany, the distance between NATO forces and St. Petersburg was about a thousand miles, but after the Baltics were admitted into NATO, the distance was about one hundred miles. This sense of being encircled, diminished, and encroached upon shapes Russian behavior going forward.

RUSSIAN FEARS

With NATO on its doorstep, the Russians understandably became alarmed. From their point of view, this alliance was first and foremost military, and however kindly its disposition might be at the moment, its future intentions were unpredictable. The Russians knew all too well how easily moods can swing, recalling painfully how Germany had gone from being a chaotic, poor, and barely armed country in 1932 to becoming the dominant military force in Europe six years later. Russia saw no reason for the West to expand NATO unless sooner or later the West wanted NATO to be in a position to strike. After all, the Russians argued, they were certainly not about to invade Europe.

There were those in NATO, particularly the Americans and the former satellites of the Soviet Union, who wanted to take advantage of the opportunity to expand for strategic reasons. But others, particularly the Europeans, had started thinking of NATO in a different way. Rather than seeing NATO as a military alliance focused on war, they saw it as a regional United Nations, designed to incorporate friendly, liberal democracies into an organization whose primary function was to maintain stability.

The inclusion of the Baltics was the high-water mark of NATO expansion, after which events began to intervene. Vladimir Putin's rise to power created a very different Russia from the one that had existed under Boris Yeltsin in the 1990s. Meanwhile, the one institution that had never stopped functioning was the intelligence services. Having held Russia and its empire together for generations, they operated through the 1990s almost as an autonomous state or crime organization. Putin had been trained in the KGB, and as a result he saw the world geopolitically rather than ideologically. In his mind, a strong state was essential to Russian stability, so from the moment he took power in 2000, he started the process of restoring Russian muscle.

For more than a century, Russia had been trying to become an industrial power that could compete with the West. Seeing that Russia could never catch up, Putin shifted the nation's economic strategy to focus on developing and exporting natural resources such as metals, grain, and particularly energy. The strategy was brilliant in that it created an economy that Russia could sustain and that would sustain Russia. It strengthened the Russian state by making Gazprom an arm of the Russian government with a monopoly on natural gas. And it created European dependence on Russian energy, thus making it less likely that the Europeans—particularly the Germans—would seek or support confrontation.

The turning point in relations between the United States and Russia came in 2004, when events in Ukraine convinced the Russians that the U.S. intended to destroy or at least tightly control them. A large nation, Ukraine covers the entire southwestern frontier of Russia, and from the Russian point of view, it is the key to Russian national security.

The Russian territory lying between Ukraine and Kazakhstan is only three hundred miles wide, and all of Russia's influence in the Caucasus—

Ukraine-Kazakhstan Gap

along with a good deal of the oil in the pipelines to the south—flows through this gap. At the center of the gap is Volgograd, formerly Stalingrad. During World War II, the Soviets sacrificed one million lives in the battle to keep that gap from being closed by the Germans.

The initial winner of the Ukrainian election in 2004, President Viktor Yanukovich, was accused of widespread electoral fraud, of which he was no doubt guilty, and demonstrations took place to demand that the election be annulled, that Yanukovich step down, and that new elections be held. This uproar, known as the Orange Revolution, was seen by Moscow as a pro-Western, anti-Russian uprising designed to take Ukraine into NATO. The Russians also charged that rather than being a popular uprising, it was a carefully orchestrated coup, sponsored by the CIA and the British MI6. According to the Russians, Western nongovernmental organizations and consulting groups had flooded Ukraine to stage the demonstrations, unseat a pro-Russian government, and directly threaten Russian national security.

Certainly the Americans and the British had supported these NGOs, and the consultants who were now managing the campaigns of some of the pro-Western candidates in Ukraine had formerly managed elections in the United States. Western money from multiple sources clearly was going into the country, but from the American point of view, there was nothing covert or menacing in any of this. The United States was simply doing what it had done since the fall of the Berlin Wall: working with democratic groups to build democracies.

This is where the United States and Russia profoundly parted company. Ukraine was divided between pro-Russian and anti-Russian factions, but the Americans merely saw themselves as supporting democrats. That the factions seen as democratic by the Americans were also the ones that were anti-Russian was, for the Americans, incidental.

For the Russians, it was not incidental. They had vivid memories of the containment policy the United States had long practiced vis-à-vis the Soviet Union, only now the container appeared smaller, tighter, and far more dangerous. They saw U.S. actions as a deliberate attempt to make Russia indefensible and as an encroachment on vital Russian interests in the Caucasus, a region in which the United States already had a bilateral agreement with Georgia.

Containment was indeed the American strategy, of course, however benignly it was expressed. The fundamental American interest is always the balance of power, and having refrained from trying to destroy the Russian Federation in the 1990s, the United States moved to create a regional balance in 2004, with Ukraine as its foundation and with the clear intent to include most of the former Soviet Union countries in this counterweight to Russian power.

Russian fears were compounded when they saw what the United States was doing in Central Asia. Even so, when the United States decided in the wake of September 11 to bring down the Taliban government in Afghanistan quickly, the Russians cooperated in two ways. First, they provided access to the Northern Alliance, a pro-Russian faction going back to the Russian occupation and the civil war that followed it. Second, Russia used its influence to obtain air and ground bases in the three countries bordering Afghanistan—Uzbekistan, Tajikistan, and Turkmenistan—from which the United States could support its invasion forces. Russia also granted flight privileges over its territory, which was extremely useful for travel from the West Coast or Europe.

It was Russia's understanding that these bases in the bordering countries were temporary, but after three years, the Americans showed no signs of leaving anytime soon. In the interim the invasion of Iraq had taken place, over Russian objections, and the United States was now bogged down in what was clearly a long-term occupation. It was also heavily involved in Ukraine and Georgia and was building a major presence in Central Asia. Whereas these actions might not seem so harmful to Moscow's interests when viewed individually, taken together they looked like a concerted effort to strangle Russia.

In particular, the U.S. presence in Georgia could be seen only as a deliberate provocation, because Georgia bordered on the Russian region of Chechnya. The Russians feared that if Chechnya seceded from the Russian Federation, the entire structure would disintegrate as others followed its lead. Chechnya is also located on the extreme northern slope of the Caucasus, and Russian power had already retreated hundreds of miles from its original frontiers deep in those mountains. If the Russians retreated any farther, they would be out of the Caucasus entirely, on flat ground that is hard to defend. Moreover, a significant oil pipeline went through Grozny, the Chechnyan capital, and its loss (although it is currently inoperative due to Chechnyan sabotage) would have a significant impact on the Russian energy export strategy.

Going back to the 1990s, the Russians believed that the Georgians were permitting a flow of weapons into Chechnya through what was called the Pankisi Gorge. They also believed that the United States, which had Special Forces advisers in Georgia, was at best doing nothing to stop the traffic and at worst encouraging it.

Proceeding from its core policy, the United States was trying to build friendships in the region, especially in Georgia, but it was obvious to all that the U.S. was no longer capable of serious power projection. It still had naval and air power in reserve, but on the ground its forces were tapped out in Iraq and Afghanistan.

This was significant enough psychologically, but then the Iraq war created a huge political effect as well. The split that developed between the United States and France and Germany over Iraq, and the general European antipathy toward the Bush administration, meant that Germany in particular was far less inclined than it had been to support American plans for NATO expansion or confrontations with Russia. In addition, the Russians had made Germany dependent on Russian natural gas by supplying nearly half of Germany's needs, so the Germans were in no position to seek confrontation. The combination of military imbalance and diplomatic tension severely limited American options, yet by habit the United States continued to try to increase its influence.

In his state-of-the-nation address on April 25, 2005, Putin declared the fall of the Soviet Union to be the "greatest geopolitical catastrophe of the century." This was his public announcement that he intended to act to reverse some of the consequences of that fall. While Russia was no longer a global power, within the region it was—absent the United States—overwhelmingly powerful. Given the wars in Iraq and Afghanistan, the United States was now absent. In light of this, Putin moved to increase the capability of his military. He also moved to strengthen his regime by increasing revenues from commodity exports, a fortuitous decision given the rise of commodity prices. He used the intelligence capabilities of the FSB and SVR, heirs to the KGB, to identify and control key figures in the former Soviet Union. Since most had been politically active under the Soviet regime, they were either former Communists or at least well known to the FSB from their files. Everyone has vulnerabilities, and Putin used his strongest resource to exploit those weaknesses.

In August 2008, the Georgian government, for reasons that have never been completely clear, attacked South Ossetia. Once part of Georgia, this region had broken away and had been effectively independent since the 1990s, and it was allied with Russia. Putin responded as if Russia had been expecting the attack: he struck back within hours, defeating the Georgian army and occupying part of that country.

The main point of the attack was to demonstrate that Russia could still project power. The Russian army had collapsed in the 1990s, and Putin needed to dispel the perception that it was no longer relevant. But he also wanted to demonstrate to the countries of the former Soviet Union that American friendship and guarantees had no meaning. It was a small attack against a small nation, but a strike against a nation that had drawn very close to the United States. The operation stunned both the region and eastern Europe, as did the lack of an American response, along with the effective indifference of the Europeans. U.S. inaction, limited to diplomatic notes, drove home the fact that America was far away and Russia was very close, and as long as the United States continued to commit its ground forces to the Middle East, its inability to act would persist. Russian supporters in Ukraine, aided by Russian intelligence, began the process of reversing the results of the Orange Revolution. In 2010, elections replaced the pro-Western government with the man whom the Orange Revolution had overthrown.

By moving too slowly, the United States allowed the Russians to regain their balance, just as the U.S. was losing its own strategic balance in Iraq. At the very moment that it needed to concentrate power on the Russian periphery to lock into place its containment system, the United States had its forces elsewhere, and its alliances in Europe were too weak to be meaningful. It is to avoid such missteps and missed opportunities that the American president will need to adopt a new and more consistent strategy in the decade ahead.

THE REEMERGENCE OF RUSSIA

In the long run, Russia is a weak country. Putin's strategy of focusing on energy production and export is a superb short-term tool, but it works only if it forms the basis for major economic expansion. To achieve this larger objective, Russia has to deal with its underlying structural weaknesses, yet these weaknesses are rooted in geographical problems that are not readily overcome.

Unlike much of the industrial world, Russia has both a relatively small population for its size and a population that is highly dispersed, tied together by little more than a security apparatus and a common culture.

Even the major cities, such as Moscow and St. Petersburg, are not the centers of a giant megalopolis. They are stand-alone entities, separated from each other by vast distances of farmland and forest. Leaving apart the fact that the Russian population is in decline, the current distribution of population makes a modern economy, or even efficient distribution of food, difficult, if not impossible. The infrastructure connecting farming areas to the city is poor, as is the infrastructure connecting industrial and commercial centers.

The problem in connectivity stems from the fact that Russia's rivers go the wrong way. Unlike American rivers, which connect farming country to ports where food can be distributed, Russian rivers merely create barriers. Neither the czars and their railway bonds nor Stalin with his enforced starvation ever came close to overcoming the problem, and the cost of building a connective tissue for the Russian economy—extensive

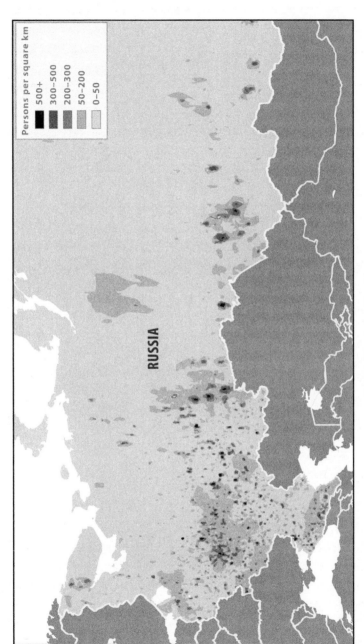

Russian Population Density

rail systems and roads—remains staggering. Russia has always wielded a military force that outstripped its economy, but it cannot do so forever.

Russia must concentrate on the short term while it has the twin advantages of German dependence on its energy and America's distraction in the Middle East. It must try to create lasting structures—some of them domestic, some foreign—that can hold together even in the face of economic limitations.

The domestic structure is already emerging, with Russia, Belarus, and Kazakhstan having reached agreement on an economic union and now discussing a common currency. Armenia, Kyrgyzstan, and Tajikistan have expressed interest in joining in, and Russia has floated the idea of Ukraine joining as well. This is a relationship that will evolve into a political union of some sort, like the European Union, an alignment that will go far in re-creating the central features of the former Soviet Union.

The international structure Russia needs is perhaps more important and problematic. It begins with a relationship with Europe, particularly Germany. Russia needs access to technology, which the Germans have in abundance, while Germany needs access to Russian natural resources. Germany fought two wars to get hold of these resources but failed. Its interest in these resources has not diminished, but its means are now diplomatic rather than military. The desire to exploit this complementary relationship will be at the heart of Russian strategy during the next ten years.

Germany is the driving force of the European Union, which, as we will see, carries with it unexpected burdens. Germany has little interest in American operations in the Middle East and no interest whatever in expanding NATO, and with it American influence, to the Russian periphery. It wants to keep its distance from the United States, and it needs options other than the EU. Closer cooperation with Russia is not a bad idea from Germany's point of view, and it is an outstanding idea from Russia's point of view. Putin knows the Germans well enough to understand their fear and distrust of Russia. But he also knows them well enough to realize that they have outgrown the postwar world, are facing serious economic problems of their own, and need Russian resources.

The simultaneous reconstruction of a Russian-dominated sphere of influence and the creation of structural relations with Germany is an idea that Russia needs to push, and push quickly, since time is not on its side. It must convince Germany that it can be a reliable partner without taking any steps to disrupt the EU or Germany's relations with it. These developments will be a ballet backed by real, if transitory, power.

To have any chance for maneuvering in the coming years, Russia must split the United States from Europe. At the same time, it will do everything it can to keep the United States bogged down in Iraq, Afghanistan, and, if possible, Iran. From the Russian point of view, the U.S.-jihadist war is like Vietnam: it relieves Russia of the burden of dealing with the American military, and it actually makes the Americans dependent on Russian cooperation in measures such as imposing sanctions on countries like Iran. The Russians can play the Americans indefinitely by threatening to ship weapons to anti-American groups and to countries such as Iran and Syria. This locks the United States in place, trying to entice the Russians when in fact the only thing the Russians want the Americans to do is to remain permanently bogged down in the war.

This Russian strategy reveals the price of the American overcommitment to the war on terror. It also shows that it is imperative for the United States to find an effective response to radical Islam, as well as an effective response to the Russians. Lurking behind each Russian move is a potential geopolitical nightmare for the Americans.

THE AMERICAN STRATEGY

The American interest in Eurasia—understood as Russia and the European peninsula—is the same as U.S. interest everywhere: for no single power or coalition to dominate. The unification of Russia and Europe would create a force whose population, technological and industrial capability, and natural resources would at the very least equal America's, and in all likelihood outstrip them.

During the twentieth century, the United States acted three times to prevent the kind of Russian-German entente that could unify Eurasia and threaten fundamental American interests. In 1917, Russia's separate peace with the Germans turned the tide against the Anglo-French in World War I. The U.S. intervened in World War II, supplying the British and especially the Soviets, who bled the Wehrmacht and prevented a German takeover of the vast Russian territories. In 1944, the United States then invaded Western Europe, blocking not only the Germans but the Soviets as well. From 1945 to 1991, the United States devoted enormous resources to preventing the Soviets from dominating Eurasia.

The response of the United States to a Russian-German entente must be the same during the next ten years as it was in the twentieth century. The United States must continue to do everything it can to block a German-Russian entente and to limit the effect that Russia's sphere of influence might have on Europe, because the very presence of a militarily powerful Russia changes the way Europe behaves.

Germany is the European center of gravity, and if it shifts its position, other European countries will have to shift accordingly, with perhaps enough countries moving to tilt the balance of the entire region. As Russia reconstitutes and solidifies its hold on the countries of the former Soviet Union, it will be able to take most of those countries along. However informal the relationship might be at the beginning, it will solidify into something more substantial over time, because the parts simply fit together too neatly for it to be otherwise. This would be a historic redefinition of U.S.-European relations, a fundamental shift not only in the regional but also in the global balance of power, with outcomes that are highly unpredictable.

While I see a confederation between Belarus and Russia as likely, such a move would bring the Russian army to the frontiers of Europe. Indeed, Russia already has a military alliance with Belarus. Add to that Ukraine, and Russian forces would be on the borders of Romania, Hungary, Slovakia, Poland, and the Baltic countries—all former Russian satellites—thus re-creating the Russian empire, albeit in different institutional form.

Yet the countries behind the front tier are more concerned about the United States than they are about Russia. They see the Americans more as economic competitors than as partners, and as a force pulling them into conflicts that they want no part of. The Russians, on the other hand, seem to be economically synergistic with the advanced European countries.

The European nations also see the former Russian satellites as a physical buffer against Moscow, further guaranteeing that they can work with Russia and still be secure in their own region. They understand the concern the eastern Europeans have but believe that the economic benefits of the relationships, as well as the eastern Europeans' dependence on the economy of the rest of Europe, will keep the Russians in line. The Europeans could diminish their relationship with the Americans, build a new, mutually beneficial relationship with the Russians, and still have the benefit of a strategic buffer as an insurance policy. This would pose a profound risk to the United States. Therefore the American president must act to contain Russia, allowing that nation's long-term, inherent weaknesses to take their toll. He can't wait until the U.S.-jihadist war ends. He must act immediately.

If Germany and Russia continue to move toward alignment, then the countries between the Baltic Sea and the Black Sea—what used to be called the Intermarium countries—become indispensable to the United States and its policy. Of these countries, Poland is the largest and the most strategically placed. It is also the one with both the most to lose and a keen awareness of that potential for loss. Membership in the European Union is one thing to the Poles, but being caught in a Russo-German entente is another. They and the other eastern Europeans are terrified of being drawn back into the spheres of influence of one or both of their historic enemies.

Most of these countries were not independent until World War I brought the collapse of the Austro-Hungarian, Russian, Ottoman, and German empires. In general, they were divided, subjugated, and exploited. In cases such as Hungary, the oppression was mild. In other cases, it was brutal. But all these nations remember occupation by the

Nazis and later by the Soviets, and those occupations were monstrous. It is true that the German and Russian regimes today are different, but for the eastern Europeans, occupation wasn't so long ago, and the memory of what it meant to be caught in the German-Russian force field has shaped their national character. It will continue to shape their behavior in the decade to come.

This is particularly true for Poland, which at various times has been absorbed into Germany, Russia, and Austria. The historical compromise, when there were compromises to be made, was the partition of Poland, which remains Poland's nightmare going forward. When the country became independent after World War I, it had to fight a war to prevent Soviet encroachment. Twenty years later, the Germans and Soviets invaded simultaneously, based on a secret pact to do just that. The following half century of Cold War communism was an unmitigated nightmare.

The Poles have suffered in direct relation to the strategic importance of their location, bordering both Germany and Russia and occupying the North European Plain, which extends like a thoroughfare from the French Atlantic coast to St. Petersburg. The other eastern European countries share the Polish view, but they are geographically safer, behind the Carpathian Mountains.

Exposed on either side, Poland will have little choice but to go along with whatever the Germans and Russians decide, which would be disastrous for the United States. It is therefore in the American interest to guarantee Poland's independence from Russia and Germany, not only formally but by creating a viable and vibrant Polish economy and military that can serve as the model and driver for the rest of eastern Europe. Poland is the historical bone in the throat of both Germany and Russia, and it is in the American interest to make sure that it is firmly lodged there. A Poland aligned with Germany is a threat to Russia, and the reverse is true as well. Poland must remain a threat to both, because the United States cannot let either feel too secure.

Over the next ten years, an American relationship with Poland would serve two functions: it might prevent or limit the Russo-German

North European Plain

entente, but failing that, it could create a counterbalance. The United States urgently needs Poland, because there is no alternative strategy for balancing an alliance between Russia and Germany. From the Polish point of view, friendship with the Americans would serve to protect it from its neighbors, but here there is a special problem. The Polish national mentality was seared by the failure of Britain and France to come to Poland's defense against Germany at the beginning of World War II, despite guarantees. Poland's hypersensitivity to betrayal will cause it to prefer accommodation with hostile powers to alignment with an unreliable partner. For this reason, the president must avoid appearing tentative or hesitant in his approach. This means making a strategic decision that is in some ways unhedged—always an uncomfortable stand, because good presidents always look to keep their options open. But insisting on too much maneuvering room might close the Polish option immediately.

When the George W. Bush administration set out to create a ballistic missile defense system for eastern Europe, the United States hedged. It decided to build a system that would defend against small numbers of missiles fired by rogue countries, particularly Iran. It planned to place a radar system in the Czech Republic and made plans to install the missiles in Poland. This was in addition to sending the Poles sophisticated weapons such as the F-16 fighter and Patriot Missiles. The system could have been located anywhere; it was located in Poland in order to make it clear that Poland was essential to American strategic interests and to intensify U.S.-Polish cooperation outside the context of NATO. The Russians understood this and tried to do everything they could to block it.

The Russians opposed placing the missiles in Poland, even though the system could defend against only a few missiles and the Russians had overwhelming numbers. In reality, the issue for the Russians was never missile defense—it was the fact that the United States was placing strategic systems on Polish soil. A strategic system has to be defended, and the Russians understood that the BMD system was just the beginning of a significant American commitment to Poland.

When the Obama administration came in, its leaders wanted to "reset" their relations with the Russians. The Russians made it clear that while they did not want to go back to Cold War hostilities, things could go forward only if the BMD system was withdrawn from Poland. By that time, the Poles regarded the system as a symbol of America's commitment to them. This, despite the fact that the BMD system did not actually protect Poland from anything and might even make it a target. Nevertheless, the Poles, sensitive to betrayal, urgently wanted the relationship with Washington. When Obama decided to shift the BMD system from Poland to ships offshore, the Poles panicked, believing that the United States was about to make a deal with the Russians. The United States had not shifted its position on Poland at all, but the Poles were convinced that it had.

If Poland believes that it is a bargaining chip, it will become unreliable, and thus in the course of the next decade the United States might get away with betraying Poland only once. Such a move could be contemplated only if it provided some overwhelming advantage, and it is difficult to see what that advantage could be, given that maintaining a powerful wedge between Germany and Russia is of overwhelming interest to the United States.

The condition of the Baltic countries is a different matter. They represent a superb offensive capability for the United States, pointing, as they do, like a bayonet at St. Petersburg, the second largest city of Russia, and with the eastern border of Lithuania only about one hundred miles from Minsk, the capital of Belarus.

Nonetheless, the United States hasn't the force or the interest to invade Russia. And given that the American position is strategically aggressive and tactically defensive, the Baltics become a liability. About three hundred miles long and nowhere more than two hundred miles wide, they are almost impossible to defend. They do, however, serve to block the Russian navy in St. Petersburg. So the Baltics remain an asset, but one that might be too expensive to maintain. The American president must therefore appear to be utterly committed to the Baltics to deter the Russians, while extracting maximum concessions from the Russians for an American agreement to withdraw from the region. Given Polish skittishness, such a maneuver should be delayed as long as possible. Unfortunately, the Russians will be aware of this fact and will probably bring pressure to bear on the Baltics sooner rather than later, making this a clear and early point of friction.

Whatever happens to Germany, it is of extreme importance to the United States to maintain a strong bilateral relationship with Denmark, whose waters block the exits from the Baltic Sea. Norway, whose North Cape provides facilities to block the Russian fleet in Murmansk, has value to the United States, as does Iceland, a superb platform from which to search for Russian submarines. Neither country is a member of the European Union, and Iceland is resentful of Germany because of economic actions taken during the 2008 financial crisis. Thus both can be gathered in at relatively low cost.

The rest of the frontier with Russia will be the Carpathian Mountains, behind which lie Slovakia, Hungary, and Romania. It is a strategic imperative for the United States to maintain friendly relations with these three countries and to help them develop their military capability. But given the obstacle that the Carpathians present to an invader, the military capability required is minimal. Because these countries are less at risk than Poland and therefore freer to maneuver, there also will be a greater degree of political complexity. But so long as the Russians don't move past the Carpathians and the Germans do not reduce these countries to complete economic dependency, the United States can manage the situation with a simple strategy: strengthen these economies and militaries, make it advantageous to remain pro-American, and wait. Do nothing to provoke the Russians in their sphere of influence. Do nothing to sabotage Russian economic relations with the rest of Europe. Do nothing to worry the rest of the Europeans that the U.S. is going to drag them into a war.

In the Caucasus, the United States is currently aligned with Georgia, a country that remains under Russian pressure and whose internal politics are in the long run unpredictable, to say the least. The next line of countries, Armenia and Azerbaijan, is also problematic. The former is a Russian ally, the latter closer to Turkey. Because of historical hostility to Turkey, Armenia is always closer to Russia. Azerbaijan tries to balance among Turkey, Iran, and Russia.

It is one thing for the United States to stake out a position in Poland, a country of 40 million people. Remaining committed to Georgia, a country of only 4 million that is far less developed than Poland, is much more difficult. And defeat in Georgia, in the form of a pro-Russian government that would ask U.S. advisers and forces to leave, would not only unravel the American position in the Caucasus but create a crisis of confidence in Poland as well.

The situation in the Caucasus can be handled only by Turkey. Whereas Russia's border moved north, unveiling the three historic states of Armenia, Azerbaijan, and Georgia, Turkey's border has remained stable. For the United States, it does not matter where the Russian tier is, so long as it is somewhere in the Caucasus. The only disastrous outcome would be a Russian occupation of Turkey, which is inconceivable, or a Russo-Turkish alliance, which is a more realistic danger.

Turkey and Russia have been historical rivals, two empires on the Black Sea, both competing in the Balkans and the Caucasus. More important, the Russians look at the Bosporus as their blocked gate to the Mediterranean. Turkey may well collaborate with the Russians in the next decade, particularly given dependency on Russian oil, but the idea that it would shift its own border in the Caucasus southward or abandon the Bosporus in any way is out of the question. Simply by existing, then, Turkey serves American interests in relation to Russia. And since the United States has no interest in the specifics of where Russia is contained in the Caucasus, as long as it *is* contained, it follows that a vast American commitment to Georgia makes little sense. Georgia is a drain on the United States with little benefit. So the American strategy in Georgia should be eliminated. It is left over from the period in which the Americans believed that such positions were risk- and cost-free. At a time when risks and costs are rising, the United States must manage its exposure more carefully, recognizing that Georgia is more liability than asset.

In the next decade there will be a small window in which the United States can extract itself from Georgia and the Caucasus without causing psychological damage to its new coalition. But most likely, abandoning Georgia would create psychological uncertainty in Poland and in the Intermarium that could very quickly cause those countries to recalculate their stance. Waiting until Poland and Russia confront each other would simply increase the magnitude of the stress. Therefore, rethinking Georgia as soon as possible has four advantages. First, it gives the United States time to stabilize the Intermarium's psychology. Second, it makes it clear that the United States is making this move for its own reasons, not because of Russian pressure. Third, it will demonstrate to the Turks that the United States can shift positions, making an increasingly confident Turkey more wary of the United States—and sometimes wary is good. Fourth, the United States can ask for Russian concessions in Central Asia in return for backing off in the Caucasus.

As long as the United States is still fighting in Afghanistan, it needs unfettered access to the nearby countries it relies on for logistical support. American oil companies also need access to Central Asian oil and gas deposits. In the long run, the United States is leaving Afghanistan, and in the long run, the United States can't be a dominant force in the region. Geography simply precludes American dominance, and the Russians know that.

The United States made promises to Georgia that it now isn't going to keep. But when we look at the broader picture, this betrayal increases America's ability to keep other commitments. Georgia is of little importance to the United States, but it is of enormous importance to the Russians, guaranteeing the security of their southern frontier. The Russians would be prepared to pay a substantial price for Georgia, and U.S. willingness to exit voluntarily and soon should command a premium.

That price would be not to supply Iran with weapons and to join in an effective sanctions regime if the U.S. overture to Iran fails. If the overture succeeds, then the United States can demand that Russia halt weapons shipments into the region, particularly to Syria. If made simultaneously with the overture to Iran, an agreement like this would lend the overture greater weight. It would give the United States more credibility and expanded options. It could also buy time in Poland to build up American assets there.

As a U.S. foothold in the Caucasus, Georgia is much less viable than Azerbaijan, which not only borders Russia and Iran and maintains close relations with Turkey but is a major source of oil. Whereas Armenia is a Russian ally and Georgia lacks a strong economic foundation, Azerbaijan has economic resources and can be a platform for American operations. So in the next decade there will need to be a strategy of withdrawal and a strategy of realignment. Both will do. The current strategy will not.

If the United States convinces Russia that its withdrawal from Georgia is elective, phased, and above all reversible, it can extract concessions that have real meaning while rationalizing its strategic position. In a sense it is a bluff, but a good president needs to be able to bluff, as well as to rationalize a betrayal.

HOW TO MANAGE RUSSIA

Russia does not threaten America's global position, but the mere possibility that it might collaborate with Europe and particularly Germany opens up the most significant threat in the decade, a long-term threat that needs to be nipped in the bud. The United States can't expect Germany to serve the role it played in the Cold War as the frontier set against the Soviet empire. In the next decade, the United States must work to make Poland what Germany was in the 1950s, although the Russian threat will not be as significant, forceful, or monochromatic as it was then. At the same time that the geopolitical confrontation goes on, the United States and Russia will be engaged in economic and political collaboration elsewhere. This is not your daddy's Cold War. The two countries might well collaborate in Central Asia or even the Caucasus while confronting each other in Poland and the Carpathians.

In the long run, the Russians are in trouble and can't sustain a major role in international affairs. Their dependence on commodity exports fills their coffers but doesn't build their economy. Their population is in severe decline. Their geographic structure is unchanged. But in geopolitics, a decade is not the long run. The mere collapse of the Soviet Union took a decade to run its course. For this decade, the threat of Russia and Europe will persist, and it will preoccupy the president as he attempts to restore balance to U.S. global strategy.

CHAPTER 9

EUROPE'S RETURN TO HISTORY

Contemporary Europe is a search for an exit from hell. The first half of the twentieth century was a slaughterhouse, from Verdun to Auschwitz. The second half was lived under threat of a possible U.S.-Soviet nuclear war fought out on European soil. Exhausted by blood and turmoil, Europe began to imagine a world in which all conflicts were economic and bureaucrats in Brussels managed them. They even began to talk of "the end of history," in the sense that all Hegelian conflicts of ideology had been resolved. For the twenty years following the collapse of the Soviet Union, it appeared to them that they had found their utopia, but now the future is much less certain. Looking ahead to the next ten years, I do not see a return to trenches and concentration camps, but I do see geopolitical tensions on the continent growing, and with them the roots of more serious conflict.

Two problems make up the European dilemma for the decade ahead. The first is defining the kind of relationship Europe will have with a resurgent Russia. The second is determining the role that Germany,

Europe's most dynamic economy, will play. The paradox of Russia—weak economy and substantial military force—will persist, as will the dynamism of Germany. The remainder of the European states must define their relationship with these two powers as a prerequisite for defining their relationships with one another. The strain of this process will lead to the emergence of a very different sort of Europe in the next decade, and it will present a significant challenge to the United States. To understand what needs to be done in terms of U.S. policy, we first have to consider the history that has brought us to this juncture.

Europe has always been a bloody place. After 1492, when new discoveries fueled the competition for far-flung empires, the continent hosted a struggle for world domination involving Spain, Portugal, France, the Netherlands, and Britain, countries that bordered either the Atlantic

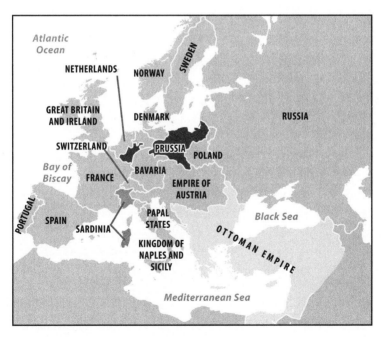

Europe—1815

Ocean or the North Sea. Austria-Hungary and Russia were left out of the contest for colonial empires, while Germany and Italy remained clusters of feudal principalities, fragmented and impotent.

For the next two centuries Europe consisted of four regions—Atlantic Europe, Scandinavia, southeastern Europe, and Russia—with a buffer zone in the center running from Denmark to Sicily. This buffer was a region fragmented into tiny kingdoms and duchies, unable to defend itself but inadvertently providing Europe with a degree of stability.

Then Napoleon redefined Europe. When he pushed east into Germany and south into Italy, he wrecked the complex balance that had existed in those two inchoate nations. Worse, from his point of view, he energized Prussia, goading it into becoming a major European power. It was the Prussians, more than anyone, who engineered Napoleon's defeat at the Battle of Waterloo. A half century later, after a brief and successful war with France in 1871, Prussia united the rest of Germany into a cohesive state. The unification of Italy was by and large completed at about the same time.

Suddenly there was a new geopolitical reality from the North Sea to the Mediterranean. Germany in particular was troublesome, because of its enormous productivity and rapid growth and also because its geography made it profoundly insecure. History had placed Germany on the north of the North European Plain, an area with a few rivers to serve as defenses, but some of the most productive parts of this new nation-state were on the opposite bank of the Rhine, completely unprotected. To the west was France. To the east was Russia. Both had enjoyed the centuries when Germany was fragmented and weak, but now there was a frightening new Germany, economically the most dynamic country in Europe, with a powerful military and with a deep sense of insecurity.

Germany in turn was frightened by its neighbors' fears. Germany's leaders knew their nation could not survive if it was attacked simultaneously by France and Russia. They also believed that at some point such an attack would come, because they understood how intimidating they appeared to their neighbors. Germany could not permit France and Russia to start a war at the time or place of their choosing, and thus Germany, driven by its own fear, devised a strategy of preemption coupled with alliances.

Europe in the twentieth century was defined by these fears, which, being imposed by geography, were both rational and unavoidable. To no one's surprise, that same geography is in place today. The Europeans tried to abolish the consequences of geography by eliminating nationalism, but as we have already begun to see, nationalism is not easily suppressed, and geography must have its due. These issues remain particularly compelling in the case of Germany, which is once again, as in the nineteenth and twentieth centuries, the economic engine of Europe, profoundly insecure and surrounded by nations with potentially divergent interests. The question going forward is whether the geopolitical logic that led to the wars of the past will have the same result or whether, in the years to come, Europe can pass the test of comity it failed so often before.

Both world wars were launched according to a single scenario: Germany, insecure because of its geographical position, swept across France in a lightning attack. The goal in both cases was to defeat France quickly, then deal with Russia. In 1914, the Germans failed to defeat France quickly, the troops dug in, and the conflict became a protracted war. The Germans found themselves fighting France, Britain, and Russia simultaneously in both the east and the west. At the same time that it appeared the Bolshevik revolution would save Germany by taking Russia out of the war, the United States sent troops to Europe, playing its first major role on the world stage and blocking German ambitions.

In 1940 Germany succeeded in overrunning France, only to discover that it still could not defeat the Soviet Union. One reason for that was the second act of America's dramatic emergence. The United States provided aid to the Soviets that kept them in the war until the Anglo-American invasion of France three years later could help destroy Germany for the second time in a quarter century.

Germany emerged from World War II humiliated by defeat but also morally humiliated by its unprecedented barbarism, having committed atrocities that had nothing to do with the necessities of geopolitics. Germany was divided and occupied by the victors.

Germany was physically devastated, but its actions had resulted in the devastation of something far more important. For five hundred years, Europe had dominated the world. Before the wave of self-destruction that began in August 1914, Europe directly controlled vast areas of Asia and Africa and indirectly dominated much of the rest of the planet. Tiny countries like Belgium and the Netherlands controlled areas as vast as the Congo or today's Indonesia.

The wars that followed the creation of Germany destroyed these empires. In addition, the slaughter of the two wars, the destruction of generations of workers and extraordinary amounts of capital, left Europe exhausted. Its empires dissolved into fragments to be fought over by the only two countries that emerged from the conflict with the power and interest to compete for what was left, the United States and the Soviet Union. However, both primarily pursued the fragments of empire as a system of alliances and commercial relations rather than formal imperial domination.

Europe went from being the center of a world empire to being the potential battleground for a third world war. At the heart of the Cold War was the fear that the Soviets, having marched into the center of Germany, would seize the rest of the continent. For Western Europe, the danger was obvious. For the United States, the greatest threat was that Soviet manpower and resources would be combined with European industrialism and technology to create a power potentially greater than the U.S. Fearing the threat to its interests, the United States focused on containing the Soviet Union around its periphery, including Europe.

Two issues converged, setting the stage for the events that will be played out over the next ten years. The first was the question of Germany's role in Europe, which ever since its nineteenth-century unification had been to trigger wars. The second was the shrinking of European power. By the end of the 1960s, not a single European country save the Soviet Union was genuinely global. All the rest had been reduced to

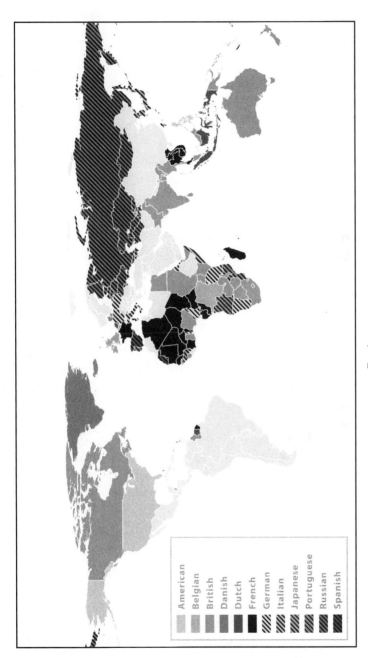

Empires—1900

regional powers, in a region where their collective power was dwarfed by the power of the Soviet Union and the United States. If Germany had to find a new place in Europe, Europe had to find its new place in the world.

The two World Wars and the dramatic reduction of status that followed had a profound psychological impact on Europe. Germany entered a period of deep self-loathing, and the rest of Europe seemed torn between nostalgia for its lost colonies and relief that the burdens of empire and even genuine sovereignty had been lifted from it. Along with European exhaustion came European weakness, but some of the trappings of great-power status remained, symbolized by permanent seats for Britain and France on the United Nations Security Council. But even the possession of nuclear weapons by some of these nations meant little. Europe was trapped in the force field created by the two superpowers.

The German response to its diminished position was in microcosm the European response: Germany recognized its fundamental problem as being that of an independent actor trapped between potentially hostile powers. The threat from the Soviet Union was fixed. However, if Germany could redefine its relationship with France, and through that with the rest of Europe, it would no longer be caught in the middle. For Germany, the solution was to become integrated with the rest of Europe, and particularly with France.

For Europe as a whole, integration was a foregone conclusion—in one sense imposed by the Soviet threat, in another by pressure from the United States. The American strategy for resisting the Soviets was to organize its European allies to defend themselves if necessary, all the while guaranteeing their security with troops already deployed to the continent. There was also the promise of more troops if war broke out, and ultimately the promise to use nuclear weapons if absolutely necessary. The nuclear weapons, however, would be kept under American control. Conventional forces would be organized into a joint command, within the North Atlantic Treaty Organization. This organization created a multilateral, unified defense force for Europe that was, in effect, controlled by the United States.

The Americans also had a vested interest in European prosperity. Through the Marshall Plan and other mechanisms, the United States created a favorable environment in which to revive the European economy while also creating the foundations for a European military capability. The more prosperity was generated through association with the United States, the more attractive membership in NATO became. The greater the contrast was between living conditions in the Soviet bloc and in Western Europe, the more likely that contrast was to generate unrest in the east. The United States believed ideologically and practically in free trade, but more than that, it wanted to see greater integration among the European economies, both for its own sake and to bind the potentially fractious alliance together.

The Americans saw a European economic union as a buttress for NATO. The Europeans saw it as a way not only to recover from the war but to find a place for themselves in a world that had reduced them to the status of regional powers at best. Power, if there was any to be regained, was to be found in some sort of federation. This was the only way to create a balance between Europe and the two superpowers. Such a federation would also solve the German problem by integrating Germany with Europe, making the extraordinary German economic machine a part of the European system. One of the key issues for the next ten years is whether the United States will continue to view European integration in the same way.

In 1992 the Maastricht Treaty established the European Union, but the concept was in fact an old European dream. Its antecedents reach back to the early 1950s and the European Steel and Coal Community, a narrowly focused entity whose leaders spoke of it even then as the foundation for a European federation.

It is coincidental but extremely important that while the EU idea originated during the Cold War, it emerged as a response to the Cold War's end. In the west, the overwhelming presence of NATO and its controls over defense and foreign policy loosened dramatically. In the east, the fall of the Berlin Wall and the collapse of the Soviet Union found sovereign nations coming out of the shadows. It was at this point that Europe regained the sovereignty it had lost but that it is now struggling to define.

The EU was envisioned to serve two purposes. The first was the integration of western Europe into a limited federation, solving the problem of Germany by binding it together with France, thereby limiting the threat of war. The second was the creation of a vehicle for the reintegration of eastern Europe into the European community. The EU turned from a Cold War institution serving western Europe in the context of east-west tensions into a post–Cold War institution designed to bind together both parts of Europe. In addition, it was seen as a step toward returning Europe to its prior position as global power—if not as individual nations, then as a collective equal to the United States. And it is in this ambition that the EU has run into trouble.

THE CRISIS OF THE EU

In the late eighteenth century, when thirteen newly liberated British colonies formed a North American confederation, it was as a practical solution to economic and political issues. But the United States of America, as that confederation came to be known, was also seen as a moral mission dedicated to higher truths, including the idea "that all men are created equal and that they are endowed by their creator with certain inalienable rights." The United States was also rooted in the idea that with the benefits of liberal society came risks and obligations. As Benjamin Franklin put it, "They who can give up essential liberty to obtain a little temporary safety, deserve neither liberty nor safety." In the United States, with such sentiments at its core, the themes of material comfort and moral purpose went hand in hand.

The United States was also created as a federation of what might be called independent countries, sharing a common language but profoundly different in other ways. When those differences led to secession, most of the remaining states of the United States waged war to preserve the Union. That willingness to sacrifice would have been impossible unless the United States was seen as a moral as well as a practical project.

In the United States, the Civil War established that the federal government was sovereign, and absolutely sovereign in foreign affairs. The federal victory put to rest the claims of the Confederate states that sovereignty rested with each of them individually.

In the European Union, by contrast, the confederate model is still in place, and sovereignty rests with each individual nation-state. Even at the level of its most basic premise, then, the European Union sets severe limits on its claims to authority and its right to command sacrifice. This union is stranger still, in that not all Europe is part of it. Some of its members share a currency; others don't. There is no unified defense policy, much less a European army. Moreover, each of the constituent nations has its own history, unique identity, and individual relationship to the idea of sacrifice. The military authority to act internationally, an indispensable part of global power, is also retained by the individual states. The EU remains an elective relationship, created for the convenience of its members, and if it becomes inconvenient, nations can leave. There is no bar on withdrawal.

Fundamentally, the EU is an economic union, and economics, unlike defense, is a means for maximizing prosperity. This limitation means that sacrificing safety for a higher purpose is a contradiction in terms, because the European Union has conflated safety and well-being as its moral purpose. There is simply no basis for the kind of inspiring rhetoric that could induce anyone to fight and die to preserve the ideals of the European Union.

As we look toward the decade ahead, the delicate balance of power established to contain Germany is coming apart—not because Germany wants it to, but because circumstances have changed dramatically.

The dissolution started during the financial crisis of 2008. Germany had been one of the leading economic powers since the 1960s, when the western portion successfully emerged from the devastation of World War II. The collapse of communism in 1989 forced the prosperous west to assimilate the impoverished east, an economic liability. While this was painful, over the next decade Germany absorbed its poor remnant and remained the most powerful country in Europe, content with the economic and political arrangements of the EU. Germany was its leading power, yet still one of many. It had no appetite for further dominance, nor any need for it.

When the financial crisis of 2008 hit, Germany suffered, as did others, but its economy was robust enough to roll with the shock. The first wave of devastation was most severe in eastern Europe, the region that had only recently emerged from Soviet domination. The banking system of many of the countries there had been created or acquired by western European countries, particularly banks in Austria, Sweden, and Italy, but also by some German banks. In one country, the Czech Republic, the banking system was 96 percent owned by other European countries. Given that the EU had accepted many of these countries—the Czech Republic, Poland, Slovakia, Hungary, Romania, and Bulgaria, as well as the Baltic nation-states of Latvia, Lithuania, and Estonia—there seemed to be no reason to be troubled by this. But although these eastern European countries were part of the EU, they still had their own currencies. Those currencies were not only weaker than the euro, they also had higher interest rates.

In an earlier chapter we discussed the problem created by the housing boom and eastern European mortgages denominated in euros, Swiss francs, and even yen. Banks in other EU countries owned many of the eastern European banks. Those banks in western Europe used euros and were under the financial oversight of the European Central Bank and the EU banking system. The eastern European countries were in the strange position of not owning their domestic banking systems. Rather than simply being supervised by their own governments, their banks were under foreign and EU supervision. A nation that doesn't control its own financial system has gone a long way to losing its sovereignty. And this points to the future problem of the EU. The stronger members, like Germany, retained and enhanced their sovereignty during the financial crisis, while the weaker nations saw sovereignty decline. This imbalance will have to be addressed in the decade to come.

Given that the European Union was a single economic entity, and given the fact that the eastern European countries had few resources and limited control over their own banks, the expectation was that the European Union's healthier countries would bail out the eastern banks. This was the expectation not only in the east, but also of the European countries who invested there. Germany had the strongest economy and banking system, so it was expected to take the lead.

But Germany balked. It did not want to underwrite the rescue of eastern Europe. There was far too much money involved, and Germany simply didn't want to shoulder the burden. Instead, the Germans encouraged the eastern Europeans to go to the International Monetary Fund for a bailout. This would reduce the German and European burden, diluting their responsibility with contributions from the Americans and other benefactors of the IMF.

This fallout from the 2008 crisis underscored just how far Europe was from being a single country. It also called attention to the fact that Germany was the prime decision-maker in Europe. If Germany had wanted a bailout, Europe would have had one.

But the financial ripples didn't end there. As recession hit Europe, tax receipts fell and borrowing for social services rose. Some countries were caught in a tremendous squeeze, their troubles compounded by domestic political pressure. For those who used the euro, some of the basic tools for managing a problem like this didn't exist. For example, a declining currency makes imports more expensive and exports cheaper and more competitive. That hurts on the consumption side but helps create jobs and increases tax revenue. Adjusting the value of your currency is a core mechanism for managing recession, but countries such as Greece didn't control their own currency; they didn't even *have* their own currency. Their asymmetry of power turned the EU into a battleground. Germany didn't want the responsibility for bailing out weaker countries, but the weaker countries didn't have full control over their economies so they couldn't take control of their own destiny. The question going forward is whether the EU, especially in light of European history, can withstand this centrifugal force. The answer lies in part in whatever the Germans choose to do.

The euro serves a series of countries in different stages of development and in different parts of their business cycle, and the currency that helps one country doesn't necessarily help another. Obviously, the European Central Bank is more worried about the condition of the German economy than about that of a smaller country, and that affects valuation decisions.

From its founding in 1993 until 2008, the EU enjoyed a period of unprecedented prosperity, and for a while that prosperity submerged all of the issues that had never been fully resolved. The measure of a political entity is how it handles adversity, and with the crisis of 2008, all the unresolved issues emerged, and with them the nationalism that the federation was intended to bury. At times this nationalism became quite powerful politically. The majority of Germans opposed help for Greece. A majority of Greeks preferred bankruptcy to submitting to EU terms, which they saw as German terms. The situation calmed down after the financial crisis eased, but in 2010 we got a glimpse of the forces churning and bubbling beneath the European calm.

The European Union will not disappear, certainly not within the next ten years. It was founded as a free trade zone and will remain one. But it will not evolve into a multinational state that can be a major player on the world stage. There is not enough common interest among the nations to share military power, and without military power Europe does not have what I have called "deep power." The Europeans struggled between national sovereignty and a European solution to the economic crisis. The challenge that finances posed for European unity blocks military integration even more intensely. Ultimately, there is a European bureaucracy but no European state.

On the other hand, it is not clear at all that many of the economic controls the EU has now will survive the decade. As the smaller countries discovered, those controls put them at a severe disadvantage. They are managed by a system that is in the control of larger countries. For citizens of the larger countries, working to build political coalitions to help other countries that run into trouble is a tough sell. Devaluing the currency is a much simpler way of making cheaper exports and more expensive imports and thus improving the economy. But once again, Greece, for example, didn't have this option, because it didn't have its own currency.

In the years immediately ahead, serious economic constraints will no doubt persist. The hardship will not be unprecedented or unmanageable, but it will remain a factor, posing different problems for different nations. Certainly economic stress will drive wedges among these nations and raise serious questions of the benefits of a single currency. I have no doubt that the EU will survive, but I would be very surprised if some members of the eurozone didn't drop out, with others placing caveats on the degree to which they will cede control to the Brussels bureaucracy.

We have already seen the high-water mark of European integration. As the tide goes out over the ten years to come, what will be exposed above all else is the power of Germany.

THE REEMERGENCE OF GERMANY

Germany was born out of a war with France, and it was crushed twice after invading France. Its postwar resolution was to align itself closely with France economically and become the new axis of Europe. But while the German military impulse seems to have been set aside, the problem of the power dynamic persists. If France and Germany stand together, they remain the European center of gravity. If Germany and France collide, that collision rips apart the fabric of Europe, leaving the federated nations to divide and realign in some new configuration.

I'm leaving Britain out of this equation for historical, geographical, and economic reasons. The English Channel has always allowed Britain to step back and engage Europe selectively. But beyond this geographical reality, from the Spanish Armada to the German Blitz, Britain has viewed continental powers as a threat to its survival and has chosen to stand apart. Part of its drive for empire was the desire to avoid being entirely dependent on Europe. Britain normally didn't build a wall against Europe (although it did in extreme cases), but it limited its involvement. Geography made this possible.

While Europe as a whole remains Britain's largest trading partner, its largest export target among nations is the United States. When Britain is drawn deeply into Europe, the cause is more often war than economics. British strategy has always been to block a unified Europe as a threat to its national security, not least because the idea of a Europe militarily dominated by France and Germany is intolerable. For Britain to be the junior partner in such an alignment is neither prudent nor necessary.

For all these reasons, British grand strategy is incompatible with an open-ended commitment to Europe. Rather, the British strategy has been to align militarily with the United States. Britain never had the weight to block the Soviets by itself, nor to manage events in Europe. Its alignment with the United States allows it to influence the major imperial power at relatively low cost. Over the next decade, Britain will continue to hedge its bets on all sides, while tilting, as the French and Germans say, to the Anglo-Saxon bloc and culture.

The Franco-German alignment has its own problems. There are two areas of tension today between France and Germany, and the first one is economic. Germany is much more disciplined fiscally than France, which means that the two countries are rarely in sync when it comes to financial cooperation. The second tension revolves around defense policy. The French, and particular the Gaullists, have always seen a united Europe as a counter to the United States, and this would require European defense integration, which inevitably would mean a force under Franco-German control.

The Germans of course value what integration with France and Europe brings, but they have no desire to take on either France's economic problems or the creation of a European military force set against the Americans. They simply don't want the potential burdens of the former or the risks of the latter.

Another problem facing the Germans is that once again, owing largely to the financial crisis and the U.S. war in Iraq, their relations with the United States have declined. Germany is an exporting country, and the United States is a major non-European customer. The Obama administration created a stimulus package to get the American economy out of recession, but the Germans took no such measures. Instead they relied on the American stimulus to generate demand for German products. This meant that the United States went into debt to jump-start its economy while (at least from the American point of view) the Germans got a free ride. The Germans also wanted the Americans to participate in the bailout of European countries through the IMF. But beyond these substantial economic disagreements between the two countries, there was a real geopolitical split. The Americans, as we've seen, have significant issues with the Russians, but Germans wanted nothing to do with U.S. efforts to contain them. Beyond their aversion to encouraging another Cold War, the Germans, as we've already seen, depend on Russia for a large part of their energy needs. In fact, they need Russian energy more than the Russians need German money.

U.S. relations with both Russia and Germany will vary over the next ten years, but we can anticipate a fundamental shift. Whatever the atmospherics, Russia's growing presence to the east of the European peninsula threatens American interests. Similarly, the more the United States sees its global interests dragging it into wars in places like Afghanistan, the more Germany is going to want to distance itself from its Cold War ally. The greater the U.S. level of concern about Russia, the greater the distance between the Germans and the United States. The sixty-five-year relationship that began at the end of World War II will not survive the decade ahead unchanged.

Germany can afford to distance itself from America, in part because its traditional problem of being squeezed from both sides is gone and it has a close and friendly relationship with France. Germany no longer borders Russia but now has Poland as a buffer. Germany needs natural gas, which the Russians have in abundance, and the Russians need technology and expertise, both of which Germany has to spare.

In addition, significant population decline will soon affect Germany's industrial plant, as a labor shortage, combined with an aging population, creates a formula for economic disaster. Even with its own decline, Russia will still have a surplus of labor that Germany can utilize, both by importing Russian workers and by moving production to Russia. The only way to counteract population decline is by encouraging immigration, but immigration and national identity in Europe are at odds.

If Germany doesn't want to bring workers to its factories, it can move its factories to where the workers are. Russia is also undergoing a decline in population, but because it has such a weak economy focused on primary commodities, it still has a surplus workforce, meaning people who are unemployed or underemployed. If the Russians want to move beyond simply exporting energy and grain and develop a modern industrial economy, they need technology and capital, and the Germans have both of those. The Germans want workers to man their factories and natural resources to fuel their economy. German businesses of all sizes are already deeply involved in Russia, adding to the new reality of a Moscow-Berlin relationship that soon will be the pivot of Europe, more dynamic if not more significant than the other relationships each country has.

With France at Germany's back—tied there by economic interests—Russia will move closer to the European core, setting off a new dynamic in the EU. Tension between the core and the periphery is already rife. The core is Germany, France, the Netherlands, and Belgium, the advanced industrial heartland of Europe. The periphery is Ireland, Spain, Portugal, Italy, Greece, and eastern Europe. Still in the early stages of economic development, these smaller countries need looser monetary policies than their more advanced neighbors and will have wider economic swings, so they will be more vulnerable to instability.

Meanwhile, France has hedged its bets, positioning itself as both a northern European power and a Mediterranean power, even to the point of considering the formation of a Mediterranean Union alongside the EU. In French thinking, this would include southern European countries, North African countries, Israel, and Turkey. This is an attractive idea in the abstract, but in reality the difference in developmental stages between Libya and Italy is so profound that it dwarfs the difference between Germany and Greece. Still, we can expect the French to dabble in the Mediterranean, trying to compensate for being Germany's junior partner in the north.

Germany is uncomfortable in the role that was pressed on it during the 2008–2010 crises. As the Germans reconsider their interest in the EU periphery, the peripheral countries raise questions about the economic benefit of integrating with the Germans. They resent losing control over vast areas of their economies, such as the banking sector, especially when they are expected to stand on their own if a crisis occurs. That those on the periphery are expected to sustain their economies with a monetary policy designed for the core adds to the pressure on both sides.

The old periphery, from Greece to Ireland, is firmly focused on economics. The new periphery, the Intermarium—and Poland in particular—is deeply concerned about Russia. And as we have seen, Poland is especially uneasy over being a neutral buffer between Germany and Russia, a role that historically has never ended well for it.

Also uncomfortable with this alignment is Britain. The UK could live with a Paris-Berlin axis as long as it was countered by the United States, with Britain as the balance point midway. But including Moscow puts too much weight on the European mainland, posing a challenge to British commercial and strategic interests.

As the next decade unfolds, Germany will resume its place on the North European Plain, but allied this time with its historic enemies, France and Russia. Britain will move even closer to the United States. Countries on the old periphery will be left to sort their way through the complexities, but it will be the new periphery—eastern Europe—that will be the focus of activity. The European Union will continue to function, as will the euro, but it will be difficult for the EU to be the organizing principle of Europe when there are so many centrifugal forces.

THE AMERICAN STRATEGY

A fairly extraordinary policy lapse since the collapse of communism is that the United States has never developed a strategy toward Europe. This will soon change. During the 1990s, the United States simply assumed a commonality of interests with the Europeans, but that assumption was never tested during the benign conditions of that decade. The emergence of the EU was never seen as a challenge to the United States, but simply as a natural evolution that posed no problem. Whereas the United States once proceeded out of habit, the decade ahead will require focused rethinking and planning.

When the American response to September 11 opened up the first significant breach with the Franco-German bloc, it also revealed a serious split in Europe. The United States wanted far more direct military help in Afghanistan than it got, and it wanted at least political cover for the war in Iraq. On the votes taken by NATO—such as guaranteeing support for Turkey if it supported the U.S. in Iraq—the overwhelming majority of countries sided implicitly with the United States, but only four countries voted against that support: Germany, France, Belgium, and Luxemburg. It should be noted that any NATO action requires unanimity. Nonetheless, many of the nations that supported the resolution sent at least token forces to Iraq, while Britain made major contributions.

The geography of this support is extremely important. The European heartland, with the exception of the Netherlands, opposed the United States. Most of the periphery—the Intermarium countries in particular—supported the United States, at least initially. Many of the countries that fell in with the United States did so not because they genuinely endorsed the American action but because of uneasiness with the Franco-German bloc. They did not want to be merely subordinate members of Europe, and they saw the United States as an important counterweight to the French and Germans. There was a particularly interesting confrontation between French president Jacques Chirac and the representatives of the Intermarium countries, who had signed a letter rejecting the Franco-German stand and supporting the United States. When that letter appeared, Chirac scolded them for being, in his terms, "badly brought up." At that point, the breach between these countries and France—and Germany, for that matter—could not have been deeper. The split in Europe over the Iraq war will, I think, become a rough framework for strategic disagreements in Europe, and will redefine U.S. alliances there in the decade ahead.

Tension between the United States and France has varied, but even after Barack Obama took office, the Germans were resolute on the subject of confrontation with Islam. They did not like Obama's management of the conflict any more than they liked Bush's, and they did not want to be drawn into it. As should be obvious by now, the United States and the Franco-German bloc simply have different interests.

It is difficult to imagine the Americans convincing the Germans to return to their prior relationship with the United States, or Germany convincing the United States to be indifferent to the rise of Russia. In the next ten years, an ideal solution from the American point of view would be to split the Franco-German bloc, and in fact the president should work to open as wide a breach as possible between the two countries. Still, this can't be the foundation of his strategy. The United States has little to offer France, while its relationship with Germany provides that country both security and economic advantages.

The United States must focus on limiting the power of the center while simultaneously doing all it can to thwart a Russo-German entente. In other words, it must apply the principle of balance of power to Europe, much as Britain did. Ironically, the first phase of this U.S. strategy must be to retain its current relationship with Britain. The two countries share economic interests, and both are maritime nations dependent on the Atlantic. The geographical position that benefited Britain can now be used by the United States with continuing benefits for Britain. In return, Britain provides the United States with an ally inside the European Union, as well as a platform for influencing other countries on the Atlantic periphery, from Scandinavia to Iberia, where Britain has close trading and political ties. These would include Sweden,

Denmark, and the Netherlands. In the decade to come, American and British national strategies will coincide to a great extent.

This U.S. balancing act in Europe also requires that the United States cultivate its relationship with Turkey. As we discussed in the chapter on the Middle East, a strong alliance with Turkey gives the United States influence in the Black Sea and counters any Mediterranean strategy that France might wish to develop. One of the things that will aid this alliance will be European immigration policy. Europeans' fear of Turkish immigration will cause them to block Turkey's entrance into the EU. Turkey is certainly going to become stronger over the next decade, but it is not ready to operate on its own. The region around it is too unstable, and threats from Russia in the Caucasus will force it to maintain a strong relationship with the United States. This will not be entirely to the Turks' liking, but they have little choice.

Whatever the United States does on the periphery of Europe, the question of Germany remains paramount and will dominate the foreign policy of many nations in the coming years. The United States must avoid the appearance of being hostile to Germany or indifferent to Europe. It must not abandon NATO, regardless of its ineffectiveness, but must treat all multilateral institutions with respect and all European countries as if they are significant powers. In other words, the United States must create a sense of normality in Europe, lest it stampede the periphery into the Franco-German camp. If the United States drives the relationship to a crisis too soon, it will only strengthen Germany's hand in the region. The inherent tension between Germany (or France and Germany) and the other European countries will mature on its own. There is no need for the United States to rush things along, because it is Germany that is under pressure, not the Americans.

At the same time, the United States must, in this relatively friendly context, take the necessary steps to deal with the possibility of a Russo-German entente. To do this, the president must begin moving toward bilateral relations with some key European countries, and he must do so outside the usual framework of multilateral relations. The model to use is Britain, a part of NATO and the EU, yet with a robust relationship with the United States on its own. Over the next few years the United States must emphasize bilateral relations with countries on the periphery of Europe, bypassing NATO while paying lip service to it.

The choice of relationships can be somewhat random, serving as they do mostly to reinforce the image of the United States as benign and content with whatever Germany does. But some countries are genuinely important to American interests. Denmark controls access to the Atlantic for the Russians while providing access to the Baltic for the United States. Italy is a country that has both a substantial economy and a strategic position in the Mediterranean. Norway, always closer to Britain than to the rest of Europe, can provide strategic advantages for the United States, from military bases to the prospect of partnerships in the Norwegian oil industry. And of course a relationship with Turkey provides the United States with options in the Balkans, the Caucasus, Central Asia, Iran, and the Arab world. But the United States should not focus on these valuable countries by themselves. It should reach out to a range of countries, some of which might be much more a burden than an advantage. The Germans and French both look down on the United States as unsophisticated. The United States should take advantage of this in the next decade by making purposeful moves along with some that seem arbitrary. Everything must be done to lead the Germans and perhaps the French to a sense that the United States is unfocused in its actions.

These relationships are not ends in themselves—they are a cover for the crucial prize of Poland and the Intermarium (Slovakia, Hungary, and Romania), which provide the geography for containing Russia. And here the American strategy once again needs to be consciously deceptive. It must lull Europe into a sense that the United States is simply drawing closer to those countries that want to be drawn closer, and that among these countries are Poland, the rest of the Intermarium, and the Baltics. Any indication that the United States is directly seeking to block Germany or to create a crisis with Russia will generate a counterreaction in Europe that might drive the periphery back into the arms of the center. Europe as a whole does not want to be drawn into a confrontation. At the same time, the desire to have an alternative to a Paris-Berlin-Moscow axis will be strong, and if the cost is low, the periphery will be attracted to the United States—or Britain—as that alternative. At all costs, the United States must prevent the geographical amalgamation of Russia and the European peninsula, because that would create a power the United States would be hard-pressed to contain.

Credibility will be the key point, particularly for Poland. The United States must make a twofold argument to overcome Poland's historical scars. First, it must argue that the Poles deluded themselves in believing that the French and British could defend them against the Germans in 1939, which was geographically impossible. Second, the United States must offer the unpleasant reminder that the Poles did not resist long enough for anyone to come to their assistance—they collapsed in the first week of a German conquest that took only six weeks to complete. Poland, and the rest of the EU countries, cannot be helped if they can't help themselves.

This is the challenge for the American president as we enter the next decade. He must move with misdirection in order not to create concern in Moscow or Berlin that might make those governments increase the intensity of their relationship before the United States can create a structure to limit it. At the same time, the United States must reassure Poland and other countries of the seriousness of its commitment to their interests. These things can be done, but success will require the studied lack of sophistication of a Ronald Reagan and the casual dishonesty of an FDR. The president must appear to be not very bright yet be able to lie convincingly. The target of this charade will not be future allies but potential enemies. The United States needs to buy time.

The ideal American strategy will be to supply aid to support the development of indigenous military power that can deter attackers, or that can at least hold out long enough for help to arrive. U.S. aid can also create an environment of economic growth, both by building the economy and by providing access to American markets. During the Cold War, this is how the United States induced West Germany, Japan, and South Korea, among others, to take the risk of resisting the Communists.

Whatever argument the United States makes to Poland in the next few years, the Poles' willingness and ability to serve American purposes will depend on three things. The first is U.S. economic and technical support to build a native Polish military force. The second is the transfer of military technology to build up domestic industry, both in support of national defense and for civilian use. The third is to supply sufficient American forces in Poland to convince the Poles that the American stake in their country is entirely credible.

This relationship must focus on Poland but be extended to the other Intermarium countries, particularly Hungary and Romania. Both of these are critical to holding the Carpathian line, and both can respond effectively to the kinds of incentives the United States is making available to them. The Baltics represent a separate case. They are indefensible, but if war can be avoided, the Baltics make an attractive bone to place in the Russians' throat.

In all of this maneuvering, the point is first to avoid a war and second to limit a relationship between Russia and Germany that could, in succeeding decades, create a power that could challenge American hegemony. The present intentions of the Russians and Germans would be much more modest than that, but the American president must focus not on what others think now but what they will think later, when circumstances change.

CHAPTER 10

FACING THE WESTERN PACIFIC

The Western Pacific is a region that does not present an immediate crisis for the United States, but this happy state of affairs will not go on indefinitely. Asia was one of the key trouble spots in the world for a good part of the preceding century, and the relative tranquillity of the past thirty years has been the exception, not the rule. That is why the president's task during the next decade will be to prepare carefully and at leisure for the inevitable crises that loom just over the horizon.

There is a great deal of concern about the Indo-Chinese balance of power, but India and China are divided by a wall—the Himalayas—that makes sustained conflict and high-volume overland trade virtually impossible. Their interaction is economic and by sea. The central and long-standing opposition in this region is actually that between China and Japan, the two nations locked in a tie for the world's second largest economy. There is substantial economic competition. Economics affect a balance of power only when geography permits other kinds of competition. All other regional powers—including South Korea, a substantial economic force in its own right—exist within the framework of the China-Japan-U.S. balance. It is in terms of maintaining and manipulating that balance that the United States will define its policy during the next decade.

It is difficult to imagine two nations more different than China and Japan, and economic friction has made them hostile to each other since their first modern war, in 1895, when Japan defeated China's navy. Japan is a maritime industrial power, utterly dependent on imports of raw materials for its survival. China, with its huge population and geography, is wedded to the land. From the moment Japan first began to industrialize, it has needed Chinese markets, raw material, and labor and has wanted these on the most favorable terms. The Chinese have needed foreign capital and expertise but have not wanted to fall under Japanese control. This wary interdependence of two economies led them into a brutal war in the 1930s and 1940s, during which Japan occupied a good deal of the Chinese mainland. The relationship between these two countries never fully recovered from that war, and hostility and distrust have been kept under control in part by the presence of the United States.

During the Cold War, the United States maintained complex relations with each country. It needed Japan's industrial power to support the U.S. in the Korean War and beyond, as well as its geography to block the Soviet fleet from entering the Pacific. Japan willingly gave both. In return, the United States gave the Japanese access to American markets for its industrial products and did not require Japan to make a military commitment to American ventures around globe.

During the same era, the United States spent nearly thirty years in marked hostility to Communist China. Then, when it had dissipated its global power in Vietnam and needed a counterweight to the Soviets, it turned to China. China, afraid of the Soviet Union and seeing the United States as a guarantor of its own security, accepted the overture.

Neither China nor Japan was comfortable with the U.S relationship with the other, but the United States managed the triangulation without difficulty, because each country had more important issues to consider. China's concerns were geopolitical: largely the fear of the Soviet Union.

Japan's were economic: its postwar economic boom. Each country needed the United States for its own reasons.

When the Cold War ended, the nature of the balance changed. Japan's period of rapid growth stalled out as China, having adopted Japan's focus on economics, was undergoing a prolonged boom. Japan remained the larger economy, but China became the most dynamic—a situation that the United States saw as quite satisfactory. Focused primarily on economic issues, the United States did not look at either country from a genuinely geopolitical point of view. In general, Asia was a matter for the Treasury Department and for managers of trade relations, not something of concern to the Department of Defense.

The stability of the western Pacific and southeast Asia since the 1980s is all the more notable when we consider that from Indochina to Indonesia, China, and elsewhere, Asia appeared to be one of the most unstable and unpromising regions in the world, a caldron of war, civil war, and general instability throughout the 1960s and '70s.

The president must bear in mind that Asia is an extraordinarily changeable place, and in the next ten years we will undoubtedly see some things that are now regarded as immutable being utterly transformed. For example, the Chinese economy will face harsh tests while Japan begins recovering from its failures. The consensus in 1970 was that Asia was inherently violent and unstable; the consensus today is that it is peaceable and stable. These contradictory assessments suggest the challenges in determining what Asia will look like over the next decade, how the Sino-Japanese dynamic will play itself out, and what American policy should be toward the region.

CHINA, JAPAN, AND THE WESTERN PACIFIC

When we talk about east Asia, we are really talking about a string of islands stretching from the Kuriles to Indonesia, as well as their relations with one another and with the mainland. When we talk about the mainland, more than anything else we are talking about China.

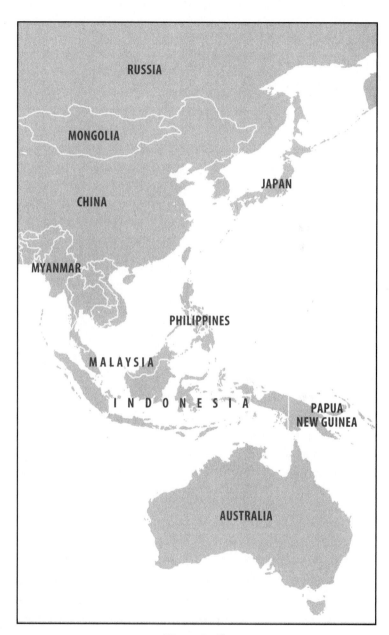

Western Pacific

China stretches twenty-five hundred miles inland and borders on fourteen countries. While China faces an ocean on only one side, it may be useful to think of it as a fairly narrow island clinging to the edge of the Pacific, isolated to the north, west, and south by virtually impenetrable barriers.

The image of an island holds up when we consider that the vast majority of China's population lives in the eastern part of the country, within about four hundred miles of the coast. The reason for this concentration is the availability of water. The area between the line bisecting the map (facing page) and the coast marks the area in which more than fifteen inches of rain a year falls—the minimum needed to maintain large numbers of people. Since the western part of China is too arid to maintain a large population, more than a billion people are crammed into a region about the size of the United States east of the Mississippi, not including New England. This is Han China, the land of the ethnic Chinese.

Western China is a vast and quite empty near-desert surrounded by four non-Chinese buffer states: Tibet, Xinjiang, Inner Mongolia, and Manchuria. These anchor China at its geographical limits, with the Himalayas to the southwest, minimally passable but certainly not by armies and not by trade in any volume. Siberia lies to the north, a huge wasteland with no north-south transportation. Jungles and rugged hills lie to the south, stretching from Myanmar to the Pacific, isolating China from southeast Asia.

Geographically, Japan is a much simpler place, consisting of four main islands and a series of much smaller islands to the north and south. It is being an archipelago that makes Japan by necessity a maritime nation, a fact compounded by an extraordinary geological reality: Japan is almost entirely devoid of the minerals needed by industry. Industrialization has always meant importing resources, including oil, which Japan gets primarily from the Persian Gulf. This means that Japan, by definition, has widespread global interests and vulnerabilities. Unlike China, which imports raw materials but has enough supplies of its own

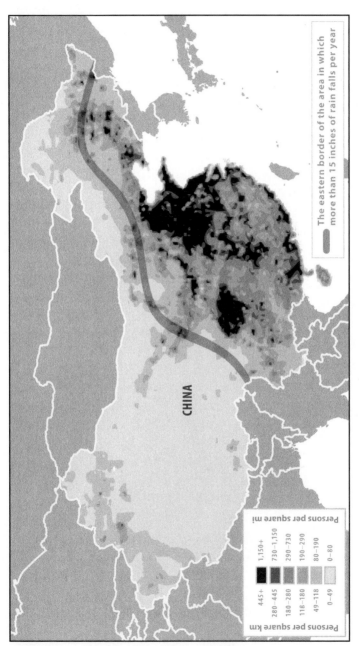

Chinese Rainfall and Population Density

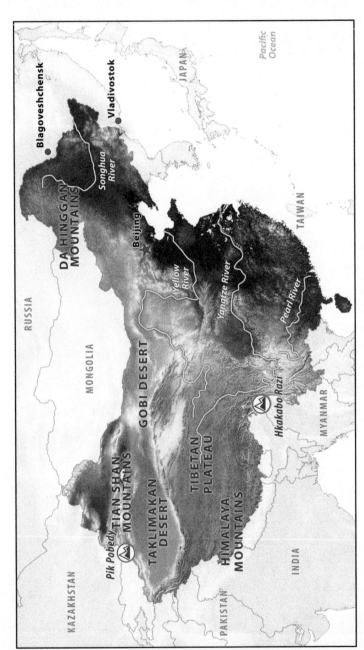

China's Terrain

to survive if necessary, Japan would collapse in a matter of months if its imports were disrupted.

Partly because of its isolation and partly because it industrialized rapidly in the nineteenth century, Japan avoided the experience that China suffered at the hands of Europeans. The Europeans provided Japan with assistance in the form of industrial technology and military training. The British organized the Japanese navy, the Germans the army, and thus Japan evolved rapidly into a power that could challenge Europeans. Indeed, it defeated the Russians in 1905.

The country most alarmed by Japan's sudden emergence was the only other industrialized power in the Pacific: the United States. Prior to World War II, the Japanese imported raw materials mostly from southeast Asia and the East Indies. In order to secure access to these supplies, Japan needed a substantial military force, particularly a navy. The United States, which became a significant maritime power only at the end of the nineteenth century, saw Japan's naval buildup as something that might one day drive the U.S. out of the Pacific. Simply by becoming an industrial and naval power, Japan appeared to threaten the security of the United States. By expanding its naval force to defend itself against Japan, the United States threatened the security of Japan.

The result of this mutual intimidation was World War II in the Pacific. The United States defeated Japan not just because of the atom bomb and the success of its island-hopping strategy, but because its submarines cut off the supply of raw materials from the south and crippled Japan's ability to wage war. Japan continued to resist, but once the U.S. submarine campaign placed a stranglehold on its supplies, its position was hopeless.

Today Japan is just as dependent on maritime trade as it was in the 1930s and '40s. It still must import all of its oil, and it must do so through waters controlled by the United States Navy. That means that Japan's industrial position depends on the willingness of the United States to guarantee the sea-lanes. It also depends on the United States' willingness not to take risks along Japan's line of supply—particularly through the Strait of Hormuz.

Thus Japan is trapped in a subordinate relationship with the United States. It cannot afford to alienate the United States without first building up a military force able to secure its own supply lines, but this is an undertaking far more ambitious and expensive than Japan wants to attempt during the next ten years. Nonetheless, its inherent insecurity because of import dependency, along with American unpredictability, will certainly drive Japan to become less dependent and exposed than it has been.

Like Japan, the Chinese can ill afford to alienate the Americans. They depend on the United States less for the flow of raw materials (although Chinese ships also pass through waters controlled by the United States) than as a consumer of Chinese industrial products. China, like Japan before it, has become a huge exporter to the United States, so much so that the ability and willingness of the United States to buy is one of the foundations of the Chinese economy along with the European market. China must have access to both. Over the next ten years, China, like Japan, will be focused on preparing for what it sees as the worst-case scenario vis-à-vis its American trading partner, a political decision to limit Chinese access to the American market.

To the extent that the regional balance will continue, it will do so not so much because of Japanese-Chinese relations but because of the relationship each Asian nation has with the United States. As China and Japan both become stronger, each will inevitably notice the other's rise and become concerned.

All other things being equal, Japan's relationship with the United States will remain stable, but with China the story will be different. Exports stabilize China's economy and society, but it is not enough to have buyers; it is also essential that the sale of exports build Chinese prosperity. If exporting to the United States no longer fits Chinese requirements, then Chinese interest in the relationship with the United States will shift and China will move away from dependency. Over the next decade, as China becomes more of an economic free agent, although not always a particularly prosperous one, Japan will have to have the United States guarantee its interests against China or shift its posture as well. Thus the balance that rests on the U.S.-Chinese relationship actually depends on how the Chinese economy functions over the next several years.

CHINA AND JAPAN

Part of the reason China was able to grow so dramatically in the 1980s is that Mao restrained growth just as dramatically up until that moment. When Mao died and was ultimately replaced by Deng Xiaoping, the mere shift of ideology freed China for an extraordinary growth spurt based on pent-up demand, combined with the native talents and capabilities of the Chinese people.

Historically, China has cycled between opposites: either isolation combined with relative poverty or an openness to trade combined with social instability. From the 1840s, when Britain forced China to open its ports, to 1947 and the Communist takeover, China was open, prosperous in at least some regions, and violently fragmented. When Mao went on the Long March and raised a peasant army to expel the Westerners, he once again imposed relative isolation and reduced the standard of living for everyone, but he created a stability and unity that China had not experienced in almost a century.

This oscillation between openness and instability and enclosure and unity is based in part on the nature of China's primary economic asset, cheap labor. When outside powers are allowed to invest in China, they build the kinds of factories and businesses that take advantage of China's abundant human capital. And yet the primary purpose of these factories is not to sell in China but to produce goods that can be sold in other countries. Accordingly, the primary focus of investment is near large ports and in areas with good transportation to these harbors. Because the population is concentrated in the coastal region, there is little reason to build infrastructure deeper within the country. Indeed, the vast majority of the factories are within a hundred miles of the coast. Even as China prospered and the factories became Chinese-owned, the pattern continued.

According to the People's Bank of China sixty million Chinese—a population equivalent to that of a large European country—live in middle-class households (those earning more than $20,000 a year). But with China's population of 1.3 billion people, 60 million middle-class citizens represent less than 5 percent of the total population, and the overwhelming majority of those live in the coastal region or in Beijing.

Six hundred million Chinese live in households earning less than $1,000 a year, or less than $3 a day for the family. Another 440 million Chinese live in households earning between $1,000 and $2,000 a year, or $3 to $6 a day. This means that 80 percent of China lives in conditions that compare with the poverty of sub-Saharan Africa. Even in the belt within one hundred miles of the coast, home to the 15 percent of Chinese who are the industrial workers, China is an extraordinarily poor country. Its narrow zone of prosperity creates a chasm that is social as well as geographic. The region around the ports profits from trade, and the rest of China does not. The coastal region's interests are in fact much more closely aligned with those of China's foreign trading partners than with the interests of the rest of the country, or even with the interests of the central government.

It is along these fault lines that China fragmented in the nineteenth century, and it is here that it may fragment in the future. Beijing balances between the impoverished majority and the prosperous minority. Supported by foreign interests, the well-off Chinese in the coastal areas will resist the central government. Attempts to transfer wealth either weakens the central government or forces it to become dictatorial. The Qing Dynasty weakened after the British incursion. Mao's solution in the 1940s and '50s was extensive repression, the expulsion of foreigners, and the expropriation and redistribution of wealth to the impoverished interior.

During periods of relative prosperity and growth, the problem can be managed by the state. Even as inequality increases, the absolute standard of living for most Chinese rises, and that increase, however minimal, goes a long way toward keeping people passive. But what happens when the economy weakens and standards of living decline overall? For those in the middle class and above, this is inconvenient. For the more than one billion Chinese living in abject poverty, even a small contraction in living standards can be catastrophic. That is where China is heading in the very near future—toward a relatively small decline of growth, but one that will pyramid economically and socially, generating resistance to the central government.

Given that China has a producer economy completely out of proportion to its consumer economy, the problem is inevitable. The iPods and clothing that China manufactures are not sold to its own impoverished masses. And yet China no longer has a wage advantage over countries like Pakistan and the Philippines. Given a limited pool of semiskilled labor (as opposed to its limitless supply of untrained peasants), the price of labor has risen. Pressed by competition, China has reduced prices, which has decreased the profitability of exports. In the face of increasing competition and of sluggish growth among some of its customers, China's ability to compete will decline, increasing the difficulty of repaying business loans and thus increasing pressure on the entire financial system.

The stark reality is that China simply can't afford unemployment. Large numbers of peasants have moved to the cities to get jobs, and if they lose their jobs, they either stay in the cities and cause instability or return to their villages and increase the level of rural poverty. China can keep its people employed by encouraging banks to lend to enterprises that should be out of business, by subsidizing exports, or by building state-owned enterprises, but these efforts hollow out the economic core.

Over the next decade, China will have no choice but to increase its internal security. The People's Liberation Army is already huge. In the end, the PLA is what will hold the country together, but this assumes that this force, drawn heavily from the poorest segments of society, will itself hold together and remain loyal. To quell class resentments, China will have to tax the coastal region and the 60 million well-to-do Chinese, then transfer the money to the PLA and the peasants. Those being taxed will resist, and the revenues will be insufficient for those the government intends to benefit, but it should be enough to retain the compliance of the army.

The long-term question, which will be answered in the decade to come, is whether the Chinese will attempt to solve their problem as Mao did—by closing off the country and destroying the coastal businessmen and expelling foreign interests—or by following the pattern of regionalism and instability of the late nineteenth and first half of the twentieth centuries. The only certainties are that the Chinese government will be absorbed with internal problems, working carefully to balance competing forces and increasingly paranoid about the intentions of the Japanese and the Americans.

In 1990, Japan went through the kind of decline that the Chinese are beginning to experience now. Japan has a much stronger degree of informal social control than most outsiders can see, and at the same time the large corporate conglomerates, called *keiretsu*, retained a great deal of latitude. Having grown rapidly after World War II, the Japanese succumbed to a financial crisis made inevitable by their failure to develop a market system for capital. Their economy operated through informal cooperation among the *keiretsu* and the government. This cooperation was designed so that there would be no losers, and therein lay its fatal flaw.

The capital problem was exacerbated by Japan's not having a retirement plan worth mentioning, which meant that citizens were forced to save heavily, putting their money in government post office banks, which paid very low interest rates. The money was then loaned by the government to the large "city banks" linked to the *keiretsu*. This system gave Japan a huge advantage in the 1970s and 1980s, when U.S. interest rates were in the double digits and Japanese corporations could borrow at less than 5 percent. But the money was not being loaned to businesses that were inherently profitable. Most profit was derived from the added margin provided by cheap money. And the need for the Japanese to save a huge amount in order to retire meant that they were reluctant consumers. Thus the heart of the Japanese economy, like the Chinese economy today, was in exports, particularly to the United States.

As competition from other Asian countries increased, the Japanese cut prices, which reduced profits. Lower profits meant that businesses had to borrow more money in order to grow, then found it increasingly difficult to pay back their loans. What followed was an economic crash that wasn't noticed by the Western media until several years after it happened.

Like the Chinese, the Japanese had to avoid unemployment, but for different reasons. In Japan, the reluctance to downsize was based on the social contract whereby a worker committed himself to one company for life and the company reciprocated. The Japanese honored the tradition by maintaining near full employment while allowing the growth rate to slip to almost nothing.

Western economists dubbed the twenty years during which the Japanese economy stagnated the "lost decades," but this is a misunderstanding of Japanese objectives, or rather the imposition of a Western point of view on Japanese values. Sacrificing growth in order to maintain full employment was for this highly cohesive society not to lose a decade but to retain a core interest.

At the same time, Japan's birthrate dropped well below the 2.1 children per woman needed to maintain its population. Now, with each generation smaller than the one before, the economy can no longer support retirees. In this way, debt and demography have created an enormous crisis for Japan.

During the next ten years, the Japanese will no longer be able to maintain full employment by exorbitantly increasing their debt, both public and private. Like the Chinese, they will have to shift economic models. But the Japanese have one overwhelming advantage: they do not have a billion people living in poverty. Unlike the Chinese, they can absorb austerity, should it be required, without inviting instability.

Japan's fundamental weakness remains its lack of natural resources for industry, from oil to rubber to iron ore. To remain an industrial power,

Japan has to buy and sell globally, and if it loses access to the sea-lanes, it loses everything. If trouble arises and it lacks the option of turning inward, Japan is far more likely to become assertive once again.

THE SINO-JAPANESE BALANCE OF POWER

For the past thirty years or so, relations between China and Japan have been secondary to each country's relationship with the United States. The United States maintained the regional balance by maintaining mutually beneficial relations with each country, but those relations will shift in the decade ahead. First, China's economic problems will alter its relationship to the world while transforming the country's internal workings. Similarly, Japan's internal problems and the solutions it chooses will transform the way it operates.

Even when passive and dependent on other countries to guarantee access to world markets, Japan always remains deeply embedded in the world. China is embedded as well, but not as irrevocably as Japan. The loss of imported raw materials does not represent an existential threat to China the way it does to Japan. Similarly, while China depends on exports, it could reconfigure itself if necessary, albeit painfully.

China, then, has less of a temptation to become assertive; it also has less of an ability to do so. China's main access to the world is by sea, but it does not have a substantial navy relative to geography and the United States. Building a naval power takes generations, not so much to develop the necessary technology as to pass along the accumulated experience that creates good admirals. It will be a long time before China can challenge either the United States or even Japan at sea. There has been a great deal of discussion of the development of China's navy. Certainly, significant development is under way, but there is a huge gap between the present level of effort and what China has to do to challenge U.S. naval power even in the waters near China. The most significant developments are in land-based anti-ship missiles. But the Chinese have a very long way to go before naval vessels can hope to defeat an American fleet. And even the anti-ship missiles are highly vulnerable to U.S. air and missile strikes. China's navy will not force the United States out of regional waters in the next decade.

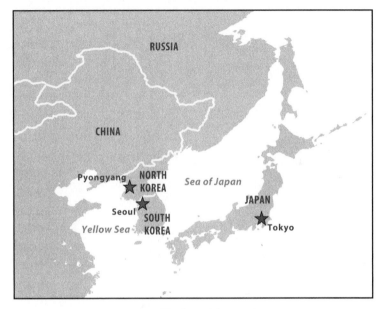

Northeast Asia

Today Japan is formally a pacifist power, barred by Article 9 of its constitution from having an offensive armed force, but this has not prevented it from maintaining the most capable navy in the western Pacific, nor from having a substantial army and air force. It has, however, managed to avoid using those forces, relying instead on the United States to protect its international interests, particularly its access to natural resources.

Japanese submission to the United States after World War II proved beneficial because the United States needed Japan's help in the Cold War and wanted Japan to be as strong as possible. Things have now subtly changed. The United States still controls Japan's sea-lanes and is still prepared to guarantee access, but its willingness to take risks with that access has put Japan in a potentially dangerous position. So far, during the U.S.-jihadist war, the United States has been cautious in not endangering the oil route through the Strait of Hormuz that Japan depends on, but it could easily miscalculate. Simply put, the United States can endure risks that Japan can't afford, so the two countries' perspectives on the world and their national interests diverge.

The internal problem for the Japanese is that they have gone as far as they can in this economic cycle. They must either accept austerity and unemployment or allow the economy to begin to overheat. Their great weakness remains capital markets, which still don't operate freely, and yet the Japanese don't have effective central planning either. This situation cannot be sustained. Moving to a free market in capital might solve the Japanese problem in the long run, but only at the cost of instability now. Because they can't afford a true market economy, they will move toward an economy in which the state imposes greater efficiencies (never as efficient as a market, but more efficient than what they have now) and in which the *keiretsu* decline in importance. This will mean that the Japanese state will concentrate more power in itself and take a greater role in managing finance.

Japan's other great problem is demographic. It is an aging country that needs more workers but is socially unable to manage large-scale immigration, which moves counter to the cohesiveness of Japanese culture. The solution is not to have workers that come to the factories but to have factories that go to the workers. Over the next ten years, Japan will be even more aggressive in exploiting labor markets outside its own borders, including those in China, depending on the evolution of events there.

Whatever the future holds, the Japanese will want to continue their core strategic relationship with the United States, including their reliance on the U.S. to secure their sea-lanes. For Japan, this is both more cost-effective and far less dangerous than striking out on its own.

THE AMERICAN STRATEGY: PLAYING FOR TIME

The United States does not have the resources or the policy bandwidth to deal with every regional balance of power at the same time. It will be preoccupied with Russia and the Middle East, which does not leave it much in the way of resources to deal with the western Pacific. By default, then, American strategy in this region must be to delay and deflect. The United States cannot really control the vast processes that are under way, so the best it can hope to do is to shape them a bit. Fortunately, this is one region in which the processes at play have the countries on a relatively benign path toward the United States, at least for now. Therefore U.S. policy should be to stall while laying the groundwork for what comes after.

The American danger does not rest in an alliance forged between Japan and China. These two nations compete with each other in too many ways, and differ from each other too profoundly, for close cooperation. Having reached the limits of this economic cycle, Japan will no longer be the quietly passive giant it has been for the past twenty years. China, on the other hand, will be less than the economic juggernaut that it has been. The challenge for the United States will be to manage its relationship with both players in this western Pacific system, each in its own different phase. At the same time, the United States must step back from being the center and let these two Asian powers develop more direct relationships with each other, finding their own point of balance.

Neither China nor Japan will emerge as a regional hegemon in the coming decade. The Chinese economic miracle will subside, as all economic miracles do, and China will focus on maintaining stability without rapid growth. Japan will restructure itself internally while beginning to align its foreign policy with its global interests. But it will be Japan that the United States will have to watch.

As Japan increases its power, it must necessarily increase its maritime strength. It is a fundamental principle of the United States to oppose the rise of maritime powers, but obviously the United States isn't going to go to war with Japan over this issue in 2015 or 2020 the way it did in 1941. Still, it will have to develop a strategy to deal with a more assertive Japan.

The first step in the U.S. strategy toward Japan must be to ensure that China doesn't splinter, because the weaker China becomes, the freer Japan will be to flex its muscles. To the extent possible, the United States should relieve pressure on China by facilitating its exports to the United States. This is a reversal, of course, and there are obvious political problems in doing this. The president will have to be very clever in justifying his generosity at a time of high U.S. unemployment. But anything that constrains Japan, even marginally, is valuable to the United States.

Only a stable China can control foreign investments in its economy, and both stability and control will be necessary to fend off Japan's designs on Chinese factories and workers. Constraining Japanese expansion will in turn delay Japan's ability to cope with its problems, and anything that slows down Japan's economic resurgence benefits the United States, if only to the extent that it buys time.

The second step in U.S. strategy must be to keep relations with the Japanese as cordial as possible. The more confident Japan is in its access to raw materials, the less it will be motivated to build its own naval force. The Japanese, always painfully aware of the imbalance of power, have never been as comfortable as they might appear in their deferential relationship with the United States. At the same time, they have never wanted to confront the enormous amounts of money and risk needed to create an alternative.

In the long run, a country as economically large and vulnerable as Japan will have to search for a way to secure its own interests. That doesn't have to be in the next decade, however, and the American strategy must be to prolong Japan's dependency as long as possible. The longer the Japanese remain dependent on the United States, the more influence the U.S. has over Japanese policy and the more it can shape that policy. Pushed hard enough, Japan might choose a new course that returns to the destructive policies of the 1930s, when it was a nation both economically statist and driven by an emphasis on national defense. The United States must be careful not to push.

Two things will make this Asian strategy easier to sell to the American public. The first is that other matters will preoccupy them. The second is that American moves in the western Pacific will be incremental rather than sudden. The president will have the advantage of not having to declare a change in policy, and his actions will not have decisive effect, because the United States is important but not central to either of these Asian powers.

At the same time, the United States must be building relationships for the next phase of history, in which it might wish to recruit Japan, China, or both to cooperate against threats from Russia or other powers. The appetite for risk within these two countries is not very great, and the United States must realize that pressing them without inducements probably won't work.

This is where Korea may play a critical role. It is already the thorn in the side of both parts of the Sino-Japanese balance, but it is particularly irksome for the Japanese. For historical reasons, Korea despises the Japanese and distrusts the Chinese. It is not particularly comfortable with the United States, for that matter, but at least geography has made it dependent on the U.S.

As Japan increases in power and China weakens, the Koreans will need the United States more than ever, and the United States will rely on Korea to increase U.S. options for dealing with both countries. Fortunately, the U.S.-Korean relationship already exists, and for that reason extending it would not cause significant concern to either Japan or China.

Korea also has become a significant technological center. China in particular will be hungry for that technology, and having some control over the rate of transfer would increase U.S. leverage with China. For their part, the Koreans will need help in dealing with the North Korean nuisance, particularly in handling the financial aspects of reunification when it inevitably comes. A unified Korea would want special trade opportunities with the United States, and even though Korea has nowhere else to turn, the American president should make such concessions, because over the next ten years Korea may well be the most important relationship the United States has in the western Pacific. But reunification is not the core issue. North Korea, for all its bluster, is a cripple, and its nuclear facilities exist only as long as others permit it. North Korea's nuclear program has bought it time by deflecting pressure. It cannot stabilize North Korea permanently. South Korea, in contrast, remains a dynamic power on its own and will remain a dynamic power whatever happens in the north.

The second important relationship the United States will have in the region is with Australia. One of the last landmasses to fall under European control, it is certainly on the margins of the world geographically, and most of its population remains confined to a relatively small area of the country's southeast.

Geopolitically, Australia is misunderstood and misunderstands itself. It appears to be isolated and secure, yet its isolation is an illusion and its vulnerability real. For example, its nearest neighbor is Indonesia, a highly fragmented and weak country, separated from Australia by hundreds of miles of water. During World War II, Indonesia and its eastern neighbor, New Guinea, served an important strategic function for Australia, soaking up the Japanese attack and leaving the Japanese too weak to think about extending themselves farther south. Interestingly, World War II and Australia's island buffers to the north have reinforced its sense of security, in spite of creating worries about boat people.

Despite the appearance of standing alone and secure, Australia is actually quite dependent on international trade, particularly the sale of food products and industrial minerals such as iron ore, to sustain its economy. These goods are shipped by sea, and Australia has no control whatever over the security of its sea-lanes. In a sense, then, Australia is like a creature whose arteries and veins are located outside its body, unprotected and constantly at risk.

Australia's strategy for dealing with this vulnerability has been to ally itself with the dominant naval power in the western Pacific—once Britain, now the United States. All alliances bear costs, and the British and Americans wanted the same quid pro quo: Australia's participation in their wars. Australians sacrificed heavily in the Boer War, both world wars, and in Korea and Vietnam. Between 1970 and 1990 the Australians pulled back from this role as military partner, but during this period there were few calls for their participation. In 1990, in Desert Storm, they returned to their strategy of assisting in military operations, and they then went on to fight in both Afghanistan and Iraq.

Along with the security of sea-lanes, Australia's well-being depends on an international trading regime that allows terms it can manage. Australia's strategy of being of service to its Anglo-American cousins has bought it a seat at the table alongside the great powers. This has provided influence and security to its trade, something that Australia never could have achieved on its own.

During World War II, Australia served Britain by sending troops to North Africa. It served the United States by acting as a depot for building up U.S. forces for the Pacific theater. Certainly Australian forces fought as well, but if no forces had been available, Australia's tremendous

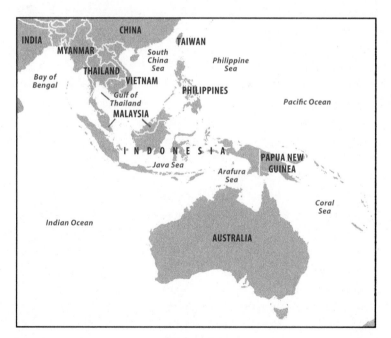

Southeast Asia

value was its location, behind the geographic shield of Indonesia and New Guinea. Should any great power emerge in the western Pacific to challenge the United States, Australia will once again be the strategic foundation for America's Pacific strategy. The caveat is that building the infrastructure for a rear depot took several years in World War II, and any future conflict might not allow that kind of lead time.

For the United States, maintaining a relationship with Australia shouldn't be difficult. Australia has only two strategic options. One is to withdraw from alliance commitments and assume that its interests will be addressed in passing. The other is to participate in the alliance and have more formal commitments from the United States. The former is cheaper but riskier. The latter is more expensive but more reliable.

If a major threat developed, Australia would most likely return to the U.S. fold. If a western Pacific power suddenly gained control of the sea-lanes, however, there is always a chance that Australia would make a deal, if it calculated that such compliance would achieve its ends with less risk than fighting alongside the Americans. Therefore, having prior commitments from and installations in Australia serves the American interests best by limiting Australia's options.

Even if Australia is hostage to U.S. protection, its strategic importance is such that the United States should be as generous and seductive as possible. Being sparing in what it asks of Australian military commitments also makes sense, because the United States may need Australia more—and more broadly—in the future than it needs Australian troops now.

Of similar strategic importance for the United States is the city of Singapore, created by the British at the tip of the Malay Peninsula as a base from which to control the Strait of Malacca. This narrow passageway is still the primary route between the Indian and Pacific Oceans, particularly for oil headed for China and Japan from the Persian Gulf. U.S. warships on the way to the Persian Gulf also must pass through this strait. Along with Gibraltar and the Suez Canal, it is one of the world's great maritime choke points. Whoever controls it can shut off trade at will, or guarantee that it will flow.

Singapore is now an independent city-state, enormously prosperous because of its geographical position and because of its technology industry. It needs the United States as a customer, but also to protect its sovereignty. When Malaya was given independence, the primarily ethnic-Chinese Singapore split from the predominantly Muslim Malaysia. Relations have varied, and there has not been much threat of annexation, but Singapore understands two geopolitical realities: that the worst thing in the world is to be rich and weak, and that security is never a sure thing. What Malaysia or, for that matter, Indonesia might want to do in a generation or two can't be predicted.

The United States cannot simply control Singapore; instead it must have cooperative relations with it. As in his dealings with Korea and Australia, the president should be more generous with Singapore than he needs to be in order to assure the alliance. The price is small and the stakes are very high.

Indonesian Sea-Lanes

INDIA

It is in the context of the western Pacific that we should consider India. Despite its size, its growing economy, and the constant discussion of India as the next China, I simply do not see India as a significant player with deep power in the coming decade. In many ways, India can be understood as a very large Australia. Both countries are economically powerful—obviously in different ways—and in that sense they have to be taken quite seriously.

Like Australia, India is a subcontinent isolated geographically, although Australia's isolation, based on thousands of miles of water, is much more visible. But India is in its own way an island, surrounded by land barriers perhaps less easily passable than oceans. The Himalayas block access from the north, and hilly jungles from the east. To the south, it is surrounded by the Indian Ocean, which is dominated by the United States Navy.

The biggest problem for India lies to the west, where there is desert, and Pakistan. That Islamic nation has fought multiple wars with the predominantly Hindu India, and relations range from extremely cool to hostile. As we saw in my discussion of Afghanistan, the balance of power between Pakistan and India is the major feature of the subcontinent. Maintaining this balance of power is a significant objective for the United States in the decade to come.

India is called the democratic China, which, to the extent that it is true, exacts a toll in regional power. One of the great limitations on Indian economic growth, impressive as it has been, is that while India has a national government, each of its constituent states has its own regulations, and some of these prevent economic development. These states jealously guard their rights, and the leadership guards its prerogatives. There are many ways in which these regions are bound together, but the ultimate guarantor is the army.

India maintains a substantial military that has three functions. First, it balances Pakistan. Second, it protects the northern frontier against a Chinese incursion (which the terrain makes difficult to imagine). Most

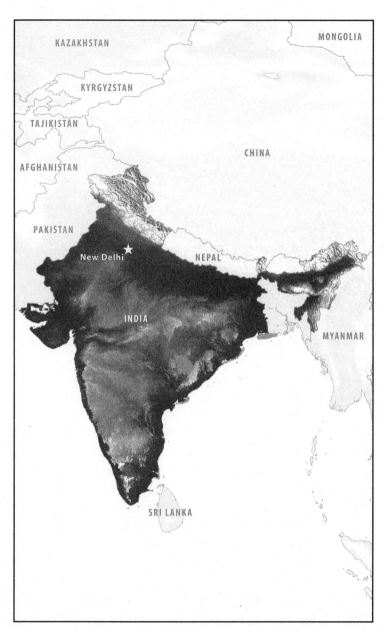

India's Terrain

important, the Indian military, like the Chinese military, guarantees the internal security of the nation—no minor consideration in a diverse country with deeply divided regions. There is currently a significant rebellion by Maoists in the east, for instance, just the sort of thing that it is the army's job to prevent or suppress.

On the seas, the Indians have been interested in developing a navy that could become a major player in the Indian Ocean, protecting India's sea-lanes and projecting Indian power. But the United States has no interest in seeing India proceed along these lines. The Indian Ocean is the passageway to the Pacific for Persian Gulf oil, and the United States will deploy powerful forces there no matter how it reduces its presence on land.

To keep Indian naval development below a threshold that could threaten U.S. interests, the United States will strive to divert India's defense expenditure toward the army and the tactical air force rather than the navy. The cheapest way to accomplish this and preempt a potential long-range problem is for the United States to support a stronger Pakistan, thus keeping India's security planners focused on the land and not the sea.

By the same token, India is interested in undermining the U.S.-Pakistani relationship or, at the very least, keeping the United States in Afghanistan in order to destabilize Pakistan. Failing that, India may reach out to other countries, as it did to the Soviet Union during the Cold War. Pakistan does not represent an existential threat to India, even in the unlikely event of a nuclear exchange. But Pakistan is not going to simply collapse, and therefore will remain the persistent problem that India's strategic policy will continue to pivot on.

India lags behind China in its economic development, which is why it is not yet facing China's difficulties. The next decade will see India surging ahead economically, but economic power by itself does not translate into national security. Nor does it translate into the kind of power that can dominate the Indian Ocean. American interests are not served by making India feel overly secure. Therefore, U.S.-Indian relations will deteriorate over the next ten years, even as the United States leaves Afghanistan and even as U.S.-Indian trade continues.

THE ASIAN GAME

In the decade to come, while the United States is preoccupied with other issues, the two major Asian powers, China and Japan, will be only minimally subject to outside influence. They will move as their internal processes dictate. Given that pace, the United States should not invest heavily in managing the Chinese-Japanese relationship. To the extent possible, the United States should help maintain a stable China and work to maintain its relationship with Japan.

Nonetheless, the peace of the western Pacific will not hold together indefinitely, and the United States should work to cement strong relations with three key players: Korea, Australia, and Singapore.

These three countries would prove essential allies in the event of war with any western Pacific country, particularly Japan, and preparations cannot begin too soon. Building the Korean navy, creating facilities in Australia, and modernizing Singapore's forces will not arouse great anxiety. These are steps that, taken in this decade, will create the framework for managing any conflict that might arise.

CHAPTER 11

A SECURE HEMISPHERE

G iven that the United States shares a hemisphere and quite a bit of history with Latin America and Canada, some might assume that this region has a singular importance for the U.S. Indeed, many Latin Americans in particular see the United States as obsessed with dominating them, or at least obtaining their resources. But with few exceptions—primarily in the case of Mexico and Cuba—what happens in Latin America is of marginal importance to the United States, and the region has rarely held a significant place in American thinking. Part of this has to do with distance. Washington is about a thousand miles farther from Rio de Janeiro than it is from Paris. And unlike European and Asian powers, the United States has never had an extensive war with the Latin world south of Panama. This isn't to say that there isn't mutual distrust and occasional hostility. But in the end—and again excepting Mexico and Cuba—the fundamental interests of the United States simply don't intersect with those of Latin America.

The United States has had limited concern with the region in part because of the fragmentation there, which has prevented the rise of a transcontinental power. South America looks like a single geographical entity, but in fact the continent is divided by significant topographic barriers. First, running north and south are the Andes, a chain of mountains much taller than the Rockies or the Alps and with few readily traversable passes. Then, in the center of the continent, the vast Amazonian jungle presents an equally impenetrable barrier.

There are actually three distinct regions in South America, each cut off from the others to the extent that basic overland commerce is difficult and political unity impossible. Brazil is an arc along the Atlantic Coast, with the inhospitable Amazon as its interior. A separate region lies to the south of Brazil along the Atlantic, and it consists of Argentina, Uruguay, and Paraguay, the latter not on the coast but part of this bloc of nations. To the west are the Andean nations of Chile, Bolivia, Peru, Ecuador, Colombia, and Venezuela. Off the mainland and not completely Latin are, of course, the Caribbean islands, important as platforms but without weight themselves.

The only connection between Brazil and the southern nations is a fairly narrow land bridge through Uruguay. The Andean nations are united only in the sense that they all share impenetrable geographies. The southern region along the Atlantic could become integrated, but there is really only one significant country there, Argentina. In addition, there is no passable land bridge between North and South America because of Central America's jungle terrain, and even if there were a bridge, only Colombia and perhaps Venezuela could take advantage of it.

The key to American policy in Latin America has always been that for the United States to become concerned, two elements would have to converge: a strategically significant area (of which there are few in the region) would have to be in the hands of a power able to use it to pose a threat. The Monroe Doctrine was proclaimed in order to make it clear that just such an eventuality was the single unacceptable geopolitical development as far as the United States was concerned.

During World War II, the presence of German agents and sympathizers in South America became a serious issue among strategists in

Terrain Barriers in South America

Washington, who envisioned German troops arriving in Brazil from Dakar, across the Atlantic. Similarly, during the Cold War, the United States became genuinely concerned about Soviet influence in the region and intervened on occasion to block it. But neither the Germans nor the Soviets made a serious strategic effort to dominate South America, because they understood that in most senses the continent was irrelevant to U.S. interests. Instead, their efforts were designed merely to irritate Washington and divert American resources.

The one place where outside involvement has been seen as a threat to be taken seriously is Cuba, and its singular importance is based on its singularly strategic location.

Cuba and the Caribbean

Early in the nineteenth century, American prosperity was founded on the river system that enabled farmers in the Louisiana and Ohio territories to ship their agricultural output to the East Coast and Europe. All of these goods first flowed to the city of New Orleans and were then transferred from barges to oceangoing vessels. The United States fought to keep New Orleans safe, first at the Battle of New Orleans in 1814, and then during the Texan war of independence. New Orleans and nearby ports remain the largest by tonnage in the United States, enabling mid-western grain to be shipped out and steel and other industrial goods to be shipped in.

Because a naval force in Cuba could control the sea-lanes in and out of the Gulf of Mexico and thereby could control New Orleans, the United States has always been obsessed with the island. Andrew Jackson contemplated invading it, and in 1898 the United States intervened to drive out the Spaniards. A half century later, when a pro-Soviet government emerged there under Fidel Castro, Cuba became a centerpiece of U.S. strategy. An anti-American Cuba without the Soviets was a trivial matter. An anti-American Cuba with Soviet missiles was a mortal threat.

As we look toward the decade ahead, Cuba has no great power patron, so the president can craft his Cuban policy in response to American political opinion. But he must bear in mind that if the United States faces a global competitor, Cuba will be the geographic point at which that competitor can put the greatest pressure on the United States. This makes Cuba the prize it will aim for.

In the long run, bringing Cuba back under American influence is a rational, preemptive policy, and it is highly desirable to do so before a global competitor emerges to raise the stakes and the price. Fidel and Raúl Castro will die or retire during the decade we're considering, and the political and intelligence elites who control the island are both younger and more cynical than the founding generation of the Castro regime. Rather than gambling on whether they can survive the deaths of the founders, they will be open to accommodation, amenable to deals that allow them to retain their position while granting America increasing power over their foreign policy. The transition will be the moment for the United States to try to deal. Before the Castros leave power they might be open to a deal that preserves their legacy while conceding to American influence. If that fails, the insecurity of the transition might be the moment to approach their heirs. The American interest is simple and has nothing to do with human rights or regime change. It is to have guarantees that regardless of future challenges, Cuba will not become a base for foreign powers. Having achieved that, the United States will have achieved much.

Venezuela is another Latin American country that has managed to attract attention by appearing to be a significant threat to the United States. It is not. First, the Venezuelan economy depends on exporting oil, and the realities of geography and logistics make it inevitable that Venezuela will export its oil to the United States. Second, Venezuela's physical isolation—with the Amazon to the south, the Caribbean (dominated by the U.S. Navy) to the north, and a hostile and stable Colombia to the west, on the other side of mountains and jungle—renders the country otherwise irrelevant, even if Islamist terrorists, say, showed up and tried to exploit its current rift with the United States. Even if a new global challenger sought to align with Venezuela and use it as a launching pad for mischief, the country's location does not allow for a significant air or naval base. Obviously, it would be desirable to have Venezuela shift its strategic outlook by the 2030s, but that is not essential to U.S. interests.

Venezuela is a case in which U.S. foreign policy should discipline itself to ignore ideology and annoyance and focus on strategy. In all likelihood, Hugo Chávez will lose power within the regime he created. Indeed, if the United States were to cut a deal with Cuba at the right time, part of that deal might be the withdrawal of Cuban support for Chávez. But even if he remains in power, he presents no threat to anyone but his own people.

BRAZIL AND THE ARGENTINE STRATEGY

There is only one Latin American country with the potential to emerge as a competitor to the United States in its own right, and that is Brazil. It is the first significant, independent economic and potentially global power to develop in the history of Latin America, and it has hedged its bets nicely.

Brazil is the world's eighth largest economy and the fifth largest country both in size and in population. Like most developing countries, it is heavily oriented toward export, but its exports are well balanced. Two-thirds are primary commodities (agricultural and mineral) and the rest are manufactured products. The geographic distribution of its exports is impressive as well, with about equal amounts going to Latin America, the European Union, and Asia. A relatively small but not insignificant amount goes to the United States. This balanced export posture means that Brazil is less vulnerable to regional economic downturns than are more focused economies.

Right now Brazil is not a power that is particularly threatening or important to the United States, nor does the United States represent a challenge to Brazil. There is minimal economic friction, and geography prevents Brazil from easily challenging the United States. Brazilian expansion northward would be irrational, because the terrain to the north is extremely hard to traverse, and there is nothing to the north that

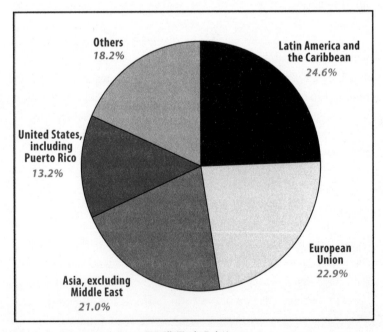

Brazil's Trade Relations

Brazil needs. Venezuelan oil, for instance, cannot be easily shipped to Brazil because of the terrain, and Brazil has ample supplies of its own anyway.

The only challenge that Brazil could pose to the United States would be if its economic expansion continued enough for it to develop sufficient air and naval power to dominate the Atlantic between its coast and West Africa, a region not heavily patrolled by the United States, unlike the Indian Ocean or South China Sea. This would not happen in the next decade, but as Brazilian wage rates rise, the geographical factors are such that Brazilian investments in Africa might carry lower transportation costs than investments in other parts of Latin America. Thus there would be advantages for Brazil in developing relations with sub-Saharan countries, particularly Angola, which, like Brazil, is Portuguese-speaking. This could lead to a South Atlantic not only dominated by Brazil but with Brazilian naval forces based on both the Brazilian and the African coasts.

Even though Brazil is not yet in any way a threat to American interests, the underlying American strategy of creating and maintaining balances of power in all areas requires that the United States begin working now to create a countervailing power. There is no rush in completing the strategy, but there is an interest in beginning it.

In the next decade, while maintaining friendly relations with Brazil, the United States should also do everything it can to strengthen Argentina, the one country that could serve as a counterweight. It should be remembered that early in the twentieth century Argentina was the major power in Latin America. Its current weakness is not inevitable. The United States should work toward developing a special relationship with Argentina in the context of a general Latin American development plan that also includes resources devoted to Uruguay and Paraguay.

This is a region where modest amounts of money now can yield substantial benefits later. Argentina's geography is suited for development; it has an adequate population and room for still more people. It has a strong agricultural base and a workforce capable of developing an industrial base. It is protected from all military incursions except those from Brazil, which should give it an incentive to play the role that the United States wants it to play.

The challenge in Argentina is political. Historically, its central government has been focused on addressing social problems in ways that actually undermine economic development. In other words, politicians tend to gain popularity by spending money they don't have. Argentina has also gone through periods of military and other dictatorship with imposed austerity, a cycle in which it does not differ fundamentally from other Latin American countries, including Brazil.

The Brazilians will see a long-term threat in U.S. support for Argentina, but ideally they will be preoccupied with their own development and the internal stresses it generates. Nevertheless, the United States should be prepared for the Brazilians to offer Argentina economic incentives that would tie its economy closer to their own. Still, two factors play in the Americans' favor. First, Brazil still needs to preserve its investment capital for domestic use. Second, Argentina has long feared Brazilian dominance, so given a choice between Brazil and the United States, it will opt for the latter.

The American goal should be to slowly strengthen Argentina's economic and political capabilities so that over the next twenty to thirty years, should Brazil begin to emerge as a potential threat to the United States, Argentina's growth rivals Brazil's. This will require the United States to provide incentives for American companies to invest in Argentina, particularly in areas outside of agricultural products, where there is already sufficient investment. The United States also should be prepared to draw the American military closer to the Argentine military, but through the civilian government, so as not to incite fears that the U.S. is favoring the Argentine military as a force in the country's domestic politics.

The American president must be careful not to show his true intentions in this, and not to rush. A unique program for Argentina could generate a premature Brazilian response, so Brazil should be included in any American program, if it wishes to participate. If necessary, this entire goodwill effort can be presented as an attempt to contain Hugo Chávez in Venezuela. It will all cost money, but it will be much cheaper, in every sense, than confronting Brazil in the 2030s or 2040s over control of the South Atlantic.

Like Cuba, Mexico is a special case in U.S. relations, and the obvious reason is that it shares the long U.S. border stretching from Texas to California. And yet Mexico is a society at a very different stage of development from Canada, the neighbor to the north, and it therefore interacts with the United States very differently. Nowhere else do domestic politics and geopolitics intersect more directly and perhaps more violently than along the desert frontier south and west of El Paso.

These two countries have had a complex and violent relationship throughout their history. In 1800, if a reasonable person had asked which would be the dominant power in North America in two hundred years, the logical answer would have been Mexico. It was far more developed and sophisticated (and better armed) than the United States at the time. But after vastly expanding its territory through the Louisiana Purchase, the United States pushed Mexico to its current borders, first by seizing Texas and then by waging the Mexican-American War, which forced Mexico out of its holdings as far north as today's Denver and San Francisco.

The reason for American success in appropriating those western lands was ultimately geographical. Compared to the area around Mexico City, the northern part of the country is underpopulated, and it was even more so in the nineteenth century. The reason is that the land running from the border both north into the United States and south into Mexico is intensely dry and desolate, and it is especially inhospitable on the Mexican side. That meant that the Mexicans found it difficult to settle and support populations north of the desert, and even harder to move armies northward. During the uprising of Anglo settlers in Texas, the Mexican president and military leader Santa Anna moved an army of peasants north through the desert to San Antonio. A period of cold weather then crippled many of his soldiers, who were from the jungles of the south and had no shoes. Santa Anna's army was exhausted by the time it arrived, and while it defeated the defenders of the Alamo, it was itself defeated at San Jacinto, near the present city of Houston, by a force that had only two virtues: it was not exhausted and it was not shoeless.

The creation of a new border between the United States and Mexico created a new reality in which the populations on both sides are able to move freely back and forth, migrating with economic opportunities and engaging in smuggling whatever is illegal on the other side. These turbulent borderlands exist throughout the world, between any countries whose political boundaries and cultural boundaries don't match up, usually because, as in this case, the border has moved. Sometimes, as in the case of Germany and France, the issue of the borderland generates war. At other times, as between the United States and Canada, the border is a matter of little importance. The situation of Mexico and the United States in the next decade will be somewhere between the two extremes.

Mexico is a country of 100 million people, most of whom live hundreds of miles away from the United States. It is now the world's fourteenth largest economy—counting only legal commerce—with a GDP of over $1 trillion. It annually exports about $130 billion worth of goods to the United States and imports about $180 billion worth, making it the second largest trading partner with the U.S., after Canada. The United States obviously can't afford to disengage from Mexico, certainly not in less than a generation. Nor does it want to.

But the United States faces two problems: Mexico's illegal export of immigrant workers and Mexico's illegal export of drugs. In both cases the underlying issue is the appetite of the American economic system for the commodities in question. Without the appetite, the exports would be pointless. Because of the appetite—and particularly in the case of drugs, because of their illegality—the export is advantageous to individual Mexicans and to Mexico as a whole.

It is important to understand that Mexican immigration is fundamentally different from immigration from distant countries such as

China and Poland. In those cases, people are breaking their tie with a homeland that is thousands of miles away. Some degree of assimilation is inevitable, because the alternatives are isolation or a life within a culturally segregated community. Although immigrants have frightened Americans ever since the Scots-Irish arrived to unsettle the merchants and gentry of eighteenth-century America, there is a fundamentally geopolitical reason not to compare Mexican immigration with those precedents.

Not only is Mexico adjacent to the United States, but in many cases the land the migrants are moving into is land that once belonged to Mexico. When Mexicans move northward, they are not necessarily breaking ties with their homeland. Indeed, within the borderland, which can extend hundreds of miles into both countries, the movement north can require minimal cultural adjustment. When Mexicans move to distant cities, they react as traditional immigrants have done and assimilate. Within the borderland, they have the option of retaining their language and their national identity, distinct from whatever legal identity they adopt. This state of affairs can create serious tension between the legal border and the cultural border.

This is the root of the profound anxiety within the United States today about Mexican illegal immigration. Critics say that American concern is really an aversion to all Mexican immigration, and they are not altogether wrong, but this analysis does not fully appreciate the roots of the fear. Non-Mexicans within the borderland and even beyond are afraid of being overwhelmed by the migrants and finding themselves living culturally in Mexico. They are also afraid that the movement north is the precursor to Mexicans reclaiming formerly Mexican territories. The fears may be overwrought, but they are not irrational; nor can they be avoided.

The irony, of course, is that the American economy requires these migrants as low-wage workers. The only reason that individuals take the risk of coming to the United States illegally is the certainty that they will be able to get jobs. If migrants were not required in order to fill these jobs, the jobs would be filled already and the migrants would not come.

The counterargument—that migrants take jobs from others, or that their claims on social services outweigh whatever economic advantages they provide—is not entirely frivolous, but it has some weaknesses. First, 10 percent unemployment in the United States translates into about 15 million people out of work. The Pew Hispanic Center estimates that there are about 12 million illegal immigrants in the United States. If the replacement theory were correct, then getting rid of illegal immigrants would create 12 million job openings, leaving only 3 million unemployed and an unemployment rate of only about 2 percent. That such a replacement scenario seems intuitively illogical argues to the point that most of the low-cost, unskilled labor that is imported does not compete with the existing workforce. The American economy requires additional workers but doesn't want to increase the pool of citizens dramatically. The Mexican economy has surplus labor it needs to export. The result is predictable.

And this problem will only intensify, because the fertility of nonimmigrant women has fallen below the rate of replacement, and this at a time when life expectancy has expanded. This means that we will have an aging population with a shrinking workforce—a condition overtaking the advanced industrial world in general. That means that countries will be importing labor both to care for the aged and to expand the workforce. Rather than subsiding, the pressure to import workers will increase, and even while Mexico improves its domestic economy, it will continue to have an abundance of exportable labor.

Compounding the turbulence along the border are the law of supply and demand and the cost of goods applied to the American appetite for narcotics. Heroin, cocaine, and marijuana, the drugs of choice, originate as extremely low-cost agricultural products—weeds, essentially, that require almost no cultivation. Because the drugs are illegal in the United States, normal market forces don't apply. The legal risk of selling drugs drives efficient competitors out of the market, enabling criminal organizations to create regional monopolies through violence that further suppresses competition, which further inflates the cost of the drugs.

Illegality means that merely moving a product a few hundred miles from Mexico to Los Angeles will increase the price to the user by extremely high multiples. Official estimates of the amount of money flowing into Mexico from the sales of narcotics run from $25 billion to $40 billion a year. Unofficial estimates place the amount much higher, but even assuming that the $40 billion figure is correct, the effective amount is staggeringly high. When you look at the revenue from a product, it is not the amount you sell it for that matters—it's the profit margin. For a manufactured product, such as the electronic components that Mexico exports to the United States legally, a profit margin of 10 percent would be quite high. Let's assume that this is the profit margin for all legal imports from Mexico into the United States. Mexico's exports of $130 billion would then generate about $13 billion in profit.

The profit margin on drug sales is enormously higher than 10 percent, because the inherent cost of the commodity is extremely low. Marijuana needs no processing, and processing costs on heroin and cocaine are insignificant. A reasonable and even conservative estimate for the profit margin on narcotics is 90 percent, which means that the $40 billion from the illegal trade generates a profit of about $36 billion. Drugs generate free cash, then, at a level almost three times greater than all of Mexico's $13 billion in legal exports.

Even if Mexico makes only $25 billion a year at an 80 percent margin, that still means a profit of $20 billion a year, which is still $7 billion more than the profit being made from all legal exports. Play with the numbers as much as you like—even demonstrate that drugs generate only half the profit of legal exports—and the fact still remains that drug money helps the liquidity of the Mexican financial system tremendously. Mexico is one of the few countries, for example, that continued to make loans for commercial real estate construction after the financial crisis of 2008.

It follows, therefore, that the Mexican government would be foolish to try to stop the trade. Certainly there is violence from the cartel wars, but it is generally concentrated along the border, not in the populated heartland of Mexico. On balance, the enormous amount of money pouring into the country—all of which finds its way into the banking system and the general economy in some way—benefits the country more than the violence and lawlessness harm it. As a consequence, the rational approach ought to be for the Mexican government to give the appearance of trying to stop the drug trade while making certain that all significant efforts fail. This would keep the United States mollified while making certain that the money continues to pour in.

AMERICA'S MEXICO STRATEGY

The American economy is too integrated with Mexico's ever to allow a disruption of legal commerce, which means that large numbers of trucks will be moving between the United States and Mexico indefinitely. The volume of traffic is too high for agents at the border to inspect all cargoes, and therefore even if the border is walled off, both illegal aliens and drugs will continue to slip through at international crossings and elsewhere. Given the low cost of the narcotics before they reach the United States, the interception of cargoes has very little effect on trade. Cargoes are readily replaced with little impact on aggregate revenue.

It should be much easier to stop illegal immigrants than drugs, because it is easy to detect immigrants once they are in the country. The simplest means of doing this is to institute a national identity card with special paper and embedded codes that make it extremely difficult to forge. No one could be employed until his or her employer first cleared the card via the sort of system currently used for credit card transactions. Any alien without a card would be deported. Any employer who hired him or her would be arrested and charged with a felony.

But this simple method is highly unlikely to be employed, in part because many of the people most opposed to illegal immigration also have a deep mistrust of the federal government. The national identity card could be used to track the movement of money and people—to detect tax fraud and deadbeat dads as well as to monitor political organizations—which could easily lead to government abuse. Dissension within the anti-immigrant coalition on these issues will preclude support for such a system.

But there is a deeper reason this relatively easy step won't be taken: the segment of society that benefits from large numbers of low-cost workers is greater and more influential than the segment harmed by it. Therefore, as with the Mexican government and drugs, the best U.S. strategy is to appear to be doing everything possible to stop the movement of immigrants while making certain that these efforts fail. This has been the American strategy on illegal immigrants for many years, creating a tension between short- and mid-term economic interests and long-term political interests. The long-term problem is the shift in demographics—and in potential loyalties—in the borderland. The president must choose between these options, and his only rational course is to allow the future to tend to itself. Given the forces interested in maintaining the status quo, any president who took the steps needed to stop illegal immigration would rapidly lose power. Therefore the best strategy for the president is to continue the current one: hypocrisy.

Similarly, the drug issue has a relatively simple solution that will not be implemented: legalization. If drugs were legalized and steps were taken to flood the country with narcotics, the street price would plunge, the economics of smuggling would collapse, and the violence along the border driven by all the money to be made would decline precipitously. Along with that there would be a decline in street violence among drug addicts seeking to steal enough money for a fix.

The downside of this strategy is that there would be an unknown increase in the amount of drug use and in the number of users. Existing users, no longer restricted by price, would increase their indulgence, and it is almost certain that some individuals who are unwilling to use drugs illegally would begin to use drugs once they were decriminalized.

The president—and in this case it is up to Congress as well, so it is not really a foreign policy decision—would have to calculate the benefits of stopping the flow of money to Mexico and limiting violence in the borderland against increased drug use and worse, and would have to appear to favor or at least be indifferent to that increase. No significant political coalition in the United States is prepared to embrace the principle of crushing the illegal drug trade by legalization. So, like national identity cards, legalization simply won't fly, for internal ideological reasons.

Assuming that no magical solution will emerge to quell the national appetite for narcotics, the president must accept three realities: drugs will continue to flow into the United States, vast amounts of money will continue to flow into Mexico, and violence in Mexico will continue until the cartels achieve a stable peace, as has happened with organized crime in other countries, or until a single group wipes out all the others.

The only other strategy the United States could use to deal with the struggle is intervention. Whether a small incursion by the FBI or a large military occupation of northern Mexico, this is an extraordinarily bad idea. First, it is unlikely to succeed. The United States is unable to police narcotics at home, so the idea that it could police narcotics in a foreign country is far-fetched. As for a large military occupation, the United States has learned that its armed forces are superbly positioned to destroy enemy armies but far less adept at crushing guerrillas resisting occupation on their own terrain.

An American intervention would conflate the drug cartels with Mexican nationalism, an idea that is already present in some quarters in Mexico, and thus would pose a threat on both sides of the border. Suddenly attacks on U.S. forces, even in the United States, would be not mere banditry but patriotic acts. Given the complexities the United States faces in the rest of the world, the last thing it needs is an out-and-out war on the Mexican border.

The top priority of the president must be to make certain that the violence in northern Mexico and the corruption of law enforcement officials do not move into the United States. He must therefore commit substantial forces to the northern borderland in an effort to suppress violence, even though this is a defective strategy. Its flaws include fighting a war that allows the enemy sanctuary on the other side of a border, which, as we learned in Vietnam, is a very bad idea. It is also a purely defensive strategy that does not give the United States control over events in Mexico. But given that gaining control of events in Mexico is extremely unlikely, a defensive posture may be the best available.

The American strategy will continue to be inherently dishonest. It does not intend to stop immigration and it doesn't expect to stop drugs, but it must pretend to be committed to both. To many Americans, these appear to be critical issues that affect their personal lives. They must not be told that in the greater scheme of things, their sense of what is important doesn't matter, or that the United States is incapable of achieving goals they see as important.

It is far better for the president to appear to be absolutely committed to these goals, and when they aren't met, to fall back on the failure of some underlings to act forcefully. On occasion, members of his staff or of the FBI, DEA, CIA, or military should be fired in disgrace, and major investigations should be held to identify the failures in the system that have permitted drugs and illegal aliens to continue crossing the border. Over the next ten years, the president will be engaged in constant investigations to provide the illusion of activity in a project that cannot succeed.

Stopping the violence from spreading north of the border is alone important enough to topple any president who fails to do so. Fortunately, not allowing violence to spread is in the interests of the cartels as well. They understand that significant violence in the United States would trigger a response that, while ineffective, would still hamper their business interests. In recognizing that the United States would neither move south nor effectively interfere with their trade otherwise, the drug cartels would be irrational to spread violence northward, and smugglers dealing in vast amounts of money are not irrational.

A final word must be included here about Canada, which of course shares the longest border with the United States and is America's largest trading partner. Canada has been an afterthought to the United States since British interest in continental North America declined. It is not that Canada is not important to the United States; it is simply that Canada is locked into place by geography and American power.

Looking at a map, Canada appears to be a vast country, though in terms of populated territory it is actually quite small, with its population distributed in a band along the U.S. border. Many parts of Canada have a north-south orientation rather than an east-west one. In other words, their economic and social life is oriented toward the United States in contrast to Canada, which operates on an east-west basis.

The issue for Canada is that the United States is a giant market as well as source of goods. There is also a deep cultural affinity. This creates problems for Canadians, who see themselves as and want to be a distinct culture as well as country. But as with the rest of the world, Canada is under heavy pressure from American culture, and resistance is difficult.

For the Canadians, there are multiple fault lines in their confederation, the most important being the split between French-speaking Quebec and the rest of Canada, which is predominantly English-speaking. There was a serious separatist movement in the 1960s and 1970s, which won major concessions on the use of language, but it never achieved independence. Today that movement has moderated and independence is not on the table, although expanded autonomy might be.

For the United States, Canada itself poses no threats. The greatest danger would come if Canada were to ally with a major global power. There is only one conceivable scenario for this, and that is if Canada were to fragment. Given the degree of economic and social integration, it would be hard to imagine a situation in which a Canadian province would be able to shift relationships without disaster, or one in which the United States would permit close relations to develop between a province and a hostile power while continuing economic relations. The only case in which this would be imaginable is an independent Quebec, which might forgo economic relations for cultural or ideological reasons.

In the next decade, of course, there are no global powers that can exploit an opening, and there are no openings likely to appear. That means that the relationship between the two countries will remain stable, with Canada increasing its position, as natural gas, concentrated in western Canada, becomes more important. The U.S.-Canadian relationship is of tremendous significance to both countries, with Canada far more vulnerable to the United States than the other way around, simply because of size and options. But as important as it is, it will not be one requiring great attention or decisions on the part of the United States in the next decade.

The American relation with the hemisphere divides into three parts: Brazil, Canada, and Mexico. Brazil is far away and isolated. The United States can shape a long-term strategy of containment, but it is not pressing. Canada is going nowhere. It is Mexico, with its twin problems of migration and drugs, that is the immediate issue for the United States. Outside of the legalization of drugs, which would force down the price, the only solution is to allow the drug wars to burn themselves out, as they inevitably will. Intervention would be disastrous. As for migration, it is a problem now, but as demography shifts, it will be the solution.

The United States has a secure position in the hemisphere. The sign of an empire is its security in its region, with conflicts occurring far away without threat to the homeland. The United States has, on the whole, achieved this.

In the end, the greatest threat in the hemisphere is the one that the Monroe Doctrine foresaw, which is that a major outside power should use the region as a base from which to threaten the United States. That means that the core American strategy should be focused on Eurasia, where such global powers arise, rather than on Latin America: first things first.

Above all else, hemispheric governments must not perceive the United States as meddling in their affairs, a perception that sets in motion anti-American sentiment, which can be troublesome. Of course the United States *will* be engaged in meddling in Latin American affairs, particularly in Argentina. But this must be embedded in an endless discussion of human rights and social progress. In fact, particularly in the case of Argentina, both will be promoted. It is the motive vis-à-vis Brazil that needs to be hidden. But then, all presidents must in all things hide their true motives and vigorously deny the truth when someone recognizes what they are up to.

Historically, the United States has neglected hemispheric issues unless a global power became involved, or the issues directly affected American interests, as circumstances with Mexico did in the nineteenth century. Other than that, Latin America was an arena for commercial relations. That basic scenario will not change in the next decade, save that Brazil must be worked with and long-term plans for containment must, if necessary, be laid.

CHAPTER 12

AFRICA: A PLACE TO LEAVE ALONE

The U.S. strategy of maintaining the balance of power between nation-states in every region of the world assumes two things: first, that there are nation-states in the region, and second, that some have enough power to assert themselves. Absent these factors, there is no fabric of regional power to manage. There is also no system for internal stability or coherence. Such is the fate of Africa, a region that can be divided in many ways but as yet is united in none.

Geographically, Africa falls easily into four regions. First, there is North Africa, forming the southern shore of the Mediterranean basin. Second, there is the western shore of the Red Sea and the Gulf of Aden, known as the Horn of Africa. Then there is the region between the Atlantic and the southern Sahara known as West Africa, and finally a large southern region, extending along a line from Gabon to Congo to Kenya to the Cape of Good Hope.

Using the criterion of religion, Africa can be divided into just two parts: Muslim and non-Muslim. Islam dominates North Africa, the northern regions of West Africa, and the west coast of the Indian Ocean

Islam in Africa

basin as far as Tanzania. Islam does not dominate the northern coast of the Atlantic in West Africa, nor has it made major inroads into the southern cone beyond the Indian Ocean coast.

The linguistic map probably gives us the best sense of Africa's broad regions. But language as a way of looking at Africa is infinitely more complex, because hundreds of languages are widely used and many more are spoken by small groups. Given this linguistic diversity, it is ironic that the common tongue within nations is frequently the language of the imperialists: Arabic, English, French, Spanish, or Portuguese. Even in North Africa, where Arabic lies over everything, there are areas where the European languages of past empires remain an anachronistic residue.

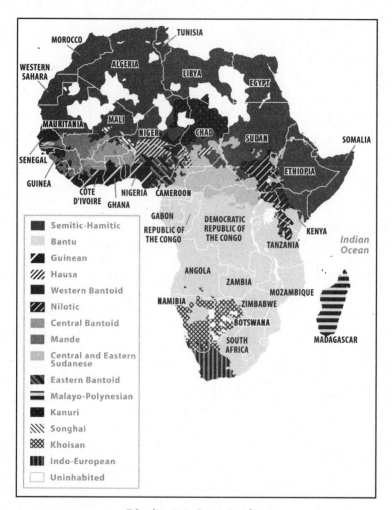

Ethnolinguistic Groups in Africa

A similar irony surrounds what is probably the least meaningful way of trying to make sense of Africa, which is in terms of contemporary borders. Many of these are also holdovers representing the divisions among European empires that have retreated, leaving behind their administrative boundaries. The real African dynamic begins to emerge when we

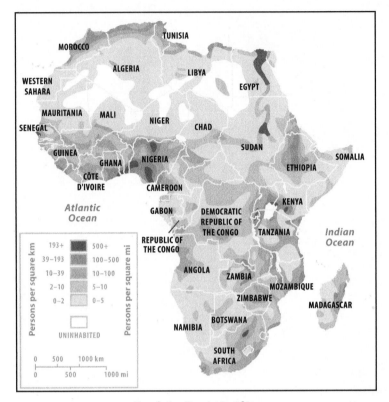

Population Density in Africa

consider that these boundaries not only define states that try to preside over multiple and hostile nations contained within, but often divide nations between two contemporary countries. Thus, while there may be African states, there are—North Africa aside—few nation-states.

Finally, we can look at Africa in terms of where people live. Africa's three major population centers are the Nile River basin, Nigeria, and the Great Lakes region of central Africa, including Rwanda, Uganda, and Kenya. These may give a sense that Africa is overpopulated, and it is true that given the level of poverty, there may well be too many people trying to extract a living from Africa's meager economy. But much of the continent is in fact sparsely populated compared to the rest of the world. Africa's topography of deserts and rain forests makes this inevitable.

Even when we look at these centers of population, we find that the political boundaries and the national boundaries have little to do with each other. Rather than being a foundation for power, then, population density merely increases instability and weakness. Instability occurs when divided populations occupy the same spaces.

Nigeria, for instance, ought to be the major regional power, since it is also a major oil exporter and therefore has the revenues to build power. But for Nigeria the very existence of oil has generated constant internal conflict; the wealth does not go to a central infrastructure of state and businesses but is diverted and dissipated by parochial rivalries. Rather than serving as the foundation of national unity, oil wealth has merely financed chaos based on the cultural, religious, and ethnic differences among Nigeria's people. This makes Nigeria a state without a nation. To be more precise, it is a state presiding over multiple hostile nations, some of which are divided by state borders. In the same way, the population groupings within Rwanda, Uganda, and Kenya are divided, rather than united, by the national identities assigned to them. At times wars have created uneasy states, as in Angola, but long-term stability is hard to find throughout.

Only in Egypt do the nation and the state coincide, which is why from time to time Egypt becomes a major power. But the dynamic of North Africa, which is predominantly a part of the Mediterranean basin, is very different from that of the rest of the continent. Thus when I use the term *Africa* from now on, I exclude North Africa, which has been dealt with in an earlier chapter.

Another irony is that while Africans have an intense sense of community—which the West often denigrates as merely tribal or clan-based—their sense of a shared fate has never extended to larger aggregations of fellow citizens. This is because the state has not grown organically out of the nation. Instead, the arrangements instituted by Arab and European imperialism have left the continent in chaos.

The only way out of chaos is power, and effective power must be located in a state that derives from and controls a coherent nation. This does not mean that there can't be multinational states, such as Russia, or even states representing only part of a nation, such as the two Koreas. But it does mean that the state has to preside over people with a genuine sense of shared identity and mutual interest.

There are three possible outcomes worth considering for Africa. The first is the current path of global charity, but the system of international aid that now dominates so much of African public life cannot possibly have any lasting impact, because it does not address the fundamental problem of the irrationality of African borders. At best it can ameliorate some local problems. At worst it can become a system that enhances corruption among both recipients and donors. The latter is more frequently the case, and truth be known, few donors really believe that the aid they provide solves the problems.

The second path is the reappearance of a foreign imperialism that will create some foundation for stable life, but this is not likely. The reason that both the Arab and the European imperial phases ended as readily as they did was that even though there were profits to be made in Africa, the cost was high. Africa's economic output is primarily in raw materials, and there are simpler ways to obtain these commodities than by sending in military forces and colonial administrators. Corporations making deals with existing governments or warlords can get the job done much more cheaply without taking on the responsibility of governing. Today's corporate imperialism allows foreign powers to go in, take what they want at the lowest possible cost, and leave when they are done.

The third and most likely path is several generations of warfare, out of which will grow a continent where nations are forged into states with legitimacy. As harsh as it may sound, nations are born in conflict, and it is through the experience of war that people gain a sense of shared fate. This is true not only in the founding of a nation but over the course of a nation's history. The United States, Germany, or Saudi Arabia are all nations that were forged in the battles that gave rise to them. War is not sufficient, but the tragedy of the human condition is that the thing that makes us most human—community—originates in the inhumanity of war.

Africa's wars cannot be prevented, and they would happen even if there had never been foreign imperialism. Indeed, they were being fought when imperialism interrupted them. Nation-building does not take place at World Bank meetings or during the building of schools by foreign military engineers, because actual nations are built in blood. The map of Africa must be redrawn, but not by a committee of thoughtful and helpful people sitting in a conference room.

What will happen, in due course, is that Africa will sort itself out into a small number of major powers and a large number of lesser ones. These will provide the framework for economic development and, over generations, create nations that might become global powers, but not at a pace that affects the next decade. The emergence of one nation-state that could introduce a native imperialism to Africa could speed up the process, but all the candidates for imperial power are so internally divided that it is hard to imagine a rapid evolution. Of all of them, South Africa is most interesting, as it combines European expertise with an African political structure. It is the most capable of Africa's countries. But that very fact leaves it with divisions that make its emergence as a regional power harder to imagine with each passing year.

Ultimately, the United States has no overwhelming interest in Africa. It obviously cares about oil from Nigeria or Angola and about controlling Islamist influence in the north as well as Somalia and Ethiopia. Thus it cares about the stability of Nigeria and Kenya, powers that might help with these issues. But America's intense involvement in Africa during the Cold War—the Congolese civil war in the early 1960s, Angola's civil war in the 1980s, Somalia and Ethiopia—was merely an attempt to block Soviet penetration. That level of intensity no longer exists.

In recent years the Chinese have become involved in Africa, purchasing mines and other natural resources. But as we have discussed, China does not represent the same order of threat that the Soviets did, both because of the limits of power projection and because of China's internal weakness. China can't exploit Africa's position strategically, as the Soviets once did, and it can't carry home the mines. The primary effect of Chinese investment is more intense exposure to Africa's instability, which leaves the United States free to remain aloof.

At the same time, U.S. corporations are as skilled as any in making the deals that allow them to get oil, other minerals, or agricultural products without a major American commitment to the region. Given all the other interests of the United States, having one region where it can remain indifferent is strategically beneficial, if only in that it allows the U.S. to conserve resources.

But there is an opportunity in Africa nonetheless. The strategic requirement for the United States to be involved in systematic manipulation in many parts of the world makes it disliked and distrusted. There is no way to avoid this through policy, but it is possible to confuse—or defuse—the issue, and Africa is the place for that.

The United States, like all nations, is brutally self-interested. But there is value in not appearing that way, and some value in being liked and admired, as long as being liked isn't mistaken for the primary goal. Giving significant amounts of aid to Africa would serve the purpose of enhancing America's image. In a decade in which the United States will need to spend hundreds of billions of dollars a year on defense, spending $10 billion or $20 billion on aid to Africa would be a proportional and reasonable attempt to buy admiration.

Again, the aid itself will not solve Africa's problems, but it might ameliorate some of them, at least for a time. It is possible that it will do some harm, as many aid programs have had unintended and negative consequences, but the gesture would redound to America's benefit, and at relatively low cost.

The fact that a president must never lift his eyes from war does not mean that he cannot be clever about it at the same time. One of Machiavelli's points is that good comes out of the ruthless pursuit of power, not out of trying to do good. But if doing some good merely convinces Europe to send more troops to the next U.S. intervention, it will be a worthwhile investment.

CHAPTER 13

THE TECHNOLOGICAL
AND DEMOGRAPHIC IMBALANCE

This book is about the imbalances of American power in the next decade and the effect of these imbalances on the world. I've focused on economic and geopolitical issues and made the argument that imbalances here are transitory and can be corrected. But the book would be incomplete without a consideration of two other major issues impinging on the decade ahead, namely demography and technology.

Economic cycles—boom and bust—can be driven by speculation and financial manipulation, as was the decade just ending. But at a deeper level, economic expansion and contraction are driven by demographic forces and by technological innovation.

During the decade to come, we will see the ebbing of the demographic tide that helped to drive the prosperity of the immediate postwar period. The age cohort known as the baby boom—the children born during the Truman and Eisenhower administrations—will be in their sixties, beginning to retire, beginning to slow down, beginning to get old. As a result, the same demographic bulge that helped create abundance a half century ago will create an economic burden in the years ahead.

In the 1950s, the baby boomers helped create demand for millions of strollers, tract houses, station wagons, bicycles, and washer-dryers. During the 1970s, they began to seek work in an economy not yet ready for them. As they applied for jobs, married and had children, bought and borrowed, their collective behavior caused interest rates, inflation, and unemployment to rise.

As the economy absorbed these people in the 1980s and as they matured in the 1990s, the boomers pushed the economy to extraordinary levels of growth. But during the next ten years, the tremendous spurts of creativity and productivity that the boomers brought to American life will draw down, and the economy will start feeling the first rumblings of the demographic crisis. The passing of the baby boomers throws into sharp relief an accompanying crisis in technological innovation that ultimately may be more salient. As the boomers age, not only will their consumption soar and their production disappear, but they will require heath care and end-of-life care at a level never seen before.

The next decade will be a period in which technology lags behind needs. In some cases, existing technologies will reach the limits of how far they can be stretched, yet replacement technologies will not be in the pipeline. Which isn't to say that there won't be ample technological change; electric cars and new generations of cell phones will abound. What will be in short supply are breakthrough technologies to solve emerging and already pressing needs, the kinds of breakthroughs that drive real economic growth.

The first problem is financial, because the development of radically new technologies is inherently risky, both in terms of implementing new concepts and in terms of matching the product to the market. The financial crisis and recession of 2008–2010 reduced the amount of capital that is available for technological development, along with the appetite for risk. The first few years of the next decade will be marked not only by capital shortages but by a tendency to deploy available capital in low-risk projects, with the available dollars flowing to more established technologies. This will ease up globally in the second half of the decade, and sooner in places like the United States. Nevertheless, given the lead time in technology development, the next generation of notable technological breakthroughs won't emerge until the 2020s.

The second problem in this rate of innovation, oddly enough, lies with the military. In the nineteenth century, the development of the steam engine and the development of the British navy (and its imperial reach) moved hand in hand. In the twentieth century, the United States was the engine of global technological development, and much of that innovation was funded and driven by military acquisitions, and almost all of that had some spin-off civilian application. The development of both aircraft and radios was heavily subsidized by the military and resulted in the subsequent birth of the airline industry and the broadcasting industry. The interstate highway system was first conceived of as a military project to facilitate the rapid movement of troops in case of Soviet attack or nuclear catastrophe. The microchip was developed for use in the small digital computers that guided both nuclear missiles and the rockets needed to put payloads in space. And of course the Internet, which entered public consciousness in the 1990s, began as a military communications project in the 1960s.

Wars are times of intense technological transformation, because societies invest—sometimes with extensive borrowing—when and where matters of life and death are at stake. The U.S.-jihadist war has driven certain developments in unmanned surveillance and attack aircraft as well as in database technology, but the profound transformations of World War II (radar, penicillin, the jet engine, nuclear weapons) and the Cold War (computers, the Internet, fiber optics, advanced materials) are lacking. The reason is that ultimately the conflicts in Afghanistan and Iraq are light-infantry wars that have required extrapolations of existing technologies but few game-changing innovations.

As funding for these wars dries up, research and development budgets will take the first hits. This is a normal cycle in American defense procurement, and growth will not resume until new threats are identified over the next three to four years. With few other countries working on breakthrough military technologies, this traditional driver of innovation will not begin bearing civilian fruit until the 2020s and beyond.

The sense of life or death that should drive technological innovation in the coming decade is the crisis in demographics and its associated costs. The decline in population that I wrote about in *The Next 100 Years* will begin to makes its appearance in a few places in this decade. However, its precursor—an aging populace—will become a ubiquitous fact of life. The workforce will contract, not only as a function of retirement but as increasing educational requirements keep people out of the market until their early or mid-twenties.

Compounding the economic effects of a graying population will be an increasing life expectancy coupled with an attendant increase in the incidence of degenerative diseases. As more people live longer, Alzheimer's disease, Parkinson's disease, debilitating heart disease, cancer, and diabetes will become an overwhelming burden on the economy as more and more people require care, including care that involves highly sophisticated technology.

Fortunately, the one area of research that is amply funded is medical research. Political coalitions make federal funding sufficiently robust to move from basic research to technological application by the pharmaceutical and biotech industries. Still, the possibility of imbalance remains. The mapping of the genome has not provided rapid cures for degenerative diseases, nor has anything else, so over the next ten years the focus will be on palliative measures.

Providing such care could entail labor costs that will have a substantial drag on the economy. One alternative is robotics, but the development of effective robotics depends on scientific breakthroughs in two key areas that have not evolved in a long time: microprocessors and batteries. Robots that can provide basic care for the elderly will require tremendous amounts of computing power as well as enhanced mobility, yet the silicon chip is reaching the limits of miniaturization. Meanwhile, the basic programs needed to guide a robot, process its sensory inputs, and assign tasks can't be supported on current computer platforms. There are a number of potential solutions, from biological materials to quantum computing, but work in these areas has not moved much beyond basic research.

Two other converging technological strands will get bogged down in the next decade. The first is the revolution in communications that began in the nineteenth century. This revolution derived from a deepening understanding of the electromagnetic spectrum, a scientific development driven in part by the rise of global empires and markets. The telegraph provided near-instantaneous communications across great distances, provided that the necessary infrastructure—telegraph lines—was in place. Analog voice communications in the form of the telephone followed, after which infrastructure-free communications developed in the form of wireless radio. This innovation subsequently divided into voice and video (television), which had a profound effect on the way the world worked. These media created new political and economic relations, allowing both two-way communications and centralized broadcast communications, a "one to many" medium that carried implicitly great power for whoever controlled the system. But the hegemony of centralized, one-to-many broadcasting has come to an end, overtaken by the expanded possibilities of the digital age. The coming decade marks the end of a sixty-year period of growth and innovation in even this most advanced and disruptive digital technology.

The digital age began with a revolution in data processing required by the tremendous challenges of personnel management during World War II. Data on individual soldiers was entered as nonelectronic binary code on computer punch cards for sorting and identification. After the war, the Defense Department pressed the transformation of this primitive form of computing into electronic systems, creating a demand for massive mainframes built around vacuum tubes. These mainframes entered the civilian market largely through the IBM sales force, serving businesses in everything from billing to payrolls.

After development of the transistor and the silicon-based chip, which allowed for a reduction in the size and cost of computers, innovation moved to the West Coast and focused on the personal computer. Whereas mainframes were concerned primarily with the manipulation and analysis of data, the personal computer was primarily used to create electronic analogs of things that already existed—typewriters, spreadsheets, games, and so on. This in turn evolved into handheld computing devices and computer chips embedded in a range of appliances.

In the 1990s, the two technological tributaries, communications and data, merged into a single stream, with information in electronic binary form that could be transmitted by way of existing telephone circuits. The Internet, which the Defense Department had developed to transmit data between mainframe computers, quickly adapted to the personal computer and the transmission of data over telephone lines using modems. The next innovation was fiber optics for transmitting large amounts of binary data as well as extremely large graphics files.

With the advent of graphics and data permanently displayed on websites, the transformation was complete. The world of controlled, one-to-many broadcasting of information had evolved into an infinitely diffuse system of "many to many" narrowcasting, and the formally imposed sense of reality provided by twentieth-century news and communications technology became a cacophony of realities.

The personal computer had become not only a tool for carrying out a series of traditional functions more efficiently but also a communications device. In this it became a replacement for conventional mail and telephone communications as well as a research tool. The Internet became a system that combined information with sales and marketing, from data on astronomy to the latest collectibles on eBay. The Web became the public square and marketplace, tying mass society together and fragmenting it at the same time.

The portable computer and the analog cell phone had already brought mobility to certain applications. When they merged together in the personal digital assistant, with computing capability, Internet access, and voice and text messaging, plus instant synchronization with larger personal computers, we achieved instantaneous, global access to data. When I land in Sydney or Istanbul, my BlackBerry instantly downloads my e-mail from around the world, then enables me to read the latest news as the plane taxis to the gate. The revolution in communications has reached an extreme point.

We are now at an extrapolative and incremental state in which the primary focus is on expanding capacity and finding new applications for technology developed years ago. This is a position similar to the plateau reached by personal computers at the end of the dot-com bubble. The basic structure was in place, from hardware to interface. Microsoft had created a comprehensive set of office applications, wireless connectivity had emerged, e-commerce was up and running at Amazon and elsewhere, and Google had launched its search engine. But it is very difficult to think of a truly transformative technological breakthrough that occurred in the past ten years. Instead of breaking new ground, the focus has been on evolving new applications, such as social networking, and on moving previous capabilities to mobile platforms. As the iPad demonstrates, this effort will continue. But ultimately, this is rearranging the furniture rather than building a new structure. Microsoft, which transformed the economy in the 1980s, is now a fairly staid corporation, protecting its achievements. Apple is inventing new devices that make what we already do more efficient. Google and Facebook are finding new ways to sell advertising and make a profit on the Internet.

Radical technological innovation has been replaced by a battle for market share—finding ways to make money by introducing small improvements as major events. Meanwhile, the dramatic increases in productivity once driven by technology, which helped in turn to drive the economy, are declining, which will have a significant impact on the challenges we face in the decade ahead. With basic research and development down and corporate efforts focused on making incremental improvements in the last generation's core technology, the primary global growth impetus is limited to putting existing technologies into the hands of more people. Since the sale of cell phones has reached the saturation point already and corporations are reluctant to invest in unnecessary upgrades, this is a problematic prescription for growth.

This is not to say that the world of digital technology is moribund.

But computing is still essentially passive, restricted to manipulating and transmitting data. The next and necessary phase is to become active, using that data to manipulate and change reality, with robotics as a primary example. Moving to that active phase is necessary for achieving the huge boost in productivity that will compensate for the economic shifts associated with the demographic change about to hit.

The U.S. Defense Department has been working on military robots for a long time, and the Japanese and South Koreans have made advances in civilian applications. However, much scientific and technological work remains to be done if this technology is to be ready when it will be urgently needed, in the 2020s.

Even so, relying on robotics to solve social problems simply begs another vexing question, which is how we are to power these machines. Human labor by itself is relatively low in energy consumption. Machines emulating human labor will use large amounts of energy, and as they proliferate in the economy (much as personal computers and cell phones did), the increase in power consumption will be enormous.

Questions of powering technological innovation in turn raise the great and heated debate about whether the increased use of hydrocarbons is affecting the environment and causing climate change. While this question engages the passions, it really isn't the most salient issue. The question of climate change raises two others that demand astute presidential leadership: first, is it possible to cut energy use? and second, is it possible to continue growing the economy using hydrocarbons, and particularly oil?

There is an expectation built into public policy that says it is possible to address the issue of energy use through conservation. But much of the recent growth of energy consumption has come from the developing world, which makes solving the problem by cutting back wishful thinking at best.

The newly industrialized countries in Asia and Latin America are not about to cut their energy use in order to solve energy issues or prevent certain island nations from being inundated by the rising waters of warmer seas. From their point of view, conservation would relegate them permanently to the Third World status they have fought long and hard to escape. In their view, the advanced industrial world of the United States, western Europe, and Japan should cut *its* energy use in order to compensate for over a century of profligate consumption.

In 2010 there was a summit in Copenhagen to address the question of energy use, or, more precisely, carbon dioxide emissions. The proposal was made to cut emissions. At a time when energy consumption is growing, cutting emissions at all poses a significant challenge. Except for a dramatic new source of energy, that sort of cut can be reached only by substantial decreases in fossil fuel consumption. Riding your bicycle to work and careful recycling will not do it.

The Copenhagen initiative collapsed because it was politically unsustainable. None of the leaders of the advanced industrial world could possibly persuade the public to accept the significant cuts in standard of living that reducing fossil fuel use would have required. For people to balk is not irrational. They are measuring a certainty against a probability. The certainty is that their lives would be significantly constrained by such reductions in consumption, which would lead to widespread economic dislocation. The probability—which is questioned by some—is that climate change will occur, with equally devastating results. That the change in the climate will be harmful rather than beneficial might well be true. But the question is whether the probable or possible effects on children and grandchildren outweigh the certainty of immediate consequences. This may be an unpleasant fact, but it explains the outcome of the Copenhagen and Kyoto meetings on climate change that failed to successfully develop strategies for reducing greenhouse emissions.

For the next decade, the assumption must be that energy use will continue to surge, and thus the issue is not whether to cut fossil fuel consumption but whether there will be enough fossil fuels to deal with rising demand. Nonfossil fuels cannot possibly come on line fast enough to substitute for energy use in the short term. It takes well over ten years to build a nuclear power plant. Wind and water power could manage only a small fraction of consumption. The same is true of solar power. For the decade ahead, whatever long-term solutions might exist, the problem is going to be finding the fuel for rising energy use while, ideally, restricting increases in carbon output.

Energy use falls into four broad categories: transportation, electrical generation, industrial uses, and nonelectrical residential uses (heating and air-conditioning). Over the next decade, energy for transportation will continue to be petroleum-based. The cost of shifting the existing global fleet to another energy source is prohibitive and won't happen within ten years. Some transportation will shift to electrical, but that simply moves fossil fuel consumption from the vehicle to the power station. Electrical generation is more flexible, as it accepts oil, coal, and natural gas. The same is possible for industrial uses. Home heating and air-conditioning can be converted, at some cost.

There is talk of global oil output having reached its historic high and now being in decline. Certainly oil production has moved to less and less hospitable areas, such as the deep waters offshore and shale, which require relatively expensive technology. That tells us that even if oil extraction has not reached its peak, all other things being equal, oil prices will continue to rise. Offshore drilling has cost and maintenance problems. As we saw with the recent BP disaster off the coast of Louisiana, an accident happening a mile under water is hard to fix. But even apart from environmental damage, wells are very expensive. Shale installations are expensive as well, and when the price of oil falls below a certain point, extraction becomes uneconomical and the investment is tied up or lost. But leaving aside broader questions of peak prices, the increased energy consumption we will see over the next decade cannot be fueled by oil, or at least not entirely.

That leaves two choices for the ten years ahead. One is coal; the other is natural gas. Widespread conservation sufficient to reduce energy consumption in absolute terms is not going to happen in the United States, let alone the world as a whole. The ability to produce more oil is limited, and the vulnerabilities in an oil economy to interdictions by countries such as Iran make it a very risky proposition. The ability of alternative energy sources to have a decisive impact in this decade is minimal at best. No nuclear power plant started now will be operational in five or six years. But a choice between more coal and more natural gas is not the choice the president will want to make. He will want a silver bullet of rapid availability, no environmental impact, and low cost. In this decade, however, he will be forced to balance what is needed against what is available. In the end, he will pick both, with natural gas having the greater surge.

The application of hydraulic fracturing, or fracking, to the production of natural gas opens the possibility of dramatic increases in energy availability. What this technology does is to recover natural gas from up to three miles beneath the earth's surface, where it is contained in rock so compressed that it does not release the gas. Fracturing the rock allows the gas to pool and be recovered, but this method, like all energy production on earth, carries environmental risks. Its virtue for the United States is that there are ample domestic supplies, and thus reliance on this source of energy reduces the chance of war. Natural gas readily substitutes for many uses of petroleum and in many cases at relatively low cost. This reduces the need to import oil, which in turn reduces the possibility that a foreign power will blockade the oil, thus triggering a war.

Fracking technology also makes it possible to get at enough quantities of natural gas in a short enough period of time to control the cost and availability of energy during this decade. We would expect other technologies to become available fifty or sixty years from now, but in the next ten years, the options come down to coal and gas.

This will be a time for addressing problems that have not yet turned into crises and for searching out solutions that do not yet exist. Consider the problem of water availability. Increased industrialization, along with a still-growing population enjoying higher standards of living, is already creating regional water shortages. These depletions have sometimes created political confrontations between nations that might well mature into wars. Add to this the possibility that climate change might alter weather patterns and that those changes might reduce rainfall in populated areas, and the problem could become a crisis.

There is, of course, no water shortage. The water is simply mixed with salt and inconveniently located, but it exists in staggeringly vast quantities. The technology needs improvement, but we do know how to desalinate water. We also know how to transport water in pipelines. The problem is that desalination and water transportation are both hugely expensive and require enormous amounts of energy. That sort of energy will not be found in available solutions. As I said in *The Next 100 Years,* we will need space-based solar generation or other very radical approaches to increase available energy by orders of magnitude.

When we look at the major problems we have to solve, such as aging population, contracting workforce, and lack of water, we find a consistent pattern. First, the problem is emerging in this decade, but it will not become an unbearable burden until later. Second, the technologies to deal with it—from cures for degenerative diseases to robotics to desalination—either exist or can be conceived of, but are not yet fully in place. Third, implementing almost all of them (save the cure for degenerative diseases) requires both a short-term solution for energy and a long-term solution.

The danger is that the problem and the solution will become unbalanced—that the problem will get to the crisis stage before the technical solutions come on line. The task of the president in addressing these issues in the next decade is not dramatic. It will be to facilitate short-term solutions while laying the groundwork for longer-term solutions and, above all, to do both rather than just one. The temptation will be to look at the long-term solution and pretend that the problem will wait or that the solution will arrive faster than it can. Long-term solutions are more attractive and cause much less controversy than short-term solutions, which will affect people who are still alive and voting. The problem that presidents in this decade will have is that the crisis won't happen on their watch but in the decade that follows. The temptation to punt the issue will be substantial. This is where another drop of wisdom from Machiavelli becomes especially important: successful rulers want to do more than rule, they want to be remembered for all time. John Kennedy didn't have time to do much, but we all remember his decision to go to the moon.

In the short term, the most crucial problem is to lay the groundwork for the energy requirements of the next decade. To do this, two things must happen. The president must choose the balance between the two available fossil fuels, coal and gas. Then he must tell the people that these are the only choices. If he fails to persuade the public of this, there will not be energy for the technologies that will emerge in the next decade. He must, of course, frame his argument within the context of global warming, climate change, and the desire to protect all species. The environmental movement has supported Obama, and every president must maintain his political base. But while appealing to his green constituents, he must make the case for enhanced natural gas and coal use for the generation of electricity. He may well be able to frame his appeal in terms of more electric cars, but however he makes it, this is his task. Otherwise, he will be seen as having neglected a crisis that he could foresee.

At the same time he must prepare for long-term increases in energy generation from nonhydrocarbon sources—sources that are cheaper and located in areas that the United States will not need to control by sending in armies. In my view, this is space-based solar power. Therefore, what should be under way, and what is under way, is private-sector development of inexpensive booster rockets. Mitsubishi has invested in space-based solar power to the tune of about $21 billion. Europe's EAB is also investing, and California's Pacific Gas and Electric has signed a contract to purchase solar energy from space by 2016, although I think fulfillment of that contract on that schedule is unlikely.

However, whether the source is space-based solar power or some other technology, the president must make certain that development along several axes is under way and that the potential for building them is realistic. Enormous amounts of increased energy are needed, and the likely source of the technology, based on history, is the U.S. Department of Defense. Thus the government will absorb the cost of early development and private investment will reap the rewards.

We are in a period in which the state is more powerful than the market, and in which the state has more resources. Markets are superb at exploiting existing science and early technology, but they are not nearly as good in basic research. From aircraft to nuclear power to moon flights to the Internet to global positioning satellites, the state is much better at investing in long-term innovation. The government is inefficient, but that inefficiency and the ability to absorb the cost of inefficiency are at the heart of basic research. When we look at the projects we need to undertake in the coming decade, the organization most likely to execute them successfully is the Department of Defense.

There is nothing particularly new in this intertwining of technology, geopolitics, and economic well-being. The Philistines dominated the Levantine coast because they were great at making armor. To connect and control their empire, the Roman army built roads and bridges that are still in use. During a war aimed at global domination, the German military created the foundation of modern rocketry; in countering, the British came up with radar. Leading powers and those contending for power constantly find themselves under military and economic pressure. They respond to it by inventing extraordinary new technologies.

The United States is obviously that sort of power. It is currently under economic pressure but declining military pressure. Such a time is not usually when the United States undertakes dramatic new ventures. The government is heavily funding one area we have discussed, finding cures for degenerative diseases. The Department of Defense is funding a great deal of research into robotics. But the fundamental problem, energy, has not had its due. For this decade, the choices are pedestrian. The danger is that the president will fritter away his authority on projects such as conservation, wind power, and terrestrial solar power, which can't yield the magnitude of results required. The problem with natural gas in particular is that it is pedestrian.

But like so much of what will take place in this decade, accepting the ordinary and obvious is called for first—followed by great dreams quietly expressed.

CHAPTER 14

THE EMPIRE, THE REPUBLIC, AND THE DECADE

In discussing American foreign policy, I have examined every continent and numerous countries, but I have by no means been exhaustive. Because of the global nature of the American empire, every country in the world is in some way important to the United States. From Niger's Islamic threat to the effect that Nepal might have on the Sino-Indian balance to Ecuador's role in the drug wars, it is difficult to imagine a country to which the United States can afford to be utterly indifferent.

There are many who would argue that the United States is overextended and that these complex international involvements ultimately are not in the American interest. This is not an unpersuasive argument, except that it isn't clear how the United States might disentangle itself from its global interests. During the next decade, the United States must manage the chaos of the Islamic world, a resurgent Russia, a sullen and divided Europe, and a China both huge and profoundly troubled. In addition it must find the path out of the current economic problems, not only for itself but for the world.

We should also remember that while the American economy might be battered at the moment, it is still almost 25 percent of the world's economy, and U.S. investments and borrowing swamp the world. Simply being the United States creates the pervasive entanglements we must strive to manage. The United States may indeed be overextended, and it might be preferable if the U.S. had never achieved imperial status, or for it now to retreat. But wishes don't make policy. Policy is made by reality, and the reality of what has been created, whether intentionally or not, can't be abandoned without breathtakingly severe consequences. The United States entered the path to global power with the Spanish-American War of 1898. It has been on this trajectory for over a century. Changing course at the velocity the United States is traveling is simply not an option. Calling for it is a fantasy.

The only option is to manage what has been created. That begins with the reconciliation of moral principles with the exercise of power. Starting with moral principles is the most practical beginning. Much of the internal conflict over waging wars is rooted in lack of clarity about the relationship between morality and power. What is needed is a common understanding of reality and morality.

The exercise of power is always morally ambiguous, yet the moral principles of the United States mean nothing if the country is destroyed. The pursuit of universal rights requires more than speeches. It requires power. "Nobody gets hurt" is unrealistic, and the best we can do is to make difficult decisions about who gets hurt and when. Lincoln had to support slavery in Kentucky. It wasn't right, but it was either that or lose the war, and if he lost the war, then his entire moral project was destroyed.

At the same time, simply pursuing power without any moral purpose leads nowhere. Nixon exercised power without purpose, and it was his lack of moral perspective that led him to Watergate and destruction. It is one thing to justify the means by the end. It is another thing for the means to become the end.

During the next decade, the United States must overcome the desire to simplify, because there is no single phrase or formula that solves the problem. The moral problem at the core of the exercise of power repeats itself in endless and unexpected forms that have to be solved each time they occur. No leader can solve them properly each time. The most that can be said about any leader is that on the whole, he or she did well, given the circumstances.

To reach this point, the American people must mature. We are an adolescent lot, expecting solutions to insoluble problems and perfection in our leaders. Churchill could not be elected president of the United States: he was, by any reasonable measure, an alcoholic, and certainly he was an elitist in the snobbish sense of the term. It is clear that Roosevelt had at least one affair while president and another before he became president. Lincoln appears to some biographers to have been suffering from bipolar disorder, a mental disease. Reagan was probably in the early stages of Alzheimer's late in his presidency. These were all men who, to say the least, did well, given the circumstances. Unless the American people can reach the maturity to discipline themselves to expect this and no more, the republic will not survive. The demands of an unintended empire and immature expectations of our leaders will bring down the regime long before militarism or corruption might.

Obviously, American society is being torn apart in rancorous discourse. This isn't new. The things said about Andrew Jackson and Franklin Roosevelt were not pleasant. Having endured the clashes over civil rights, Vietnam, and Watergate, we cannot really argue that we have reached new levels of incivility. But Iraq, Afghanistan, and the recent financial crisis have raised significant questions about the global interests of the American elite and whether they have undermined the interests of the general public. Villains and saints are sometimes difficult to distinguish, so there is no simple approach to this discussion. The Tea Party's vilification of Obama and Obama's vilification of the Tea Party don't contribute much to creating a coherent political road map.

The last decade posed challenges to the United States that it was not prepared for and that it did not manage well. It was, as they say, a learning experience, valuable because the mistakes did not threaten the survival of the United States. But the threat that will arise later in the century will tower over those of the last decade. Look back on the middle of the twentieth century to imagine what might face the United States going forward.

The United States is fortunate to have the next decade in which to make the transition from an obsessive foreign policy to a more balanced and nuanced exercise of power. By this I don't mean that the goal is to learn to use diplomacy rather than force. Diplomacy has its place, but I am saying that when push comes to shove, the United States must learn to choose its enemies carefully, make certain they can be beaten, and then wage an effective war that causes them to capitulate. It is important not to fight wars that can't be won and to fight wars in order to win. Fighting wars out of rage is impermissible for a country with such vast power and interests.

The United States has spent sixteen of the past fifty years fighting wars in Asia. After his experience in Korea, Douglas MacArthur, hardly a pacifist, warned Americans to avoid such adventures. The reason was simple: as soon as Americans set foot in Asia, they are vastly outnumbered. The logistical problems of supplying forces thousands of miles from home, and of fighting an enemy that has nowhere to go and is intimately familiar with the terrain, only compound an already overwhelming challenge. Yet the United States continues to wade in, expecting that each time will be different. Of all the lessons of the last decade, this is the most important for the decade to come.

The lesson we should have learned from the British is that there are far more effective, if cynical, ways to manage wars in Asia and Europe. One is by diverting the resources of potential enemies away from the United States and toward a neighbor. Maintaining the balance of power should be as fundamental to American foreign policy as the Bill of Rights is to domestic policy. The United States should enter a war in the Eastern Hemisphere only in the direst of circumstances, when an onerous power threatens to overtake vast territory and no one who can resist is left.

The foundation of American power is the oceans. Domination of the oceans prevents other nations from attacking the United States, permits the United States to intervene when it needs to, and gives the United States control over international trade. The United States need never use that power, but it must deny it to anyone else. Global trade depends on the oceans. Whoever controls the oceans ultimately controls global trade. The balance-of-power strategy is a form of naval warfare, preventing challengers from building forces that can threaten American control of the seas.

The American military is now obsessed with building a force that can fight in the Islamic world. Some say that we have reached a point in which all warfare will be asymmetric. Some describe the future in terms of the "long war," a conflict that will stretch for generations. If that is true, then the United States has already lost, because there is no way it can pacify more than a billion Muslims.

But I would argue that such an assessment is misguided and that such a goal is a failure of imagination. Generals, as they say, always fight the last war, and it is easy to reach the conclusion while the war is still raging that all wars in the future will look like the one you are fighting now. It must never be forgotten that systemic wars—wars in which the major powers fight to redefine the international system—happen in almost every century. If we count the Cold War and its subwars, then three systemic wars were fought in the twentieth century. It is a virtual certainty that there will be systemic wars in the twenty-first century. It must always be remembered that you can win a dozen minor wars, but if you lose the big one, you lose everything.

American forces might be called on to fight anywhere. It was hard to believe in 2000 that the United States would spend nine of the next ten years fighting a war in Afghanistan, but it has. Shaping a military to keep fighting these wars would be a tremendous mistake, as would deciding that the United States doesn't want to fight wars any longer and slashing the defense budget.

The first focus must be on the sea. The U.S. Navy is the strategic foundation of the United States, followed closely by U.S. forces in space, because it will be the reconnaissance satellites that will guide anti-ship missiles in the next decade, and shortly after that the missiles themselves will find their way into space. In an age when fielding a new weapons system can take twenty years, the next decade must be the period of intense preparation for whatever may come. The next decade is the time for transition.

The British had the Colonial Office. The Romans had the Proconsul. The United States has a chaotic array of institutions dealing with foreign policy. There are sixteen intelligence services with overlapping responsibilities. The State Department, Defense Department, National Security Council, and national director of intelligence all wind up dealing with the same issues, coordinated only to the extent that the president manages them all. To say there are too many cooks in the kitchen misses the point—and there are too many kitchens serving the same meal. Bureaucratic infighting in Washington may be fodder for comedians, but it can shatter lives around the world. It is easier to leave it as it is, but only easier for Washington. The American foreign policy apparatus simply must be rationalized. The president spends much of his time just trying to control his own team. This must change in the next decade, before things spiral out of control.

Americans like to hold everyone responsible for the problems of the United States but themselves. The problem is said to be Fox News or special interests or the liberal media. At root the problem is that there is no consensus in the United States about whether it has an empire and what to do about it. Americans prefer mutual vilification to facing up to the facts; they prefer arguing about what ought to be to arguing about what is. What I have tried to show is the reality as I see it, in terms of both the regime and the next decade. In arguing that the United States has unintentionally become an empire, I have also made the case that the empire poses a profound threat to the republic. To lose that moral foundation would make the empire pointless.

I have also made the argument for what I call the Machiavellian president, a leader who both understands power and has a moral core. The president is the only practical bulwark for the republic, because he alone is elected by all the people. It is his job to lead so that he can manage, but the president, no matter how crafty, cannot lead alone. He must have the other institutions the founders gave the republic functioning maturely, and, above all, he must have a mature public that takes responsibility for the state of the nation. The New Testament contains this passage: "When I was a child, I talked like a child, I thought like a child, I reasoned like a child. When I became a man, I put childish ways behind me." The United States has grown up. Its public must too.

Lincoln, Roosevelt, and Reagan all led fractious nations. Each was skillful enough to craft coalitions that were sufficiently strong to get through the storm. But going forward, we need not only clever leaders but also a clever public. A woman asked Benjamin Franklin after the Constitutional Convention about the kind of government the delegates had given the country. "A republic," he told her, "if you can keep it."

I genuinely believe that the United States is far more powerful than most people think. Its problems are real but trivial compared to the extent of its power. I am also genuinely frightened, not about America's survival, but about the ability of the United States to keep the republic provided by the founders. The demands and temptations of empire can easily destroy institutions already besieged by a public that has lost both civility and perspective, and by politicians who cannot lead because they are capable of neither the exercise of power nor the pursuit of moral ends.

Four things are needed. First, a nation that has an unsentimental understanding of the situation it is in. Second, leaders who are prepared to bear the burden of reconciling that reality with American values. Third, presidents who understand power and principles and know the place of each. But above all, what is needed is a mature American public that recognizes what is at stake and how little time there is to develop the culture and institutions needed to manage the republic cast in an imperial role. Without this, nothing else is possible. The situation is far from hopeless, but it requires an enormous act of will for the country to grow up.

ACKNOWLEDGMENTS

Every author of every book is indebted to many people whose thoughts and writings his own rest upon. My more immediate debts are to Rodger Baker, Peter Zeihan, Colin Chapman, Reva Bhalla, Kamran Bokhari, Lauren Goodrich, Eugene Chausovsky, Nate Hughes, Marko Papic, Matt Gertken, Kevin Stech, Emre Dogru, Bayless Parsley, Matt Powers, Jacob Shapiro, and Ira Jamshidi. Each of them helped make this book better than it might have been otherwise. I would also like to thank Ben Sledge and T. J. Lensing for producing the maps—not, I've learned, an easy task. My thanks to the Army and Navy Club Library in Washington, D.C., for all its help.

My special thanks to Jim Hornfischer, my literary agent, for his support and encouragement; to my editor at Doubleday, Jason Kaufman, for his unrelenting confidence in me and his always helpful criticism; and to Rob Bloom. Bill Patrick helped turn my turgid prose into much better prose. Susan Copeland kept me on track and organized. I am grateful to everyone at STRATFOR, including our readers, for their lively support and criticism. And, above all, I thank my wife, Meredith, as always, my rock and my guide.